# LIBERTARIANISM

*A PRIMER*

*by*

*DAVID BOAZ*

THE FREE PRESS
A Division of Simon & Schuster Inc.
1230 Avenue of the Americas
New York, NY 10020

Manufactured in the United States of America

10   9   8   7   6   5   4   3   2   1

*Library of Congress Cataloging-in-Publication Data*

Boaz, David, 1953–
   Libertarianism : a primer / by David Boaz.
      p.   cm.
   Includes bibliographical references and index.
   ISBN 0-684-83198-8
   1. Libertarianism.  I. Title.
JC585.B559   1997
320.5'12—dc20                                      96-46012
                                                       CIP

# CONTENTS

*Chapter 1*

# THE COMING LIBERTARIAN AGE

*In* 1995 Gallup pollsters found that 39 percent of Americans said that "the federal government has become so large and powerful that it poses an immediate threat to the rights and freedoms of ordinary citizens." Pollsters couldn't believe it, so they tried again, taking out the word "immediate." This time 52 percent of Americans agreed.

Later that year *USA Today* reported in a front-page story on post-baby-boom Americans that "many of the 41 million members of Generation X . . . are turning to an old philosophy that suddenly seems new: libertarianism." A front-page report in the *Wall Street Journal* agreed: "Much of the angry sentiment coursing through [voters'] veins today isn't traditionally Republican or even conservative. It's libertarian. . . . Because of their growing disdain for government, more and more Americans appear to be drifting—often unwittingly—toward a libertarian philosophy."

Writing in 1995 about the large numbers of Americans who say they'd welcome a third party, David Broder of the *Washington Post* commented,

> The distinguishing characteristic of these potential independent voters—aside from their disillusionment with Washington politicians of both parties—is their libertarian streak. They are skeptical of the Democrats because they identify them with big

1

government. They are wary of the Republicans because of the growing influence within the GOP of the religious right.

Where did this sudden media interest in libertarianism come from? As *USA Today* noted, libertarianism challenges the conventional wisdom and rejects outmoded statist ideas, so it often has a strong appeal to young people. As for myself, when I first discovered libertarian ideas in my college days, it seemed obvious to me that most libertarians would be young (even though I was dimly aware that the libertarian books I was reading were written by older people). Who but a young person could believe in such a robust vision of individual freedom? When I went to my first libertarian event off-campus, I was mildly surprised that the first person I encountered was about forty, which seemed quite old to me at the time. Then another person arrived, more the sort of person I had expected to meet, a young woman in her late twenties. But her first question was, "Have you seen my parents?" I soon learned that her sixtyish parents were the leading libertarian activists in the state, and my mistaken impressions about what kind of people would become libertarians were gone forever. I discovered that the young woman's parents, and the millions of Americans who today share libertarian beliefs, stand firmly in a long American tradition of individual liberty and opposition to coercive government.

Libertarianism is the view that each person has the right to live his life in any way he chooses so long as he respects the equal rights of others. (Throughout this book I use the traditional "he" and "his" to refer to all individuals, male and female; unless the context indicates otherwise, "he" and "his" should be understood to refer to both men and women.) Libertarians defend each person's right to life, liberty, and property—rights that people possess naturally, before governments are created. In the libertarian view, all human relationships should be voluntary; the only actions that should be forbidden by law are those that involve the initiation of force against those who have not themselves used force—actions like murder, rape, robbery, kidnapping, and fraud.

Most people habitually believe in and live by this code of ethics. Libertarians believe this code should be applied consistently—and specifically, that it should be applied to actions by governments as well as by individuals. Governments should exist to protect rights, to protect us from others who might use force against us. When governments use force against people who have not violated the rights of others, then governments themselves become rights violators. Thus libertarians condemn such government actions as censorship, the draft, price controls, confiscation of property, and regulation of our personal and economic lives.

Put so starkly, the libertarian vision may sound otherworldly, like a doctrine for a universe of angels that never was and never will be. Surely, in today's messy and often unpleasant world, government must do a great deal? But here's the surprise: The answer is no. In fact, the more messy and modern the world, the better libertarianism works compared—for instance—with monarchy, dictatorship, and even postwar American-style welfarism. The political awakening in America today is first and foremost the realization that libertarianism is not a relic of the past. It is a philosophy—more, a pragmatic plan—for the future. In American politics it is the leading edge—not a backlash, but a vanguard.

Libertarian thought is so widespread today, and the American government has become so bloated and ludicrous, that the two funniest writers in America are both libertarians. P. J. O'Rourke summed up his political philosophy this way: "Giving money and power to government is like giving whiskey and car keys to teenage boys." Dave Barry understands government about as clearly as Tom Paine did: "The best way to understand this whole issue is to look at what the government does: it takes money from some people, keeps a bunch of it, and gives the rest to other people."

Libertarianism is an old philosophy, but its framework for liberty under law and economic progress makes it especially suited for the dynamic world—call it the Information Age, or the Third Wave, or the Third Industrial Revolution—we are now entering.

## The Resurgence of Libertarianism

Some readers may well wonder why people in a generally free and prosperous country like the United States need to adopt a new philosophy of government. Aren't we doing reasonably well with our current system? We do indeed have a society that has brought unprecedented prosperity to a larger number of people than ever before. But we face problems—from high taxes to poor schools to racial tensions to environmental destruction—that our current approach is not handling adequately. Libertarianism has solutions to those problems, as I'll try to demonstrate. For now I'll offer three reasons that libertarianism is the right approach for America on the eve of the new millennium.

First, we are not nearly as prosperous as we could be. If our economy were growing at the rate it grew from 1945 to 1973, our gross domestic product would be 40 percent larger than it is. But that comparison doesn't give the true picture of the economic harm that excessive government is doing to us. In a world of global markets and accelerating technological change, we shouldn't be growing at the same pace we did forty years ago—we should be growing faster. More reliance on markets and individual enterprise would mean more wealth for all of us, which is especially important for those who have the least today.

Second, our government has become far too powerful, and it increasingly threatens our freedom—as those 52 percent of Americans told the befuddled pollsters. Government taxes too much, regulates too much, interferes too much. Politicians from Jesse Helms to Jesse Jackson seek to impose their own moral agenda on 250 million Americans. Events like the assault on the Branch Davidians, the shootings of Vicki Weaver and Donald Scott, the beating of Rodney King, and the government's increasing attempts to take private property without judicial process make us fear an out-of-control government and remind us of the need to reestablish strict limits on power.

Third, in a fast-changing world where every individual will have unprecedented access to information, centralized bureaucracies and coercive regulations just won't be able to keep up with the real economy. The existence of global capital markets means that investors won't be held hostage by national governments and their confiscatory tax systems. New opportunities for telecommuting will mean that more and more workers will also have the ability to flee high taxes and other intrusive government policies. Prosperous nations in the twenty-first century will be those that attract productive people. We need a limited government to usher in an unlimited future.

The twentieth century has been the century of state power, from Hitler and Stalin to the totalitarian states behind the Iron Curtain, from dictatorships across Africa to the bureaucratic welfare states of North America and Western Europe. Many people assume that as time goes on, and the world becomes more complex, governments naturally get bigger and more powerful. In fact, however, the twentieth century was in many ways a detour from the 2,500-year history of the Western world. From the time of the Greeks, the history of the West has largely been a story of increasing freedom, with a progressively limited role for coercive and arbitrary government.

Today, at the end of the twentieth century, there are signs that we may be returning to the path of limiting government and increasing liberty. With the collapse of communism, there is hardly any support left for central planning. Third World countries are privatizing state industries and freeing up markets. Practicing capitalism, the Pacific Rim countries have moved from poverty to world economic leadership in a generation.

In the United States, the bureaucratic leviathan is threatened by a resurgence of the libertarian ideas upon which the country was founded. We are witnessing a breakdown of all the cherished beliefs of the welfare-warfare state. Americans have seen the failure of big government. They learned in the 1960s that governments wage unwinnable wars, spy on their domestic opponents, and lie about it. They learned in the 1970s that government management of the economy leads to inflation, unemployment, and stagnation. They learned in the 1980s that government's cost and intrusiveness grew even as a succession of presidents ran against Washington and promised to change it. Now in the 1990s they are ready to apply those lessons, to make the twenty-first century not the century of the state but the century of the free individual.

These changes have two principal roots. One is the growing recognition by people around the world of the tyranny and inefficiency inherent in state planning. The other is the growth of a political movement rooted in ideas, particularly the ideas of libertarianism. As E. J. Dionne, Jr., writes in *Why Americans Hate Politics,* "The resurgence of libertarianism was one of the less noted but most remarkable developments of recent years. During the 1970s and 1980s, antiwar, antiauthoritarian, antigovernment, and antitax feelings came together to revive a long-stagnant political tendency."

Why is there a libertarian revival now? The main reason is that the alternatives to libertarianism—fascism, communism, socialism, the welfare state—have all been tried in the twentieth century and have all failed to produce peace, prosperity, and freedom.

Fascism, as exemplified in Mussolini's Italy and Hitler's Germany, was the first to go. Its economic centralization and racial collectivism now seem repellent to every civilized person, so we may forget that before World War II many Western intellectuals admired the "new forms of economic organization in Germany and Italy," as the magazine the *Nation* put it in 1934. The world's horror at National Socialism in Germany helped produce not only the civil rights movement but such harbingers of the libertarian renaissance as *The God of the Machine* by Isabel Paterson and *The Road to Serfdom* by Friedrich A. Hayek.

The other great totalitarian system of the twentieth century was communism, as outlined by Karl Marx and implemented in the Soviet Union and its satellites. Communism maintained its appeal to idealists far longer than fascism. At least until the revelations of Stalin's purges in the 1950s, many American intellectuals viewed communism as a noble if sometimes excessive attempt to eliminate the inequalities and "alienation" of capitalism. As late as the 1980s, some American economists continued to praise the Soviet Union for its supposed economic growth and efficiency—right up to the system's collapse, in fact.

When communism suddenly imploded in 1989–91, libertarians were not surprised. Communism, they had argued for years, was not only inimical to human freedom and dignity but devastatingly inefficient, and its inefficiency would only get worse over time, while the capitalist world progressed. The collapse of communism had a profound impact on the ideological landscape of the entire world: It virtually eliminated full-blown socialism as one end point of the ideological debate. It's obvious now that total statism is a total disaster, leading more and more people to wonder why a society would want to implement *some* socialism if full socialism is so catastrophic.

But what about the welfare states of the West? The remaining ideological battles may be relatively narrow, but they are still important. Shouldn't government temper the market? Aren't the welfare states more humane than libertarian states would be? Although Western Europe and the United States never tried complete socialism, such concerns did cause government control of people's economic lives to increase dramatically during the twentieth century. European governments nationalized more industries and created more state monopolies than the United States did; airlines, telephone companies, coal mines, steel manufacturers, automobile producers, and radio and television broadcasters were among the major industries that were generally private in the United States but state-owned in Western Europe. European countries also established earlier and more comprehensive "cradle-to-grave" government benefits programs.

In the United States, few industries were nationalized (the railroads Conrail and Amtrak were among the few), but regulation and restriction of economic choices grew throughout the century. And while we have not quite created a European system of "social insurance," we do have transfer payments ranging from the Women, Infants, and Children (WIC) program to Head Start to college loans to unemployment compensation and welfare to Social Security and Medicare—a pretty good start on cradle-to-grave government.

Yet today, all over the developed world, welfare states are faltering. The tax rates necessary to sustain the massive transfer programs are crippling Western economies. Dependence on government has devalued family, work, and thrift. From Germany to Sweden to Australia the promises of the welfare state can no longer be kept.

In the United States, Social Security will start running deficits by 2012—only fifteen years from now—and will be out of money by 2029. Official projections show that Medicare will be out of money as early as 2001 and will be running a deficit of $443 billion by 2006. Economists calculate that an American born in 1975 would have to pay 82 percent of his lifetime income in taxes to keep entitlement programs going, which is why young people are balking at the prospect of working most of their lives to pay for transfer programs that will eventually go bankrupt anyway. A 1994 poll found that 63 percent of Americans between eighteen and thirty-four don't believe Social Security will exist by the time they retire; more of them (46 percent) believe in UFOs than in Social Security (28 percent).

Getting out of the welfare state is going to be a tricky economic and political problem, but more and more people—in the United States and elsewhere—recognize that Western-style big government is going through a slow-motion version of communism's collapse.

Economic growth slowed down dramatically in the United States and Europe in the early 1970s. Various explanations have been offered for this phenomenon; the most compelling, I would argue, is that the burden of taxes and regulation increased substantially during the 1960s. The number of pages in the *Federal Register,* where new regulations are printed, doubled between 1957 and 1967, then tripled between 1970 and 1975. Great Britain, which had higher taxes and more socialism than the United States, suffered even more. It was the richest country in the world in the nineteenth century, but by the 1970s its economic stagnation and national malaise were known worldwide as the "British disease."

These sorts of problems led to the elections of Margaret Thatcher as prime minister of Great Britain in 1979 and Ronald Reagan as president of the United States in 1980. Thatcher and Reagan were unlike previous leaders of their respective parties. Rather than manage the welfare state a little more efficiently than the Labour and Democratic parties, they promised to roll back socialism in Britain and high taxes in the United States. Their programs were by no means consistently libertarian, but their elections did indicate that voters were growing uncomfortable with the economic burden of big government.

Unfortunately, neither Reagan nor Thatcher, despite the length of their tenure in office, did much to slow down the growth of the welfare state. Thatcher did privatize quite a few nationalized industries, including British Airways, the telephone company, public housing, and the Jaguar automobile company. But she made little headway against the middle-class entitlement state, and government spending as a percentage of GNP was not reduced. Reagan arguably accomplished even less in the economic arena. He cut income tax rates but then raised payroll taxes to preserve the cornerstone of the welfare state, Social Security. The percentage of national income going to government transfer payments kept on rising.

There was some evidence during the 1980s that a country actually had to run smack into welfare-state bankruptcy before reform would be possible. The greatest success story was not Thatcher's Britain or Reagan's America but New Zealand, whose corporatist and paternalist welfare state had run out of money. Ironically, it was the Labour Party government of Prime Minister David Lange and Finance Minister Roger Douglas that stripped away business-coddling tariffs, reduced taxes, trimmed middle-class welfare, and explored ideas like parental choice in education. According to a worldwide index of economic freedom, New Zealand soared from a dismal 4.9 out of 10 in 1985 to 9.1, the third highest rating in the world, by 1995. Chile and Argentina, two other especially profligate welfare states, also hit bottom and made major reforms in the 1990s. As in New Zealand, the reforms in Argentina came from a surprising source, President Carlos Menem of the Peronist party, which had from the 1940s to the 1970s implemented popular welfarist programs that took Argentina from one of the world's richest countries to a poor country with a bankrupt government.

## The Disillusionment with Politics

The inability of Western governments to deliver on their promises of prosperity, security, and social justice—along with the less than successful attempts at reform—has led to a profound disillusionment with the political class throughout the West. The historian Paul Johnson wrote in his book *Modern Times,*

> Disillusionment with socialism and other forms of collectivism was only one aspect of a much wider loss of faith in the state as an agency of benevolence. The state was the great gainer of the twentieth century; and the central failure. . . . Whereas, at the time of the Versailles Treaty, most intelligent people believed that an enlarged state could increase the sum total of human happiness, by the 1980s the view was held by no one outside a small, diminishing and dispirited band of zealots. The experiment had been tried in innumerable ways; and it had failed in nearly all of them. The state had proved itself an insatiable spender, an unrivalled waster. Indeed, in the twentieth century it had also proved itself the great killer of all time.

By the 1990s the political leaders in every major Western country had fallen to unprecedented lows in popularity. In the United States, it can be argued that in every presidential election since 1968 the voters have chosen the candidate who seemed to offer the greatest prospect of smaller government. Yet the largest and most complex government in history has remained virtually impervious to the public's desire for reduction of its size and power. (Note that I am certainly not claiming that the United States government is the most oppressive ever; far from it. I do think it's fair to say, however, that this government commands more resources, dispenses more favors, and promulgates more rules and regulations than any other.) By 1993 the public's dissatisfaction was starkly captured in a Gallup Poll. Gallup regularly asks people how much confidence they have in the federal government. The number has steadily fallen since the mid-1960s, with periodic ups and downs. Unsurprisingly, it reached a low in 1974, at the end of Richard

Nixon's disastrous presidency. It rose a bit and then fell even lower during the last year of Jimmy Carter's inept administration. It rose with the initial enthusiasm for Ronald Reagan's promised revolution and then resumed its fall until—remarkably—it reached an all-time low in January 1993, as Bill Clinton assumed the presidency. Never before had public confidence in government been so low at the *beginning* of a presidency. No wonder there was so little popular enthusiasm for Clinton's ambitious program of government activism: a tax increase, an economic stimulus program, national youth service, and of course his massively complicated plan to effectively nationalize medical care.

Other poll results confirmed the popular alienation from government. To the question, "Which do you favor, a smaller government with fewer services or a larger government with many services?" the percentage responding "smaller government" rose from 49 in 1984 to 60 in 1993 to 68 in 1995. (Note that the question doesn't even remind people that more services mean more taxes.) Another regular poll question asks, "How much of the time do you think you can trust the government in Washington to do what is right?" In 1964, 14 percent said "always" and 62 percent said "most of the time." By 1994, "always" had virtually disappeared, and "most of the time" was down to 14 percent. "Only some of the time" had risen from 22 percent to 73 percent, while 9 percent *volunteered* the response of "never." Given all that, it's no surprise that by mid-1995 the number of voters expressing support for creating a third party had risen to 62 percent.

Michael Ledeen of the American Enterprise Institute argues that throughout the cold war voters in the West figured they had to stick with their ruling classes to avoid a far worse fate. But in the 1990s, "the external threat having collapsed, the people are ready to reclaim control over their destiny."

Those people realize, at least intuitively, that the Age of Politics has failed to make good on its promises. They are ready for a political philosophy and a political movement that can explain why politics failed and what can replace it.

## Why Politics Fails

Much of this book will be devoted to examining the problems with coercive government, and the libertarian alternative. Here I'll offer just a brief introduction. The real problem in the United States is the same one being recognized all over the world: too much government. The bigger the government, the bigger the failure; thus state socialism was the most obvious failed policy. As libertarians warned throughout the twentieth century, socialism and other attempts to replace individual decision making with government solutions took away the freedom and dignity of the individual—the goal for which so many battles in Western civilization had been fought. Socialism also faced several insurmountable political and economic problems:

- The *totalitarian problem,* that such a concentration of power would be an irresistible temptation to abuse
- The *incentive problem,* the lack of inducement for individuals to work hard or efficiently
- The least understood, the *calculation problem,* the inability of a socialist system, without prices or markets, to allocate resources according to consumer preferences

For decades libertarian economists such as F. A. Hayek and Ludwig von Mises insisted that socialism simply couldn't work, couldn't effectively utilize all the resources and knowledge of a great society to serve consumers. And for decades social democrats in the West dismissed those claims, arguing that not only was Soviet communism surviving, its economy was growing faster than the economies of the West.

The social democrats were wrong. Although the clumsy Soviet economy could produce large quantities of low-grade steel and concrete—it practiced what the Hungarian-born philosopher Michael Polanyi called "conspicuous production"—and even put men in space, it never managed to produce anything that consumers wanted. By the late 1980s the Soviet economy was *not* two-thirds the size of the U.S. economy, as the CIA estimated; it did *not* "make full use of its manpower," as the Harvard University economist John Kenneth Galbraith said; it was *not* "a powerful engine for economic growth," as Nobel laureate

Paul Samuelson's textbook told generations of college students. It was, in fact, about 10 percent the size of the U.S. economy, as nearly as such disparate things can be compared, and it made grossly inefficient use of the educated Soviet workforce. A failure in the industrial age, it was a dinosaur in the information age, a fact obvious to everyone—except Western intellectuals—who visited the USSR.

Government intervention into society and markets in the United States suffers from the same problems, albeit in weaker form. Power always corrupts, and the power of government to tell people how to live their lives or to transfer money from those who earn it to others is always a temptation to corruption. Taxes and regulations reduce people's incentive to produce wealth, and government transfer programs reduce the incentive to work, to save, and to help family and friends in case of sickness, disability, or retirement. And though U.S. bureaucrats don't make the gross errors that socialist planners did, it is nonetheless clear that government enterprises are less efficient, less innovative, and more wasteful than private firms. Just compare the U.S. Postal Service with Federal Express. Or compare what it's like to call American Express versus the IRS to correct problems. Or compare a private apartment building with public housing. People who don't own property don't take care of it as well as owners; people who don't have their own money invested in an enterprise and won't make a profit by its success will never innovate, serve customers, and cut costs as well as profit-seeking entrepreneurs.

In his book *The Affluent Society,* Galbraith observed "private opulence and public squalor"—that is, a society in which privately owned resources were generally clean, efficient, well maintained, and improving in quality, while public spaces were dirty, overcrowded, and unsafe—and concluded, oddly enough, that we ought to move more resources into the public sector. This book suggests a different conclusion.


## Basic Political Choices

For centuries people have argued about the basic issues of politics and government. According to Aristotle, the possible political systems were tyranny, aristocracy, oligarchy, and democracy. In the middle of the twentieth century, it seemed to many that the choices were communism, fascism, and democratic capitalism. Today, all those choices have fallen from favor except democratic capitalism, and many intellectuals have embraced Francis Fukuyama's proclamation of "the end of history," meaning that the great battles over ideology have ended with the triumph of mixed-economy democracy. Even as his book appeared, however, Islamic fundamentalism was rising in one part of the world, and some Asian political leaders and intellectuals were beginning to develop a positive argument for a form of authoritarian capitalism they dubbed "Asian values."

In any case, the supposed triumph of democracy still leaves much room for contending ideologies. Even the identification of "democracy" as the Western alternative to fascism and socialism is problematic. Libertarians, as the name implies, believe that the most important political value is liberty, not democracy. Many modern readers may wonder, what's the difference? Aren't liberty and democracy the same thing? Certainly one could get that idea from the standard teaching of American history. But consider: India is the world's largest democracy, yet its commitment to free speech and pluralism is weak and its citizens are enmeshed in a web of protectionist regulations that limit their liberty at every turn. For the past several decades, Hong Kong has not been a democracy—its citizens have had no right to vote for their rulers—yet it has afforded more scope for individual choice and freedom than any other place in the world. There is a connection between liberty and democracy, but they are not identical. As my friend Ross Levatter says, if we lived in a society where everyone's spouse was chosen by majority vote of the entire community, we'd live in a democracy but we wouldn't have much liberty.

Much of the confusion stems from two different senses of the word "liberty," a distinction notably explored by the nineteenth-century French libertarian Benjamin Constant in an essay titled "The Liberty of the Ancients Compared with That of the Moderns." Constant noted that to the ancient Greek writers the idea of liberty meant the right to participate in public life, in making decisions for the entire community. Thus Athens was a free polity because all the citizens—that is, all the free, adult, Athenian men—could go to the arena and participate in the decision-making process. Socrates, indeed, was free because he could participate in the collective decision to execute him for his heretical opinions. The modern concept of liberty, however, emphasizes the right of individuals to live as they choose, to speak and worship freely, to own property, to engage in commerce, to be free from arbitrary arrest or detention—in Constant's words, "to come and go without permission, and without having to account for their motives and undertakings." A government based on the participation of the governed is a valuable safeguard for individual rights, but liberty itself is the right to make choices and to pursue projects of one's own choosing.

For libertarians, the basic political issue is the relationship of the individual to the state. What rights do individuals have (if any)? What form of government (if any) will best protect those rights? What powers should government have? What demands may individuals make on one another through the mechanism of government?

As Edward H. Crane of the Cato Institute puts it, there are only two basic ways to organize society: coercively, through government dictates, or voluntarily, through the myriad interactions among individuals and private associations. All the various political "isms"—monarchy, oligarchy, fascism, communism, conservatism, liberalism, libertarianism—boil down to a single question: Who is going to make the decision about this particular aspect of your life, you or somebody else?

Do you spend the money you earn, or does Congress?

Do you pick the school your child goes to, or does the school board?

Do you decide what drugs to take when you're sick, or does the Food and Drug Administration in Washington?

In a civil society, you make the choices about your life. In a political society, someone else makes those choices. And because people naturally resist letting others make important choices for them, the political society is of necessity based on coercion. Throughout this book we'll explore the implications of this analysis.

## Key Concepts of Libertarianism

With that background in mind, I want to spell out some of the key concepts of libertarianism, themes that will recur throughout this book. These themes have developed over many centuries. The first inklings of them can be found in ancient China, Greece, and Israel; they began to be developed into something resembling modern libertarian philosophy in the work of such seventeenth- and eighteenth-century thinkers as John Locke, David Hume, Adam Smith, Thomas Jefferson, and Thomas Paine.

*Individualism.* Libertarians see the individual as the basic unit of social analysis. Only individuals make choices and are responsible for their actions. Libertarian thought emphasizes the dignity of each individual, which entails both rights and responsibility. The progressive extension of dignity to more people—to women, to people of different religions and different races—is one of the great libertarian triumphs of the Western world.

*Individual Rights.* Because individuals are moral agents, they have a right to be secure in their life, liberty, and property. These rights are not granted by government or by society; they are inherent in the nature of human beings. It is intuitively right that individuals enjoy the security of such rights; the burden of explanation should lie with those who would take rights away.

*Spontaneous Order.* A great degree of order in society is necessary for individuals to survive and flourish. It's easy to assume that order must be imposed by a central authority, the way we impose order on a stamp collection or a football team. The great insight of libertarian social analysis is that order in society arises spontaneously, out of the actions of thousands or millions of individuals who coordinate their actions with those of others in order to achieve their purposes. Over human history, we have gradually opted for more freedom and yet managed to develop a complex society with intricate organization. The most important institutions in human society—language, law, money, and markets—all developed spontaneously, without central direction. Civil society—the complex network of associations and connections among people—is another example of spontaneous order; the associations within civil society are formed for a purpose, but civil society itself is not an organization and does not have a purpose of its own.

*The Rule of Law.* Libertarianism is not libertinism or hedonism. It is not a claim that "people can do anything they want to, and nobody else can say anything." Rather, libertarianism proposes a society of liberty under law, in which individuals are free to pursue their own lives so long as they respect the equal rights of others. The rule of law means that individuals are governed by generally applicable and spontaneously developed legal rules, not by arbitrary commands; and that those rules should protect the freedom of individuals to pursue happiness in their own ways, not aim at any particular result or outcome.

*Limited Government.* To protect rights, individuals form governments. But government is a dangerous institution. Libertarians have a great antipathy to concentrated power, for as Lord Acton said, "Power tends to corrupt and absolute power corrupts absolutely." Thus they want to divide and limit power, and that means especially to limit government, generally through a written constitution enumerating and limiting the powers that the people delegate to government. Limited government is the basic *political* implication of libertarianism, and libertarians point to the historical fact that it was the dispersion of power in Europe—more than other parts of the world—that led to individual liberty and sustained economic growth.

*Free Markets.* To survive and to flourish, individuals need to engage in economic activity. The right to property entails the right to exchange property by mutual agreement. Free markets are the economic system of free individuals, and they are necessary to create wealth. Libertarians believe that people will be both freer and more prosperous if government intervention in people's economic choices is minimized.

*The Virtue of Production.* Much of the impetus for libertarianism in the seventeenth century was a reaction against monarchs and aristocrats who lived off the productive labor of other people.

Libertarians defended the right of people to keep the fruits of their labor. This effort developed into a respect for the dignity of work and production and especially for the growing middle class, who were looked down upon by aristocrats. Libertarians developed a pre-Marxist class analysis that divided society into two basic classes: those who produced wealth and those who took it by force from others. Thomas Paine, for instance, wrote, "There are two distinct classes of men in the nation, those who pay taxes, and those who receive and live upon the taxes." Similarly, Jefferson wrote in 1824, "We have more machinery of government than is necessary, too many parasites living on the labor of the industrious." Modern libertarians defend the right of productive people to keep what they earn, against a new class of politicians and bureaucrats who would seize their earnings to transfer them to nonproducers.

*Natural Harmony of Interests.* Libertarians believe that there is a natural harmony of interests among peaceful, productive people in a just society. One person's individual plans—which may involve getting a job, starting a business, buying a house, and so on—may conflict with the plans of others, so the market makes many of us change our plans. But we all prosper from the operation of the free market, and there are no necessary conflicts between farmers and merchants, manufacturers and importers. Only when government begins to hand out rewards on the basis of political pressure do we find ourselves involved in group conflict, pushed to organize and contend with other groups for a piece of political power.

*Peace.* Libertarians have always battled the age-old scourge of war. They understood that war brought death and destruction on a grand scale, disrupted family and economic life, and put more power in the hands of the ruling class—which might explain why the rulers did not always share the popular sentiment for peace. Free men and women, of course, have often had to defend their own societies against foreign threats; but throughout history, war has usually been the common enemy of peaceful, productive people on all sides of the conflict.

These themes will be explored and developed throughout this book. It may be appropriate to acknowledge at this point the reader's likely suspicion that libertarianism seems to be just the standard framework of modern thought—individualism, private property, capitalism, equality under the law. Indeed, after centuries of intellectual, political, and sometimes violent struggle, these core libertarian principles have become the basic structure of modern political thought and of modern government, at least in the West and increasingly in other parts of the world. However, three additional points need to be made: First, libertarianism is not *just* these broad liberal principles. Libertarianism *applies* these principles fully and consistently, far more so than most modern thinkers and certainly more so than any modern government. Second, while our society remains generally based on equal rights and capitalism, every day new exceptions to those principles are carved out in Washington and in Albany, Sacramento, and Austin (not to mention London, Bonn, Tokyo, and elsewhere). Each new government directive takes a little bit of our freedom, and we should think carefully before giving up any liberty. Third, liberal society is resilient; it can withstand many burdens and continue to flourish; but it is not infinitely resilient. Those who claim to believe in liberal principles but advocate more and more confiscation of the wealth created by productive people, more and more restrictions on voluntary interaction, more and more exceptions to property rights and the rule of law, more and more transfer of power from society to state, are unwittingly engaged in the ultimately deadly undermining of civilization.

## Left or Right?

In modern American political discourse, we want to assign everyone a place along a spectrum labeled left to right, liberal to conservative. So is libertarianism left or right? Well, let's consider what those terms mean. The *American Heritage Dictionary* says that liberals favor "progress and reform," while conservatives "favor the preservation of the existing order and regard proposals for change with distrust." The *Random House Dictionary* says that people on the left advocate "liberal reform . . . usually on behalf of greater personal freedom or improved social conditions," while those on the right "advocate maintenance of the existing social, political, or economic order, sometimes by authoritarian means." Well, if those are my choices, I'll take "left." But then, by these standards, could we call, say, Ronald Reagan and Newt Gingrich conservatives? Haven't they supported significant changes in American government, which they believed would be "reform" and would "improve social conditions"? These definitions don't seem to tell us much about modern American politics.

Some political science textbooks display political ideologies along a left-right spectrum, such as this:

| Communism | Liberalism | Conservatism | Fascism |
|---|---|---|---|

But is liberalism really a mild form of communism, and conservatism a mild form of fascism? Aren't fascism and communism both totalitarian, so that they have more in common with each other than with their neighbors on the left-right spectrum?

The columnist Charles Krauthammer, trying to make sense of the words "liberal" and "conservative" around the world, suggested that we agree that the right means less government and the left means more government. His chart would look like this:

| Most Government | More Government | Less Government | Least Government |
|---|---|---|---|

But in the real world, people aren't always consistent about favoring more or less government. On Krauthammer's chart, where would you place the conservative who wants to cut taxes and censor pornography on the Internet? Or the liberal who wants to increase government regulation but repeal antigay laws?

In fact, if we look at the people in American politics who are called liberals and conservatives, we find a common pattern: liberals typically want more government intervention in our economic lives—taxes and regulation—and less government intervention in free speech and personal decisions. Conservatives typically want less government intervention in our economic lives and more intervention in issues of free speech and personal freedom. Some political scientists have suggested that those are the available options in modern America; anyone who doesn't fall into one of those categories is labeled "confused." The political scientists William S. Maddox and Stuart A. Lilie, in their book *Beyond Liberal and Conservative,* asked a simple question: Since there are two dimensions in such an approach— economic issues and personal freedoms—each with two basic positions, shouldn't we recognize four possible combinations of positions? They came up with the chart shown below.

Libertarians believe that the history of civilization is progress

|  |  | Government Intervention in Economic Affairs | |
| --- | --- | --- | --- |
|  |  | For | Against |
| Expansion of Personal Freedoms | For | Liberal | Libertarian |
|  | Against | Populist | Conservative |

toward liberty. And besides, the libertarian and "populist" ("statist" might be a better word) positions are actually more consistent than the liberal and conservative positions. So why not turn the chart to show that a consistent commitment to freedom is not just one of four choices but is in fact the pinnacle of political thought? With that reasoning, we get a chart that looks like the one on page 22.

Now we can answer the question posed a few pages back. On the contemporary American left-right spectrum, libertarianism is neither left nor right. Libertarians believe in individual freedom and limited government consistently, unlike either contemporary liberals or contemporary conservatives. Some journalists say that libertarians are conservative on economic issues and liberal on social issues, but it would make more sense to say that contemporary liberals are libertarian on (some) social issues but statist on economic issues, whereas contemporary

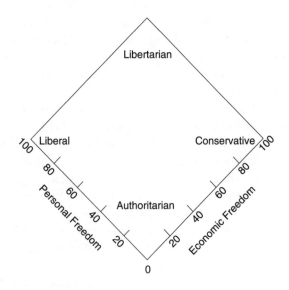

conservatives are libertarian on (some) economic issues but statist on social issues.

## A Note on Labels: Why "Libertarian"?

Some people say they don't like labels. After all, each of us is too complicated to be summed up in a word, whether it's a word like black or white, or gay or straight, or rich or poor, or an ideological term like socialist, fascist, liberal, conservative, or libertarian. But labels serve purposes; they help us to conceptualize, they economize on words, and if our beliefs are coherent and consistent, there probably is a label to describe them. In any case, if you don't label your own philosophy or movement, someone else will label it for you. (That's how the system of human creativity and progress in a free market got labeled "capitalism," a term that refers to the accumulation of money, which happens in any economy. It was capitalism's sworn enemy, Karl Marx, who gave the system its name.) So I'm willing to use the term "libertarian" to describe my political philosophy and the movement that seeks to advance it.

Why would anyone choose such an awkward term as libertarian to describe a political philosophy? It's a clunky neologism with too many syllables. It probably wouldn't be anyone's first choice. But there's a historical reason for the word.

Elements of libertarianism can be traced as far back as the ancient Chinese philosopher Lao-tzu and the higher-law concept of the Greeks and the Israelites. In seventeenth-century England, libertarian ideas began to take modern form in the writings of the Levellers and John Locke. In the middle of that century, opponents of royal power began to be called Whigs, or sometimes simply opposition or country (as opposed to court) writers.

In the 1820s the representatives of the middle class in the Spanish Cortes, or parliament, came to be called the *Liberales*. They contended with the *Serviles* (the servile ones), who represented the nobles and the absolute monarchy. The term Serviles, for those who advocate state power over individuals, unfortunately didn't stick. But the word liberal, for the defenders of liberty and the rule of law, spread rapidly. The Whig Party in England came to be called the Liberal Party. Today we know the philosophy of John Locke, Adam Smith, Thomas Jefferson, and John Stuart Mill as liberalism.

But around 1900 the term liberal underwent a change. People who supported big government and wanted to limit and control the free market started calling themselves liberals. The economist Joseph Schumpeter noted, "As a supreme, if unintended, compliment, the enemies of private enterprise have thought it wise to appropriate its label." Thus we now refer to the philosophy of individual rights, free markets, and limited government—the philosophy of Locke, Smith, and Jefferson—as classical liberalism.

But classical liberalism is not much of a name for a modern political philosophy. "Classical" sounds old, outdated, and carved in stone. (And in this era of historical illiteracy, if you call yourself a classical liberal, most people think you're an admirer of Teddy Kennedy!) Some advocates of limited government began using the name of their old adversaries, "conservative." But conservatism properly understood signifies, if not a defense of absolute monarchy and the old order, at least an unwillingness to change and a desire to preserve the status quo. It would be odd to refer to free-market capitalism—the most progressive, dynamic, and ever-changing system the world has ever known—as conservative. Edward H. Crane has proposed that today's heirs of Locke and Smith call themselves "market liberals," retaining the word liberal, with its etymological connection with liberty, but reaffirming the liberal commitment to markets. That term has been well received by market-liberal intellectuals, but it seems unlikely to catch on with journalists and the public.

The right term for the advocates of civil society and free markets is arguably *socialist.* Thomas Paine distinguished between society and government, and the libertarian writer Albert Jay Nock summed up all the things that people do voluntarily—for love or charity or profit—as "social power," which is always being threatened by the encroachment of state power. So we might say that those who advocate social power are socialists, while those who support state power are statists. But alas, the word socialist, like the word liberal, has been claimed by those who advocate neither civil society nor liberty.

In much of the world, the advocates of liberty are still called liberals. In South Africa the liberals, such as Helen Suzman, rejected the system of racism and economic privilege known as apartheid in favor of human rights, nonracial policies, and free markets. In Iran liberals oppose the theocratic state and press for Western-style "democratic capitalism." In China and Russia liberals are those who want to replace totalitarianism in all its aspects with the classical liberal system of free markets and constitutional government. Even in Western Europe, liberal still indicates at least a fuzzy version of classical liberalism. German liberals, for instance, usually to be found in the Free Democratic Party, oppose the socialism of the Social Democrats, the corporatism of the Christian Democrats, and the paternalism of both. Outside the United States, even American journalists understand the traditional meaning of liberal. In 1992, a *Washington Post* story datelined Moscow reported that "liberal economists have criticized the government for failing to move quickly enough with structural reforms and for allowing money-losing state factories to continue churning out goods that nobody needs." Liberal economists such as Milton Friedman make similar criticisms in the United States, but then the *Post* calls them conservative economists.

Here at home, though, by the 1940s the word liberal had clearly been lost to the advocates of big government. Some classical liberals resisted for a time, doggedly insisting that *they* were the true liberals and that the so-called liberals in Washington were in fact recreating the old order of state power that liberals had fought to overthrow. But others resigned themselves to finding a new term. In the 1950s Leonard Read, founder of the Foundation for Economic Education, began calling himself a libertarian. That word had long been used for the advocates of free will (as opposed to determinism); and, like liberal, it was derived from the Latin *liber* (free). The name was gradually embraced by a growing band of libertarians in the 1960s and 1970s. A Libertarian Party was formed in 1972. The term was still rejected by some of the greatest twentieth-century libertarians, including Ayn Rand, who called herself a "radical for capitalism," and Friedrich Hayek, who continued to call himself a liberal or an Old Whig.

In this book I accept the contemporary usage. I call the ideas I advocate, and the movement that seeks to advance them, libertarianism. Libertarianism may be regarded as a political philosophy that applies the ideas of classical liberalism consistently, following liberal arguments to conclusions that would limit the role of government more strictly and protect individual freedom more fully than other classical liberals would. Most of the time, I use liberal in its traditional sense; I call today's misnamed liberals welfare-state liberals or social democrats. And I should note that libertarian ideas and the libertarian movement are far broader than any political party, such as the Libertarian Party. References to libertarianism should not be taken to indicate the Libertarian Party unless that is made explicit.

The old ideologies have been tried and found wanting. All around us—from the postcommunist world to the military dictatorships of Africa to the faltering, bankrupt welfare states of Europe and North and South America—we see the failed legacy of coercion and statism. At the same time we see moves toward libertarian solutions—constitutional government in

Eastern Europe and South Africa, privatization in Britain and Latin America, democracy and the rule of law in Korea and Taiwan, and demands for tax reduction everywhere. We even see people in many parts of the world—Quebec, Croatia, Bosnia, northern Italy, Scotland, and much of Africa, not to mention the fifteen new republics of the old Soviet Union—challenging the large, intrusive, incorrigible nation-states that they find themselves in and demanding devolution of power. Libertarianism offers an alternative to coercive government that should appeal to peaceful, productive people everywhere.

No, a libertarian world won't be a perfect one. There will still be inequality, poverty, crime, corruption, man's inhumanity to man. But unlike the theocratic visionaries, the pie-in-the-sky socialist utopians, or the starry-eyed Mr. Fixits of the New Deal and Great Society, libertarians don't promise you a rose garden. Karl Popper once said that attempts to create heaven on earth invariably produce hell. Libertarianism holds out the goal not of a perfect society but of a better and freer one. It promises a world in which more of the decisions will be made in the right way by the right person: you. The result will be not an end to crime and poverty and inequality but less—often much less—of most of those things most of the time.

*Chapter 2*

# THE ROOTS OF LIBERTARIANISM

*I*n a sense there have always been but two political philosophies: liberty and power. Either people should be free to live their lives as they see fit, as long as they respect the equal rights of others, or some people should be able to use force to make other people act in ways they wouldn't choose. It's no surprise, of course, that the philosophy of power has always been more appealing to those in power. It has gone by many names—Caesarism, Oriental despotism, theocracy, socialism, fascism, communism, monarchism, ujamaa, welfare-statism—and the arguments for each of these systems have been different enough to conceal the essential similarity. The philosophy of liberty has also gone by different names, but its defenders have always had a common thread of respect for the individual, confidence in the ability of ordinary people to make wise decisions about their own lives, and hostility to those who would use violence to get what they want.

The first known libertarian may have been the Chinese philosopher Lao-tzu, who lived around the sixth century B.C. and is best known as the author of the *Tao Te Ching*. Lao-tzu advised, "Without law or compulsion, men would dwell in harmony." The Tao is a classic statement of the spiritual serenity associated with Eastern philosophy. The Tao consists of yin and yang; that is, it is the unity of opposites. It anticipates the theory of spontaneous order by teaching that harmony can be achieved through competition. And it advises the ruler not to interfere in the lives of the people.

Despite the example of Lao-tzu, libertarianism really arose in the West. Does that make it a narrowly Western idea? I don't think so. The principles of liberty and individual rights are universal, just as the principles of science are universal, even though most of the discovery of those scientific principles took place in the West.

## The Prehistory of Libertarianism

Both the two main lines of Western thought, the Greek and the Judeo-Christian, contributed to the development of freedom. According to the Old Testament, the people of Israel lived without a king or any other coercive authority, governing themselves not by force but by their mutual adherence to their covenant with God. Then, as recorded in the First Book of Samuel, the Jews went to Samuel and said, "Make us a king to judge us like all the other nations." But when Samuel prayed to God about their request, God said,

> This will be the manner of the king that shall reign over you: He will take your sons, for his chariots. And he will take your daughters, to be cooks. And he will take your fields, and your oliveyards, and give them to his servants. And he will take the tenth of your seed, and of your vineyards, and of your sheep. And ye shall be his servants.
>
> And ye shall cry out in that day because of your king which ye shall have chosen, and the Lord will not hear you in that day.

Although the people of Israel defied this awful warning and created a monarchy, the story served as a constant reminder that the origins of the state were by no means divinely inspired. God's warning resonated not just in ancient Israel but on down to modern times. Thomas Paine cited it in *Common Sense* to remind Americans that "the few good kings" in the 3,000 years since Samuel could not "blot out the sinfulness of the origin" of monarchy. The great historian of liberty, Lord Acton, assuming that all nineteenth-century British readers were familiar with it, referred casually to Samuel's "momentous protestation."

Although they installed a king, the Jews may have been the first people to develop the idea that the king was subordinate to a higher law. In other civilizations, the king *was* the law, generally because he was considered divine. But the Jews said to the Egyptian Pharaoh, and to their own kings, that a king is still just a man, and every man is judged by God's law.

## Natural Law

That concept of a higher law also developed in ancient Greece. The playwright Sophocles, in the fifth century B.C., told the story of Antigone, whose brother Polyneices had attacked the city of Thebes and been killed in battle. For his treason the tyrant Creon ordered that his body be left to rot outside the gates, unburied and unmourned. Antigone defied Creon and buried her brother. Brought before Creon, she declared that a law made by a mere man, even a king, could not override "the gods' unwritten and unfailing laws," which had existed longer than anyone could say.

The notion of a law by which even rulers could be judged endured and grew throughout European civilization. It was developed in the Roman world by the Stoic philosophers, who argued that even if the ruler is the people, they still may do only what is just according to natural law. The enduring power of this Stoic idea in the West was partly due to a happy accident: The Stoic lawyer Cicero was regarded in later years as the greatest writer of Latin prose, so his essays were read by educated Europeans for many centuries.

Shortly after Cicero's time, in a famous encounter, Jesus was asked whether his followers should pay taxes. "Render unto Caesar the things that are Caesar's and unto God the things that are God's," he replied. In so doing he divided the world into two realms, making it clear that not all of life is under the control of the state. This radical notion took hold in Western Christianity, though not in the Eastern Church, which was totally dominated by the state, leaving no space in society where alternative sources of power might develop.

*Pluralism*

The independence of the Western Church, which came to be known as Roman Catholic, meant that throughout Europe there were two powerful institutions contending for power. Neither state nor church particularly liked the situation, but their divided power gave breathing space for individuals and civil society to develop. Popes and emperors frequently denounced each other's character, contributing to a delegitimation of both. Again, this conflict between church and state was virtually unique in the world, which helps to explain why the principles of freedom were discovered first in the West.

In the fourth century the emperor Theodosius ordered the bishop of Milan, St. Ambrose, to hand over his cathedral to the empire. Ambrose rebuked the emperor, saying,

> It is not lawful for us to deliver it up nor for your majesty to receive it. By no law can you violate the house of a private man. Do you think that the house of God may be taken away? It is asserted that all things are lawful to the emperor, that all things are his. But do not burden your conscience with the thought that you have any right as emperor over sacred things. Exalt not yourself, but if you would reign the longer be subject to God. It is written, God's to God and Caesar's to Caesar.

The emperor was forced to come to Ambrose's church and beg forgiveness for his wrongdoing.

Centuries later a similar conflict took place in England. The archbishop of Canterbury, Thomas à Becket, defended the church's rights against Henry II's usurpations. Henry wished aloud that he could be rid of "this meddlesome priest," whereupon four knights rode off to murder Becket. Within four years Becket had been made a saint, and Henry had been forced to walk barefoot through the snow to Becket's church as penance for his crime and to back down from his demands on the church.

Because the struggle between church and state prevented any absolute power from arising, there was room for autonomous institutions to develop, and because the church lacked absolute power, dissident religious views were able to ferment. Markets and associations, oath-bound relationships, guilds, universities, and chartered cities all contributed to the development of pluralism and civil society.

## Religious Toleration

Libertarianism is often seen as primarily a philosophy of economic freedom, but its real historical roots lie more in the struggle for religious toleration. Early Christians began to develop theories of toleration to counter their persecution by the Roman state. One of the earliest was Tertullian, a Carthaginian known as "the Father of Latin theology," who wrote around A.D. 200,

> It is a fundamental human right, a privilege of nature, that every man should worship according to his own convictions. One man's religion neither harms nor helps another man. It is assuredly no part of religion to compel religion, to which free will and not force should lead us.

Already the case for freedom is being made in terms of fundamental, or natural, rights.

The growth of trade, of varying religious interpretations, and of civil society meant that there were more sources of influence within each community, and that pluralism led to demands for formal limitations on government. In one remarkable decade there were major steps toward limited, representative government in three widely dispersed parts of Europe. The most famous, at least in the United States, took place in England in 1215, when the barons confronted King John at Runnymede and forced him to sign Magna Carta, or the Great Charter, which guaranteed every free man security from illegal interference in his person or property and justice to everyone. The king's ability to raise revenue was limited, the church was guaranteed a degree of freedom, and liberties of the boroughs were confirmed.

Meanwhile, around 1220 the German town of Magdeburg developed a set of laws that emphasized freedom and self-government. Magdeburg law was so widely respected that it was adopted by hundreds of the newly forming towns all over central Europe, and legal cases in some central-eastern European towns were referred to Magdeburg judges. Finally, in 1222 the lesser nobles and gentry of Hungary—then very much a part of the European mainstream—forced King Andrew II to sign the Golden Bull, which exempted the gentry and clergy from taxation, granted them freedom to dispose of their domains as they saw fit, protected them from arbitrary imprisonment and confiscation, assured them an annual assembly to present grievances, and even gave them the *Jus Resistendi,* the right to resist the king if he attacked the liberties and privileges of the Golden Bull.

The principles found in these documents were far from full-fledged libertarianism; they still excluded many people from their guarantees of liberties, and both Magna Carta and the Golden Bull explicitly discriminated against Jews. Still, they are milestones in a continuing advance toward liberty, limited government, and the expansion of the concept of personhood to include all individuals. They demonstrated that people all over Europe were thinking about concepts of freedom, and they created classes of people jealous to defend their liberties.

Later in the thirteenth century, St. Thomas Aquinas, who was perhaps the greatest of all Catholic theologians, and other philosophers developed the theological argument for limits on royal power. Aquinas wrote, "A king who is unfaithful to his duty forfeits his claim to obedience. It is not rebellion to depose him, for he is himself a rebel whom the nation has a right to put down. But it is better to abridge his power, that he may be unable to abuse it." Thus was theological authority put behind the idea that tyrants could be deposed. Both John of Salisbury, an English bishop who witnessed Becket's murder in the twelfth century, and Roger Bacon, a thirteenth-century scholar—whom Lord Acton describes as the most distinguished English writers of their respective epochs—defended even the right to kill tyrants, an argument unimaginable virtually anywhere else in the world.

The sixteenth-century Spanish Scholastic thinkers, sometimes known as the school of Salamanca, built on the work of Aquinas to explore theology, natural law, and economics. They anticipated many of the themes later found in the works of Adam Smith and the Austrian School. From his post at the University of Salamanca, Francisco de Vitoria condemned the Spanish enslavement of the Indians in the New World in terms of individualism and natural rights: "Every Indian is a man and thus capable of achieving salvation or damnation. . . . Inasmuch as he is a person, every Indian has free will and, consequently, is the master of his actions. . . . Every man has the right to his own life and to physical and mental integrity." Vitoria and his colleagues also developed natural-law doctrine in such areas as private property, profits, interest, and taxation; their works influenced Hugo Grotius, Samuel Pufendorf, and through them Adam Smith and his Scottish associates.

The prehistory of libertarianism culminates in the period of the Renaissance and the Protestant Reformation. The rediscovery of classical learning and the humanism that marked the Renaissance are usually regarded as the emergence of the modern world after the Middle Ages. With a novelist's passion, Ayn Rand summed up one view of the Renaissance, that of the rationalist, individualist, secular strain of liberalism:

> The Middle Ages were an era of mysticism, ruled by blind faith and blind obedience to the dogma that faith is superior to reason. The Renaissance was specifically the *rebirth of reason,* the liberation of man's mind, the triumph of *rationality* over mysticism—a faltering, incomplete, but impassioned triumph that led to the birth of science, of individualism, of freedom.

However, the historian Ralph Raico argues that the Renaissance can be overrated as a progenitor of liberalism; the medieval charters of rights and independent legal institutions provided a more secure footing for freedom than the Promethean individualism of the Renaissance.

The Reformation contributed more to the development of liberal ideas. The Protestant reformers, such as Martin Luther and John Calvin, were by no means liberals. But by breaking the monopoly of the Catholic Church they inadvertently encouraged a proliferation of Protestant sects, some of which—such as the Quakers and Baptists—did nurture liberal thought. After the Wars of Religion people began to question the notion that a community had to have only one religion. It had been thought that without a single religious and moral authority, a community would witness an endless proliferation of moral commitments and literally fall to pieces. That profoundly con-servative idea has a long history. It goes back at least to Plato's insistence on regulating even the music in an ideal society. It has been enunciated in our own time by the socialist writer Robert Heilbroner, who says that socialism requires "a deliber-ately embraced collective moral goal" to which "every dissent-ing voice raises a threat." And it can also be heard in the fears of the residents of rural Catlett, Virginia, who told the *Washington Post* about their worries when a Buddhist temple was built in their small town: "We believe in one true God, and I guess we were afraid with a false religion like that, maybe it would have an influence on our children." Fortunately, most people noticed after the Reformation that society did *not* fall apart in the pres-ence of differing religious and moral views. Instead it became stronger by accommodating diversity and competition.

## The Response to Absolutism

By the end of the sixteenth century the church, weakened by its own corruption and by the Reformation, needed the support of the state more than the state needed the church. The church's weakness created an opening for the rise of royal absolutism, seen especially in the reigns of Louis XIV in France and the Stu-art kings in England. Monarchs began to set up their own bu-reaucracies, impose new taxes, establish standing armies, and make increasing claims for their own power. Drawing on the work of Copernicus, who proved that the planets revolve around the sun, Louis XIV called himself the Sun King because he was the center of life in France, and he famously declared, *"L'état, c'est moi"* ("I am the state"). He banned Protestantism and tried to make himself head of the Catholic Church in France. During his reign of almost seventy years, he never called a session of the representative assembly, the estates-gen-eral. His finance minister implemented a policy of mercantil-ism, under which the state would supervise, guide, plan, design, and monitor the economy—subsidizing, prohibiting, granting monopolies, nationalizing, setting wages and prices, and ensur-ing quality.

In England the Stuart kings also tried to institute absolute rule. They sought to ignore the common law and to raise taxes without the approval of England's representative assembly, Parliament. But civil society and the authority of Parliament proved more durable in England than on the Continent, and the Stuarts' absolutist campaign was stymied within forty years of James I's accession to the throne. The resistance to absolutism culminated in the beheading of James's son, Charles I, in 1649.

Meanwhile, as absolutism took root in France and Spain, the Netherlands became a beacon of religious toleration, commercial freedom, and limited central government. After the Dutch gained their independence from Spain in the early seventeenth century, they created a loose confederation of cities and provinces, becoming the century's leading commercial power and a haven for refugees from oppression. Books and pamphlets by dissident Englishmen and Frenchmen were often published in Dutch cities. One of those refugees, the philosopher Baruch Spinoza, whose Jewish parents had fled Catholic persecution in Portugal, described in his *Theologico-Political Treatise* the happy interplay of religious toleration and prosperity in seventeenth-century Amsterdam:

> The city of Amsterdam reaps the fruit of freedom in its own great prosperity and in the admiration of all other people. For in this most flourishing state, and most splendid city, men of every nation and religion live together in the greatest harmony, and ask no questions before trusting their goods to a fellow-citizen. A citizen's religion and sect is considered of no importance: for it has no effect before the judges in gaining or losing a cause, and there is no sect so despised that its followers, provided that they harm no one, pay every man his due, and live uprightly, are deprived of the protection of the magisterial authority.

Holland's example of social harmony and economic progress inspired protoliberals in England and other countries.

## The English Revolution

English opposition to royal absolutism created a great deal of intellectual ferment, and the first stirrings of clearly protoliberal ideas can be seen in seventeenth-century England. Again, liberal ideas developed out of the defense of religious toleration. In 1644 John Milton published *Areopagitica,* a powerful argument for freedom of religion and against official licensing of the press. Of the relationship between freedom and virtue, an issue that vexes American politics to this day, Milton wrote, "Liberty is the best school of virtue." Virtue, he said, is only virtuous if chosen freely. On freedom of speech, he wrote, "Who ever knew Truth put to the worse in a free and open encounter?"

During the interregnum, the time after the beheading of Charles I when England was between kings and under the rule of Oliver Cromwell, there was tremendous intellectual debate. A group known as the Levellers began enunciating the full set of ideas that would come to be known as liberalism. They placed the defense of religious liberty and the ancient rights of Englishmen in a context of self-ownership and natural rights. In a famous essay, "An Arrow against All Tyrants," the Leveller leader Richard Overton argued that every individual has a "self-propriety"; that is, everyone owns himself and thus has rights to life, liberty, and property. "No man hath power over my rights and liberties, and I over no man's."

Despite the efforts of the Levellers and other radicals, the Stuart dynasty returned to the throne in 1660, in the person of Charles II. Charles promised to respect liberty of conscience and the rights of landowners, but he and his brother, James II, again tried to extend royal power. In the Glorious Revolution of 1688, Parliament offered the crown to William and Mary of Holland (both grandchildren of Charles I). William and Mary agreed to respect the "true, ancient, and indubitable rights" of Englishmen, as put down in the Bill of Rights in 1689.

We can date the birth of liberalism to the time of the Glorious Revolution. John Locke is rightly seen as the first real liberal and as the father of modern political philosophy. If you don't know the ideas of Locke, you really can't understand the world we live in. Locke's great work *The Second Treatise of Government* was published in 1690, but it had been written a few years earlier, to refute the absolutist philosopher Sir Robert Filmer, making its defense of individual rights and representative government that much more radical. Locke asked, what is the point of government? Why do we have it? He answered, people have rights prior to the existence of government—thus we call them natural rights, because they exist in nature. People form a government to protect their rights. They could do that without government, but a government is an efficient system for protecting rights. And if government exceeds that role, people are justified in revolting. Representative government is the best way to ensure that government sticks to its proper purpose. Echoing a philosophical tradition that had been entrenched in the West for centuries, he wrote, "A Government is not free to do as it pleases. . . . The law of nature stands as an eternal rule to all men, legislators as well as others."

Locke also articulated clearly the idea of property rights:

> Every Man has a *Property* in his own *Person*. This no Body has any Right to but himself. The *Labour* of his Body, and the *Work* of his Hands, we may say, are properly his. Whatsoever then he removes out of the State that Nature hath provided, and left it in, he hath mixed his *Labour* with, and joyned to it something that is his own, and thereby makes it his *Property*.

People have an inalienable right to life and liberty, and they acquire a right to previously unowned property that they "mix their labor with," such as by farming. It is the role of government to protect the "Lives, Liberties, and Estates" of the people.

These ideas were enthusiastically received. Europe was still in the grip of royal absolutism, but thanks to their experience with the Stuarts, the English were suspicious of all forms of government. They warmly embraced this powerful philosophical defense of natural rights, the rule of law, and the right of revolution. They also, of course, began carrying the ideas of Locke and the Levellers on ships bound for the New World.

## The Liberal Eighteenth Century

England prospered under limited government. As Holland had inspired liberals a century earlier, the English model began to be cited by liberal thinkers on the Continent and eventually around the world. We might date the Enlightenment from roughly 1720, when the French writer Voltaire fled from French tyranny and arrived in England. He saw religious toleration, representative government, and a prosperous middle class. He noticed that trade was more respected than it was in France, where aristocrats looked down their noses at those involved in commerce. He also noticed that when you allow people to trade freely, their prejudices may take second place to self-interest, as in his famous description of the stock exchange in his *Letters on England:*

> Go into the London Stock Exchange—a more respectable place than many a court—and you will see representatives of all nations gathered there for the service of mankind. There the Jew, the Mohammedan, and the Christian deal with each other as if they were of the same religion, and give the name of infidel only to those who go bankrupt. There the Presbyterian trusts the Anabaptist, and the Anglican accepts the Quaker's promise. On leaving these peaceful and free assemblies, some go to the synagogue, others go to drink . . . others go to their church to wait the inspiration of God, their hats on their heads, and all are content.

The eighteenth century was the great century of liberal thought. Locke's ideas were developed by many writers, notably John Trenchard and Thomas Gordon, who wrote a series of newspaper essays signed "Cato," after Cato the Younger, the defender of the Roman Republic against Julius Caesar's quest for power. These essays, which denounced the government for continuing to infringe upon the rights of Englishmen, came to be known as *Cato's Letters.* (Names reminiscent of the Roman Republic were popular with eighteenth-century writers; compare the *Federalist Papers,* which were signed "Publius.") In France the Physiocrats developed the modern science of economics. Their name came from the Greek *physis* (nature) and *kratos* (rule); they argued for the rule of nature, by which they meant that natural laws similar to those of physics governed society and the creation of wealth. The best way to increase the supply of real goods was to allow free commerce, unhindered by monopolies, guild restrictions, and high taxes. The absence of coercive constraints would produce harmony and abundance. It is from this period that the famous libertarian rallying cry "laissez faire" comes. According to legend, Louis XV asked a group of merchants, "How can I help you?" They responded, *"Laissez-nous faire, laissez-nous passer. Le monde va de lui-même."* ("Let us do, leave us alone. The world runs by itself.")

The leading Physiocrats included François Quesnay and Pierre Du Pont de Nemours, who fled the French Revolution and came to America, where his son founded a small business in Delaware. An associate of the Physiocrats, A. R. J. Turgot, was a great economist who was named finance minister by Louis XVI, an "enlightened despot" who wanted to ease the burden of government on the French people—and perhaps create more wealth to be taxed, since, as the Physiocrats had pointed out, "poor peasants, poor kingdom; poor kingdom, poor king." Turgot issued the Six Edicts to abolish the guilds (which had become calcified monopolies), abolish internal taxes and forced labor (the *corvée*), and establish toleration for Protestants. He ran into stiff resistance from the vested interests, and he was dismissed in 1776. With him, says Raico, "went the last hope for the French monarchy," which indeed fell to revolution thirteen years later.

The French Enlightenment is better known to history, but there was an important Scottish Enlightenment as well. Scots had long resented English domination, they had suffered greatly under British mercantilism, and they had within the past century achieved a higher literacy rate and better schools than had the English. They were well suited to develop liberal ideas (and to dominate English intellectual life for a century). Among the scholars of the Scottish Enlightenment were Adam Ferguson, author of *Essay on the History of Civil Society,* who coined the phrase "the result of human action but not of human design," which would inspire future scholars of spontaneous order; Francis Hutcheson, who anticipated the utilitarians with his notion of "the greatest good for the greatest number"; and Dugald Stewart, whose *Philosophy of the Human Mind* was widely read in early American universities. But the most prominent were David Hume and his friend Adam Smith.

Hume was a philosopher, an economist, and a historian, in the days before the university aristocracy decreed that knowledge must be divided into discrete categories. He is best known to contemporary students for his philosophical skepticism, but he also helped to develop our modern understanding of the productiveness and benevolence of the free market. He defended property and contract, free-market banking, and the spontaneous order of a free society. Arguing against the balance-of-trade doctrine of the mercantilists, he pointed out that everyone benefits from the prosperity of others, even the prosperity of people in other countries.

Along with John Locke, Adam Smith was the other father of liberalism, or what we now call libertarianism. And since we live in a liberal world, Locke and Smith may be seen as the architects of the modern world. In *The Theory of Moral Sentiments,* Smith distinguished between two kinds of behavior, self-interest and beneficence. Many critics say that Adam Smith, or economists generally, or libertarians, believe that all behavior is motivated by self-interest. In his first great book, Smith made clear that that wasn't the case. Of course people sometimes act out of benevolence, and society should encourage such sentiments. But, he said, if necessary, society could exist without beneficence extending beyond the family. People would still get fed, the economy would still function, knowledge would progress; but society cannot exist without justice, which means the protection of the rights of life, liberty, and property. Justice, therefore, must be the first concern of the state.

In his better-known book, *The Wealth of Nations,* Smith laid the groundwork for the modern science of economics. He said that he was describing "the simple system of natural liberty." In the modern vernacular, we might say that capitalism is what happens when you leave people alone. Smith showed how, when people produce and trade in their own self-interest, they are led "by an invisible hand" to benefit others. To get a job, or to sell something for money, each person must figure out what others would like to have. Benevolence is important, but "it is not from the benevolence of the butcher, the brewer, or the baker, that we expect our dinner, but from their regard to their own interest." Thus the free market allows more people to satisfy more of their desires, and ultimately to enjoy a higher standard of living, than any other social system.

Smith's most important contribution to libertarian theory was to develop the idea of spontaneous order. We frequently hear that there is a conflict between freedom and order, and such a perspective seems logical. But, more completely than the Physiocrats and other earlier thinkers, Smith stressed that order in human affairs arises spontaneously. Let people interact freely with each other, protect their rights to liberty and property, and order will emerge without central direction. The market economy is one form of spontaneous order; hundreds or thousands—or today, billions—of people enter the marketplace or the business world every day wondering how they can produce more goods or get a better job or make more money for themselves and their families. They are not guided by any central authority, nor by the biological instinct that drives bees to make honey, yet they produce wealth for themselves and others by producing and trading.

The market is not the only form of spontaneous order. Consider language. No one sat down to write the English language and then teach it to early Englishmen. It arose and changed naturally, spontaneously, in response to human needs. Consider also law. Today we think of laws as something passed by Congress, but the common law grew up long before any king or legislature sought to write it down. When two people had a dispute, they asked another to serve as a judge. Sometimes juries were assembled to hear a case. Judges and juries were not supposed to "make" the law; rather, they sought to "find" the law, to ask what the customary practice was or what had been decided in similar cases. Thus, in case after case the legal order developed. Money is another product of spontaneous order; it arose naturally when people needed something to facilitate trade. Hayek wrote that "if [law] had been deliberately designed, it would deserve to rank among the greatest of human inventions. But it has, of course, been as little invented by any one mind as language or money or most of the practices and conventions on which social life rests." Law, language, money, markets—the most important institutions in human society— arose spontaneously.

With Smith's systematic elaboration of the principle of spontaneous order, the basic principles of liberalism were essentially complete. We might define those basic principles as the idea of a higher law or natural law, the dignity of the individual, natural rights to liberty and property, and the social theory of spontaneous order. Many more specific ideas flow from these fundamentals: individual freedom, limited and representative government, free markets. It had taken a long time to define them; it was still necessary to fight for them.

## Making a Liberal World

Like the English Revolution, the period leading up to the American Revolution was one of great ideological debate. Even more than the seventeenth-century English world, eighteenth-century America was dominated by liberal ideas. Indeed, we might say that there were virtually no nonliberal ideas circulating in America; there were only conservative liberals, who urged that Americans continue to peacefully petition for their rights as Englishmen, and radical liberals, who eventually rejected even a constitutional monarchy and called for independence. The most galvanizing of the radical liberals was Thomas Paine. Paine was what we might call an outside agitator, a traveling missionary of liberty. Born in England, he went to America to help make a revolution, and when his task was done, he crossed the Atlantic again to help the French with their revolution.

### Society versus Government

Paine's great contribution to the revolutionary cause was his pamphlet *Common Sense,* which is said to have sold some 100,000 copies within a few months, in a country of three million people. Everyone read it; those who could not read heard it read in taverns and participated in debating its ideas. *Common Sense* was not just a call for independence. It offered a radically libertarian theory to justify natural rights and independence. Paine began by making a distinction between society and government: "Society is produced by our wants, and government by our wickedness. . . . Society in every state is a blessing, but government even in its best state is but a necessary evil; in its worst state an intolerable one." He went on to denounce the origins of monarchy: "Could we take off the dark covering of antiquity . . . we should find the first [king] nothing better than the principal ruffian of some restless gang, whose savage manners or pre-eminence in subtlety obtained him the title of chief among plunderers."

In *Common Sense* and in his later writings, Paine developed the idea that civil society exists prior to government and that people can peacefully interact to create spontaneous order. His belief in spontaneous order was strengthened when he saw society continue to function after the colonial governments were kicked out of American cities and colonies. In his writings he neatly fused the normative theory of individual rights with the positive analysis of spontaneous order.

Neither *Common Sense* nor *The Wealth of Nations* was the only milestone in the struggle for liberty in 1776. Neither may even have been the most important event in that banner year. For in 1776 the American colonies issued their Declaration of Independence, probably the finest piece of libertarian writing in history. Thomas Jefferson's eloquent words proclaimed to all the world the liberal vision:

> We hold these truths to be self-evident, that all men are created equal, that they are endowed by their Creator with certain unalienable Rights, that among these are life, liberty, and the pursuit of happiness. That to secure these rights, governments are instituted among men, deriving their just powers from the consent of the governed. That whenever any form of government becomes destructive of these ends, it is the right of the people to alter or abolish it.

The influence of the Levellers and John Locke is obvious. Jefferson succinctly made three points: that people have natural rights; that the purpose of government is to protect those rights; and that if government exceeds its proper purpose, people have the right "to alter or abolish it." For his eloquence in stating the liberal case, and for his lifelong role in the liberal revolution that changed the world, the columnist George F. Will named Jefferson "the man of the millennium." Far be it from me to argue with that choice. But it should be noted that in writing the Declaration of Independence, Jefferson did not break much new ground. John Adams, perhaps resentful of the attention Jefferson got, said years later that "there is not an idea in [the Declaration] but what had been hackneyed in Congress for two years before." Jefferson himself said that while he "turned to neither book nor pamphlet in writing it," his goal was "not to find out new principles, or new arguments," but merely to produce "an expression of the American mind." The ideas in the Declaration were, he said, the "sentiments of the day, whether expressed in conversation, in letters, printed essays, or the elementary books of public right." The triumph of liberal ideas in the United States was overwhelming.

## Limiting Government

After their military victory, the independent Americans set about putting into practice the ideas that English liberals had been developing throughout the eighteenth century. The distinguished Harvard University historian Bernard Bailyn writes in his 1973 essay "The Central Themes of the American Revolution" that

> the major themes of eighteenth-century radical libertarianism [were] brought to realization here. The first is the belief that power is evil, a necessity perhaps but an evil necessity; that it is infinitely corrupting; and that it must be controlled, limited, restricted in every way compatible with a minimum of civil order. Written constitutions; the separation of powers; bills of rights; limitations on executives, on legislatures, and courts; restrictions on the right to coerce and wage war—all express the profound distrust of power that lies at the ideological heart of the American Revolution and that has remained with us as a permanent legacy ever after.

The Constitution of the United States built on the ideas of the Declaration to establish a government suitable for free people. It was based on the principle that individuals have natural rights that precede the establishment of government and that all the power a government has is delegated to it by individuals for the protection of their rights. Based on that understanding, the Framers did not set up a monarchy, nor did they create an unlimited democracy, a government of plenary powers limited only by popular vote. Instead, they carefully enumerated (in Article I, Section 8) the powers that the federal government would have. The Constitution, whose greatest theorist and architect was Jefferson's friend and neighbor James Madison, was truly revolutionary in its establishment of a government of *delegated, enumerated,* and thus *limited* powers.

When a Bill of Rights was first proposed, many of the Framers responded that one was not needed because the enumerated powers were so limited that government would be unable to infringe on individual rights. Eventually, it was decided to add a Bill of Rights, in Madison's words, "for greater caution." After enumerating specific rights in the first eight amendments, the first Congress added two more that summarize the whole structure of the federal government as it was created: The Ninth Amendment provides that "the enumeration in the Constitution of certain rights shall not be construed to deny or disparage others retained by the people." The Tenth Amendment says, "The powers not delegated to the United States by the Constitution, nor prohibited by it to the States, are reserved to the States respectively or to the people." Again, the fundamental tenets of liberalism: People have rights before they create government, and they retain all the rights they haven't expressly delegated to government; and the national government has no powers not specifically granted in the Constitution.

In both the United States and Europe, the century after the American Revolution was marked by the spread of liberalism. Written constitutions and bills of rights protected liberty and guaranteed the rule of law. Guilds and monopolies were largely eliminated, with all trades thrown open to competition on the basis of merit. Freedom of the press and of religion was greatly expanded, property rights were made more secure, international trade was freed.

## Civil Rights

Individualism, natural rights, and free markets led logically to agitation for the extension of civil and political rights to those who had been excluded from liberty, as they were from power—notably slaves, serfs, and women. The world's first antislavery society was founded in Philadelphia in 1775, and slavery and serfdom were abolished throughout the Western world within a century. During the debate in the British Parliament over the idea of compensating slaveholders for the loss of their "property," the libertarian Benjamin Pearson replied that he had "thought it was the slaves who should have been compensated." Tom Paine's *Pennsylvania Journal* published a stirring early defense of women's rights in 1775. Mary Wollstonecraft, a friend of Paine and other liberals, published *A Vindication of the Rights of Woman* in England in 1792. The first feminist convention in the United States took place in 1848, as women began to demand the natural rights that white men had claimed in 1776 and that were being demanded for black men. In the phrase of the English historian Henry Sumner Maine, the world was moving from a society of status to a society of contract.

Liberals also took on the ever-present specter of war. In England, Richard Cobden and John Bright tirelessly argued that free trade would bind people of different nations together peacefully, reducing the likelihood of war. The new limits on governments, and greater public skepticism toward rulers, made it more difficult for political leaders to meddle abroad and to go to war. After the turmoil of the French Revolution and the final defeat of Napoleon in 1815, and with the exception of the Crimean War and the wars of national unification, most of the people of Europe enjoyed a century of relative peace and progress.

## *The Results of Liberalism*

This liberation of human creativity created astounding scientific and material progress. The *Nation* magazine, which was then a truly liberal journal, looking back in 1900, wrote, "Freed from the vexatious meddling of governments, men devoted themselves to their natural task, the bettering of their condition, with the wonderful results which surround us." The technological advances of the liberal nineteenth century are innumerable: the steam engine, the railroad, the telegraph, the telephone, electricity, the internal combustion engine. Thanks to the accumulation of capital and "the miracle of compound interest," in Europe and America the great masses of people began to be liberated from the backbreaking toil that had been the natural condition of mankind since time immemorial. Infant mortality fell and life expectancy began to rise to unprecedented levels. A person looking back from 1800 would see a world that for most people had changed little in thousands of years; by 1900, the world was unrecognizable.

Liberal thought continued to develop throughout the nineteenth century. Jeremy Bentham propounded the theory of utilitarianism, the idea that government should promote "the greatest happiness for the greatest number." Although his philosophical premises were different from those of natural rights, he came to most of the same conclusions about limited government and free markets. Alexis de Tocqueville came to America to see how a free society worked and published his brilliant observations as *Democracy in America* between 1834 and 1840. John Stuart Mill published *On Liberty,* a powerful case for individual freedom, in 1859. In 1851 Herbert Spencer, a towering scholar whose work is unjustly neglected and often misrepresented today, published *Social Statics,* in which he set forth his "law of equal freedom," an early and explicit statement of the modern libertarian credo. Spencer's principle was "that every man may claim the fullest liberty to exercise his faculties compatible with the possession of like liberty by every other man." Spencer pointed out that "the law of equal freedom manifestly applies to the whole race—female as well as male." He also extended the classical liberal critique of war to distinguish between two kinds of societies: industrial society, where people produce and trade peacefully and in voluntary association, and militant society, in which war prevails and the government controls the lives of its subjects as means to its own ends.

In its golden age, Germany produced great writers such as Goethe and Schiller, who were liberals, and it contributed to liberal philosophy in the ideas of philosophers and scholars such as Immanuel Kant and Wilhelm von Humboldt. Kant emphasized individual autonomy and attempted to ground individual rights and liberties in the requirements of reason itself. He called for a "legal constitution which guarantees everyone his freedom within the law, so that each remains free to seek his happiness in whatever way he thinks best, so long as he does not violate the lawful freedom and rights of his fellow subjects." Humboldt's classic work *The Sphere and Duties of Government,* which heavily influenced Mill's *On Liberty,* argued that the full flourishing of the individual requires not only freedom but "a manifoldness of situations," by which he meant that people should have available to them a wide variety of circumstances and living arrangements—the modern term might be "alternative lifestyles"—which they can continually test and choose. In France, Benjamin Constant was the best-known liberal on the Continent in the early part of the century. "He loved liberty as other men love power," a contemporary said. Like Humboldt, he saw liberty as a system in which people could best discover and develop their own personalities and interests. In an important essay, he contrasted the meaning of liberty in the ancient republics—equal participation in public life—with modern liberty—the individual freedoms to speak, write, own property, trade, and pursue one's private interests. An associate of Constant was Madame de Staël, a novelist, perhaps best known for the saying, "Liberty is old; it is despotism that is new," referring to the attempt of the royal absolutists to take away the hard-won chartered liberties of the Middle Ages.

Another French liberal, Frederic Bastiat, served in Parliament as an avid free-trader and wrote a multitude of witty and hard-hitting essays attacking the state and all its actions. His last essay, "What Is Seen and What Is Not Seen," offered the important insight that whatever a government does—build a bridge, subsidize the arts, pay out pensions—has simple and obvious effects. Money is circulated, jobs are created, and people think that the government has generated economic growth. The task of the economist is to see what is not so easily seen—the houses not built, the clothes not bought, the jobs not created—because money was taxed away from those who would have spent it on their own behalf. In "The Law," he attacked the concept of "legal plunder," by which people use government to appropriate what others have produced. And in "The Petition of the Candlemakers against the Competition of the Sun," he mocked French industrialists who wanted to be protected from competition by pretending to speak on behalf of the candlemakers who wanted Parliament to block out the sun, which was causing people not to need candles during daytime—an early refutation of "antidumping" laws.

In the United States, the abolitionist movement was naturally led by libertarians. Leading abolitionists called slavery "man stealing," in that it sought to deny self-ownership and steal a man's very self. Their arguments paralleled those of the Levellers and John Locke. William Lloyd Garrison wrote that his goal was not just the abolition of slavery but "the emancipation of our whole race from the dominion of man, from the thraldom of self, from the government of brute force." Another abolitionist, Lysander Spooner, proceeded from the natural-rights argument against slavery to the conclusion that no one could be held to have given up any of his natural rights under any contract, including the Constitution, that he had not personally signed. Frederick Douglass likewise made his arguments for abolition in the terms of classical liberalism: self-ownership and natural rights.

## The Decline of Liberalism

Toward the end of the nineteenth century, classical liberalism began to give way to new forms of collectivism and state power. If liberalism had been so successful—liberating the great mass of humanity from the crushing burden of statism and unleashing an unprecedented improvement in living standards—what happened? That question has vexed liberals and libertarians throughout the twentieth century.

One problem was that the liberals got lazy; they forgot Jefferson's admonition that "eternal vigilance is the price of liberty" and figured that the obvious social harmony and abundance brought about by liberalism would mean that no one would want to revive the old order. Some liberal intellectuals gave the impression that liberalism was a closed system, with no more interesting work to be done. Socialism, especially the Marxist variety, came along, with a whole new theory to develop, and attracted younger intellectuals.

It may also be that people forgot how hard it had been to create a society of abundance. Americans and Britons born in the latter part of the nineteenth century entered a world of rapidly improving wealth, technology, and living standards; it was not so obvious to them that the world had not always been like that. And even those who understood that the world was different may have assumed that the age-old problem of poverty had been solved. It was no longer important to maintain the social institutions that had solved it.

A related problem was the separation of the issue of production from that of distribution. In a world of abundance, people began to take production for granted and discuss "the problem of distribution." The great philosopher Friedrich Hayek once told me in an interview,

> I am personally convinced that the reason which led the intellectuals, particularly of the English-speaking world, to socialism was a man who is regarded as a great hero of classical liberalism, John Stuart Mill. In his famous textbook *Principles of Political Economy,* which came out in 1848 and for some decades was a widely read text on the subject, he makes the following statement as he passes from the theory of production to the theory of distribution: "The things once there, mankind, individually or collectively, can do with them as they like." Now, if that were true I would admit that it is a clear moral obligation to see that it is justly distributed. But it isn't true, because if we did do with that product whatever we pleased, people would never produce those things again.

Besides, for the first time in history people began to question the tolerability of poverty. Before the Industrial Revolution, everyone was poor; there was no problem to study. Only when most people became rich—by the standards of history—did people begin to wonder why some were still poor. Thus Charles Dickens bemoaned the already waning practice of child labor that kept alive many children who in earlier eras would have died, as most children had from time immemorial; and Karl Marx offered a vision of a world of perfect freedom and plenty. Meanwhile, the success of science and business gave rise to the notion that engineers and corporate executives could design and run a whole society as well as a large corporation.

Bentham and Mill's utilitarian emphasis on "the greatest

good for the greatest number" caused some scholars to begin questioning the need for limited government and protection of individual rights. If the point of it all was to generate prosperity and happiness, why take the roundabout way of protecting rights? Why not just aim directly at economic growth and widespread prosperity? Again, people forgot the concept of spontaneous order, assumed away the problem of production, and developed schemes to guide the economy in a politically chosen direction.

Of course, we must not neglect the age-old human desire for power over others. Some forgot the roots of economic progress, some mourned the disruption of family and community that freedom and affluence brought, and some genuinely believed that Marxism could make everyone prosperous and free without the necessity of work in dark satanic mills. But many others used those ideas as a means to power. If the divine right of kings would no longer persuade people to hand over their liberty and property, then the power seekers would use nationalism, or egalitarianism, or racial prejudice, or class warfare, or the vague promise that the state would alleviate whatever ailed you.

By the turn of the century the remaining liberals despaired of the future. The *Nation* editorialized that "material comfort has blinded the eyes of the present generation to the cause which made it possible" and worried that "before [statism] is again repudiated there must be international struggles on a terrific scale." Herbert Spencer published *The Coming Slavery* and mourned at his death in 1903 that the world was returning to war and barbarism.

Indeed, as the liberals had feared, the century of European peace that began in 1815 came crashing down in 1914, with the First World War. The replacement of liberalism by statism and nationalism was in large part to blame, and the war itself may have delivered the death blow to liberalism. In the United States and Europe, governments enlarged their scope and power in response to the war. Exorbitant taxation, conscription, censorship, nationalization, and central planning—not to mention the 10 million deaths at Flanders fields and Verdun and elsewhere—signaled that the era of liberalism, which had so recently supplanted the old order, was now itself supplanted by the era of the megastate.

## The Rise of the Modern Libertarian Movement

Through the Progressive Era, World War I, the New Deal, and World War II, there was tremendous enthusiasm for bigger government among American intellectuals. Herbert Croly, the first editor of the *New Republic,* wrote in *The Promise of American Life* that that promise would be fulfilled "not by . . . economic freedom, but by a certain measure of discipline; not by the abundant satisfaction of individual desires, but by a large measure of individual subordination and self-denial." Even the awful collectivism beginning to emerge in Europe was not repugnant to many "progressive" journalists and intellectuals in America. Anne O'Hare McCormick reported in the *New York Times* in the first months of Franklin Roosevelt's New Deal,

> The atmosphere [in Washington] is strangely reminiscent of Rome in the first weeks after the march of the Blackshirts, of Moscow at the beginning of the Five-Year Plan. . . .
>
> Something far more positive than acquiescence vests the President with the authority of a dictator. This authority is a free gift, a sort of unanimous power of attorney. . . . America today literally asks for orders. . . . Not only does the present occupant of the White House possess more authority than any of his predecessors, but he presides over a government that has more control over more private activities than any other that has ever existed in the United States. . . . [The Roosevelt administration] envisages a federation of industry, labor and government after the fashion of the corporative State as it exists in Italy.

Although a few liberals—notably the journalist H. L. Mencken—remained outspoken, there was indeed a general intellectual and popular acquiescence in the trend toward big government. The government's apparent success in ending the Great Depression and winning World War II gave impetus to the notion that government could solve all sorts of problems.

Not until twenty-five years or so after the end of the war did popular sentiment start to turn against the megastate.

## The Austrian Economists

Meanwhile, even in the darkest hour of libertarianism, great thinkers continued to emerge and to refine liberal ideas. One of the greatest was Ludwig von Mises, an Austrian economist who fled the Nazis, first to Switzerland in 1934 and then to the United States in 1940. Mises's devastating book *Socialism* showed that socialism could not possibly work because without private property and a price system there is no way to determine what should be produced and how. His student Friedrich Hayek related the influence that *Socialism* had on some of the most promising young intellectuals of the time:

> When *Socialism* first appeared in 1922, its impact was profound. It gradually but fundamentally altered the outlook of many of the young idealists returning to their university studies after World War I. I know, for I was one of them. . . . Socialism promised to fulfill our hopes for a more rational, more just world. And then came this book. Our hopes were dashed.

Another young intellectual whose faith in socialism was dashed by Mises was Wilhelm Roepke, who went on to be the chief adviser to Ludwig Erhard, the German economics minister after World War II and chief architect of the "German economic miracle" of the 1950s and 1960s. Others took longer to learn. The American economist and bestselling author Robert Heilbroner wrote that in the 1930s, when he was studying economics, Mises's argument about the impossibility of planning "did not seem a particularly cogent reason to reject socialism." Fifty years later, Heilbroner wrote in the *New Yorker,* "It turns out, of course, that Mises was right." Better late than never.

Mises's magnum opus was *Human Action,* a comprehensive treatise on economics. In it he developed a complete science of economics, which he considered to be the study of all purposeful human action. He was an uncompromising free-marketer, who forcefully pointed out how every government intervention in the marketplace tends to reduce wealth and the overall standard of living.

Mises's student Hayek became not only a brilliant economist—he won the Nobel Prize in 1974—but perhaps the greatest social thinker of the century. His books *The Sensory Order, The Counter-Revolution of Science, The Constitution of Liberty,* and *Law, Legislation, and Liberty* explored topics ranging from psychology and the misapplication of the methods of the physical sciences in the social sciences to law and political theory. In his most famous work, *The Road to Serfdom,* published in 1944, he warned the very countries that were then engaged in a war against totalitarianism that economic planning would lead not to equality but to a new system of class and status, not to prosperity but to poverty, not to liberty but to serfdom. The book was bitterly attacked by socialist and left-leaning intellectuals in England and the United States, but it sold very well (perhaps one of the reasons the writers of academic books resented it) and inspired a new generation of young people to explore libertarian ideas. Hayek's last book, *The Fatal Conceit,* published in 1988 when he was approaching ninety, returned to the problem that had occupied most of his scholarly interest: the spontaneous order, which is "of human action but not of human design." The fatal conceit of intellectuals, he said, is to think that smart people can design an economy or a society better than the apparently chaotic interactions of millions of people. Such intellectuals fail to realize how much they don't know or how a market makes use of all the localized knowledge each of us possesses.

## The Last Classical Liberals

A group of writers and political thinkers was also keeping libertarian ideas alive. H. L. Mencken was best known as a journalist and literary critic, but he thought deeply about politics; he said his ideal was "a government that barely escapes being no government at all." Albert Jay Nock (the author of *Our Enemy, the State*), Garet Garrett, John T. Flynn, Felix Morley, and Frank Chodorov worried about the future of limited, constitutional government in the face of the New Deal and what seemed to be a permanent war footing that the United States had assumed during the twentieth century. Henry Hazlitt, a journalist who wrote about economics, served as a link between these schools. He worked for the *Nation* and the *New York Times,* wrote a column for *Newsweek,* gave Mises's *Human Action* a rave review, and popularized free-market economics in a little book called *Economics in One Lesson,* which drew out the implications of Bastiat's "what is seen and what is not seen." Mencken said of him, "He was one of the few economists in human history who could really write."

In the dark year of 1943, in the depths of World War II and the Holocaust, when the most powerful government in the history of the United States was allied with one totalitarian power to defeat another, three remarkable women published books that could be said to have given birth to the modern libertarian movement. Rose Wilder Lane, the daughter of Laura Ingalls Wilder, who had written *Little House on the Prairie* and other stories of American rugged individualism, published a passionate historical essay called *The Discovery of Freedom.* Isabel Paterson, a novelist and literary critic, produced *The God of the Machine,* which defended individualism as the source of progress in the world. And Ayn Rand published *The Fountainhead.*

## Ayn Rand

*The Fountainhead* was a sprawling novel about architecture and integrity. The book's individualist theme did not fit the spirit of the age, and reviewers savaged it. But it found its intended readers. Its sales started slowly, then built and built. It was still on the *New York Times* bestseller list two full years later. Hundreds of thousands of people read it in the 1940s, millions eventually, and thousands of them were inspired enough to seek more information about Ayn Rand's ideas. Rand went on to write an even more successful novel, *Atlas Shrugged,* in 1957, and to found an association of people who shared her philosophy, which she called Objectivism. Although her political philosophy was libertarian, not all libertarians shared her views on metaphysics, ethics, and religion. Others were put off by the starkness of her presentation and by her cult following.

Like Mises and Hayek, Rand demonstrates the importance of immigration not just to America but to American libertarianism. Mises had fled the Nazis, Rand fled the Communists who came to power in her native Russia. When a heckler asked her after a speech, "Why should we care what a foreigner thinks?" she replied with her usual fire, "I *chose* to be an American. What did you ever do, except for having been born?"

## The Postwar Revival

Not long after the publication of *Atlas Shrugged,* the University of Chicago economist Milton Friedman published *Capitalism and Freedom,* in which he argued that political freedom could not exist without private property and economic freedom. Friedman's stature as an economist, which won him a Nobel Prize in 1976, was based on his work in monetary economics. But through *Capitalism and Freedom,* his long-running *Newsweek* column, and the 1980 book and television series *Free to Choose,* he became the most prominent American libertarian of the past generation.

Another economist, Murray Rothbard, achieved less fame but played an important role in building both a theoretical structure for modern libertarian thought and a political movement devoted to those ideas. Rothbard wrote a major economic treatise, *Man, Economy, and State;* a four-volume history of the American Revolution, *Conceived in Liberty;* a concise guide to the theory of natural rights and its implications, *The Ethics of Liberty;* a popular libertarian manifesto, *For a New Liberty;* and countless pamphlets and articles in magazines and newsletters. Libertarians compared him to both Marx, the builder of an integrated political-economic theory, and Lenin, the indefatigable organizer of a radical movement.

Libertarianism got a major boost in scholarly respect in 1974 with the publication of *Anarchy, State, and Utopia* by the Harvard University philosopher Robert Nozick. With wit and fine-toothed logic, Nozick laid out a case for rights, which concluded that

> a minimal state, limited to the narrow functions of protection against force, theft, [and] fraud, enforcement of contracts, and so on, is justified; that any more extensive state will violate persons'

rights not to be forced to do certain things, and is unjustified; and that the minimal state is inspiring as well as right.

In a catchier vein, he called for the legalization of "capitalist acts between consenting adults." Nozick's book—along with Rothbard's *For a New Liberty* and Rand's essays on political philosophy—defined the "hard-core" version of modern libertarianism, which essentially restated Spencer's law of equal freedom: Individuals have the right to do whatever they want to, so long as they respect the equal rights of others. The role of government is to protect individual rights from foreign aggressors and from neighbors who murder, rape, rob, assault, or defraud us. And if government seeks to do more than that, it will itself be depriving us of our rights and liberties.

## Libertarianism Today

Libertarianism is sometimes accused of being rigid and dogmatic, but it is in fact merely a basic framework for societies in which free individuals can live together in peace and harmony, each undertaking what Jefferson called "their own pursuits of industry and improvement." The society created by a libertarian framework is the most dynamic and innovative ever seen on earth, as witness the unprecedented advances in science, technology, and standard of living since the liberal revolution of the late eighteenth century. A libertarian society is marked by widespread charity undertaken as a result of personal benevolence, not left to state coercion.

Libertarianism is also a creative and dynamic framework for intellectual activity. Today it is statist ideas that seem old and tired, while there is an explosion of libertarian scholarship in such fields as economics, law, history, philosophy, psychology, feminism, economic development, civil rights, education, the environment, social theory, bioethics, civil liberties, foreign policy, technology, the Information Age, and more. Libertarianism has developed a framework for scholarship and problem solving, but our understanding of the dynamics of free and unfree societies will continue to develop.

Today, the intellectual development of libertarian ideas continues, but the broader impact of those ideas derives from the growing network of libertarian magazines and think tanks, the revival of traditional American hostility to centralized government, and most important, the continuing failure of big government to deliver on its promises.

*Chapter 3*

# WHAT RIGHTS DO WE HAVE?

 $\mathcal{C}$ ritics on both left and right have complained that America in the 1990s is awash in talk about rights. No political debate proceeds for very long without one side, or both, resting its argument on rights—property rights, welfare rights, women's rights, nonsmokers' rights, the right to life, abortion rights, gay rights, gun rights, you name it.

A journalist asked me recently what I thought of a proposal by self-proclaimed communitarians to "suspend for a while the minting of new rights." Communitarians in late twentieth-century America are people who believe that "the community" should in some way take precedence over the individual, so naturally they would respond to rights-talk overload by saying, "Let's just stop doing it." How many ways, I mused, does that get it wrong? Communitarians seem to see rights as little boxes; when you have too many, the room won't hold them all. In the libertarian view, we have an infinite number of rights contained in one natural right. That one fundamental human right is the right to live your life as you choose so long as you don't infringe on the equal rights of others.

That one right has infinite implications. As James Wilson, a signer of the Constitution, said in response to a proposal that a Bill of Rights be added to the Constitution: "Enumerate all the rights of man! I am sure, sirs, that no gentleman in the late

Convention would have attempted such a thing." After all, a person has a right to wear a hat, or not; to marry, or not; to grow beans, or apples; or to open a haberdashery. Indeed, to cite a specific example, a person has a right to sell an orange to a willing buyer even though the orange is only $2\frac{3}{8}$ inches in diameter (although under current federal law, that is illegal).

It is impossible to enumerate in advance all the rights we have; we usually go to the trouble of identifying them only when someone proposes to limit one or another. Treating rights as tangible claims that must be limited in number gets the whole concept wrong.

But the complaint about "the proliferation of rights" is not all wrong. There is indeed a problem in modern America with the proliferation of phony "rights." When rights become merely legal claims attached to interests and preferences, the stage is set for political and social conflict. Interests and preferences may conflict, but *rights* cannot. There is no conflict of genuine human rights in a free society. There are, however, many conflicts among the holders of so-called welfare rights, which require someone else to provide us with things we want, whether that is education, health care, social security, welfare, farm subsidies, or unobstructed views across someone else's land. This is a fundamental problem of interest-group democracy and the interventionist state. In a liberal society, people *assume* risks and obligations through contract; an interventionist state *imposes* obligations on people through the political process, obligations that conflict with their natural rights.

So what rights *do* we have, and how can we tell a real right from a phony one? Let's start by returning to one of the basic documents in the history of human rights, the Declaration of Independence. In the second paragraph of the Declaration, Thomas Jefferson laid out a statement of rights and their meaning that has rarely been equaled for grace and brevity. As noted in chapter 2, Jefferson's task in writing the Declaration was to express the common sentiments of the American colonists, and he was chosen for the job not because he had new ideas but because of his "peculiar felicity of expression." Introducing the American cause to the world, Jefferson explained:

We hold these truths to be self-evident, that all men are created equal, that they are endowed by their Creator with certain unalienable Rights, that among these are life, liberty, and the pursuit of happiness. That to secure these rights, governments are instituted among men, deriving their just powers from the consent of the governed. That whenever any form of government becomes destructive of these ends, it is the right of the people to alter or abolish it.

Let's try to draw out the implications of America's founding document.

## Basic Rights

Any theory of rights has to begin somewhere. Most libertarian philosophers would begin the argument earlier than Jefferson did. Humans, unlike animals, come into the world without an instinctive knowledge of what their needs are and how to fulfill them. As Aristotle said, man is a reasoning and deliberating animal; humans use the power of reason to understand their own needs, the world around them, and how to use the world to satisfy their needs. So they need a social system that allows them to use their reason, to act in the world, and to cooperate with others to achieve purposes that no one individual could accomplish.

Every person is a unique individual. Humans are social animals—we like interacting with others, and we profit from it—but we think and act individually. Each individual owns himself or herself. What other possibilities besides self-ownership are there?

• *Someone—a king or a master race—could own others.* Plato and Aristotle did argue that there were different kinds of humans, some more competent than others and thus endowed with the right and responsibility to rule, just as adults guide children. Some forms of socialism and collectivism are—explicitly or implicitly—based on the notion that many people are not competent to make decisions about their own lives, so that the more talented should make decisions for them. But that would mean there were no universal human rights, only rights that some have and others do not, denying the essential humanity of those who are deemed to be owned.

• *Everyone owns everyone, a full-fledged communist system.* In such a system, before anyone could take an action, he would need to get permission from everyone else. But how could each other person grant permission without consulting everyone else? You'd have an infinite regress, making any action at all logically impossible. In practice, since such mutual ownership is impossible, this system would break down into the previous one: someone, or some group, would own everyone else. That is what happened in the communist states: the party became a dictatorial ruling elite.

Thus, either communism or aristocratic rule would divide the world into factions or classes. The only possibility that is humane, logical, and suited to the nature of human beings is *self-ownership*. Obviously, this discussion has only scratched the surface of the question of self-ownership; in any event, I rather like Jefferson's simple declaration: Natural rights are self-evident.

Conquerors and oppressors told people for millennia that men were *not* created equal, that some were destined to rule and others to be ruled. By the eighteenth century, people had thrown off such ancient superstition; Jefferson denounced it with his usual felicity of expression: "The mass of mankind has not been born with saddles on their backs, nor a favored few booted and spurred ready to ride them legitimately by the grace of God." As we enter the twenty-first century, the idea of equality is almost universally accepted. Of course, people are not equally tall, equally beautiful, equally smart, equally kind, equally graceful, or equally successful. But they have equal rights, so they should be equally free. As the Stoic lawyer Cicero wrote, "While it is undesirable to equalize wealth, and everyone cannot have the same talents, legal rights at least should be equal among citizens of the same commonwealth."

In our own time we've seen much confusion on this point. People have advocated public policies both mild and repressive to bring about equality of outcomes. Advocates of material equality apparently don't feel the need to defend it as a principle; ironically, they seem to take it as self-evident. In defending equality, they typically confuse three concepts:

- A right to equality before the law, which is the kind of equality Jefferson had in mind.
- A right to equality of results or outcomes, meaning that everyone has the same amount of—of what? Usually egalitarians mean the same amount of money, but why is money the only test? Why not equality of beauty, or of hair, or of work? The fact is, equality of outcomes requires a political decision about measurement and allocation, a decision no society can make without some group forcing its view on others. True equality of results is logically impossible in a diverse world, and the attempt to achieve it leads to nightmarish results. Producing equal outcomes would require treating people unequally.
- A right to equality of opportunity, meaning an equal chance to succeed in life. People who use "equality" this way usually mean equal rights, but an attempt to create true equality of opportunity could be as dictatorial as equality of results. Children raised in different households will never be equally prepared for the adult world, yet any alternative to family freedom would mean a nanny state of the worst order. Full equality of opportunity might indeed lead to the solution posed in Kurt Vonnegut's short story "Harrison Bergeron," in which the beautiful are scarred, the graceful are shackled, and the smart have their brain patterns continuously disrupted.

The kind of equality suitable for a free society is *equal rights.* As the Declaration stated clearly, rights are not a gift from government. They are natural and unchanging, inherent in the nature of mankind and possessed by people by virtue of their humanity, specifically their ability to take responsibility for their actions. Whether rights come from God or from nature is not essential in this context. Remember, the first paragraph of the Declaration referred to "the laws of nature and of nature's God." What is important is that rights are imprescriptible, that is, not granted by any other human. In particular, they are not granted by government; people form governments in order to protect the rights they already possess.

## Self-Ownership

Because every person owns himself, his body and his mind, he has the right to life. To unjustifiably take another person's life—to murder him—is the greatest possible violation of his rights.

Unfortunately, the term "right to life" is used in two confusing ways in our time. We might do better to stick to "right to self-ownership." Some people, mostly on the political right, use "right to life" to defend the rights of fetuses (or unborn children) against abortion. Obviously, that is not the sense in which Jefferson used the term.

Other people, mostly on the political left, would argue that the "right to life" means that everyone has a fundamental right to the necessities of life: food, clothing, shelter, medical care, maybe even an eight-hour day and two weeks of vacation. But if the right to life means this, then it means that one person has a right to force other people to give him things, violating their equal rights. The philosopher Judith Jarvis Thomson writes, "If I am sick unto death, and the only thing that will save my life is the touch of Henry Fonda's cool hand on my fevered brow, then all the same, I have no right to be given the touch of Henry Fonda's cool hand on my fevered brow." And if not the right to Henry Fonda's touch, then why would she have the right to a room in Henry Fonda's house, or a portion of his money with which to buy food? That would mean forcing him to serve her, taking the product of his labor without his consent. No, the right to life means that each person has the right to take action in the furtherance of his life and flourishing, not to force others to serve his needs.

Ethical univeralism, the most common framework for moral theory, holds that a valid ethical theory must be applicable for all men and women, at whatever time and place we find them. The natural rights to life, liberty, and property can be enjoyed by people under any normal circumstances. But so-called rights to housing, education, medical care, cable television, or the "periodic holidays with pay" generously proclaimed in the United

Nations' Universal Declaration of Human Rights, cannot be enjoyed everywhere. Some societies are too poor to provide everyone with leisure or housing or even food. And remember that there is no collective entity known as "education" or "medical care"; there are only specific, particular goods, such as a seat for a year in the Hudson Street School or an operation performed by kindly Dr. Johnson on Tuesday. Some person or group of people would have to provide each particular unit of "housing" or "education," and providing it to one person necessarily means denying it to other people. Therefore, it is logically impossible to make such desirable things "universal human rights."

The right to self-ownership leads immediately to the right to liberty; indeed, we may say that "right to life" and "right to liberty" are just two ways of expressing the same point. If people own themselves, and have both the right and the obligation to take the actions necessary for their survival and flourishing, then they must enjoy freedom of thought and action. Freedom of thought is an obvious implication of self-ownership; in a sense, though, it's difficult to deny freedom of thought. Who can regulate the content of someone else's mind? Freedom of speech is also logically implied by self-ownership. Many governments have tried to outlaw or restrict freedom of speech, but speech is inherently fleeting, so control is difficult. Freedom of the press—including, in modern times, broadcasting, cable, electronic mail, and other new forms of communications—is the aspect of intellectual freedom that oppressive governments usually target. And when we defend freedom of the press, we are necessarily talking about property rights, because ideas are expressed *through property*—printing presses, auditoriums, sound trucks, billboards, radio equipment, broadcast frequencies, computer networks, and so on.

## Property Rights

In fact, the ownership of property is a necessary implication of self-ownership because all human action involves property. How else could happiness be pursued? If nothing else, we need a place to stand. We need the right to use land and other property to produce new goods and services. We shall see that all rights can be understood as property rights. But this is a contentious point, not always easily understood. Many people wonder why we couldn't voluntarily share our goods and property.

Property is a *necessity*. "Property" doesn't mean simply land, or any other physical good. Property is anything that people can use, control, or dispose of. A property right means the freedom to use, control, or dispose of an object or entity. Is this a bad, exploitative necessity? Not at all.

If our world were not characterized by scarcity, we wouldn't need property rights. That is, if we had infinite amounts of everything people wanted, we would need no theory of how to allocate such things. But of course scarcity is a basic characteristic of our world. Note that scarcity doesn't imply poverty or a lack of basic subsistence. Scarcity simply means that human wants are essentially unlimited, so we never have enough productive resources to supply all of them. Even an ascetic who had transcended the desire for material goods beyond bare subsistence would face the most basic scarcity of all: the scarcity of one's own body and life and time. Whatever time he devoted to prayer would not be available for manual labor, for reading the sacred texts, or for performing good works. No matter how rich our society gets—nor how indifferent to material goods we become—we will always have to make choices, which means that we need a system for deciding who gets to use productive resources.

We can never abolish property rights, as socialist visionaries promise to do. As long as things exist, someone will have the power to use them. In a civilized society, we don't want that power to be exercised simply by the strongest or most violent person; we want a theory of justice in property titles. When socialist governments "abolish" property, what they promise is that the entire community will own all property. But since—visionary theory or no—only one person can eat a particular apple, or sleep in a particular bed, or stand on a particular spot, someone will have to decide who. That someone—the party official, or the bureaucrat, or the czar—is the real possessor of the property right.

Libertarians believe that the right to self-ownership means that individuals must have the right to acquire and exchange property in order to fulfill their needs and desires. To feed ourselves, or provide shelter for our families, or open a business, we must make use of property. And for people to be willing to save and invest, we need to be confident that our property rights are legally secure, that someone else can't come and confiscate the wealth we've created, whether that means the crop we've planted, the house we've built, the car we've bought, or the complex corporation we've created through a network of contracts with many other people.

*Original Acquisition of Property.* How do men and women come to acquire property in the first place? Perhaps if a spaceship full of men and women landed on Mars, there would seem to be no need for conflict over land. Just pick a spot and start building or planting. A cartoonist once depicted one caveman saying to another, "Let's cut the earth into little squares and sell them." Put like that, it sounds absurd. Why do that? And who would buy the little squares? And with what? But as population increases, it becomes necessary to decide what land—or water or frequency spectrum—belongs to whom. John Locke described one way to acquire property: Whoever first "mixed his labor with" a piece of land acquired title to it. By mixing his own labor with a piece of previously unowned land, he made it his own. He then had the right to build a house on it, put a fence around it, sell it, or otherwise dispose of it.

For each entity there is in fact a bundle of property rights, which can be disaggregated. There can be as many property rights attached to one entity as there are aspects of that entity. For instance, you might purchase or lease the right to drill for oil on a piece of land, but not the right to farm or build on it. You might own the land but not the water under it. You might donate your house to a charity but retain the right to live there for your lifetime. As Roy Childs wrote in *Liberty Against Power,* "Before there was a technology available to broadcast through the airwaves, certain kinds of things . . . could not have been property, because they could not have been specified by any technological means." But once we understand the physics of broadcasting, we can create property rights in the frequency spectrum. Childs went on, "As a society gets more complicated

. . . and technology advances, the kinds of ownership that are possible to people become more and more complex."

The homesteading principle—initially acquiring a property title by being the first to use or transform the property—may operate differently with different kinds of property. For instance, in a state of nature, when most land is unowned (as if men landed on a new planet), we might say that simply camping on a piece of land and remaining there is sufficient to acquire the property right. Surely laying out the foundation for a house and then beginning to build it would establish a property right. Rights to water—whether in lakes, rivers, or underground pools—have traditionally been acquired in ways different from land acquisition. When people began to use the frequency spectrum to broadcast in the 1920s, they generally adopted a homestead principle: start broadcasting on a particular frequency, and you acquire a right to continue using that frequency. (The role of government in all these cases is simply to *protect,* largely through the courts, the rights that individuals acquire on their own.) The important thing, as I'll discuss later, is that we have some way of establishing property rights and then that we allow people to transfer them to others by mutual consent.

*Property Rights Are Human Rights.* What exactly does it mean to own property? We might cite Jan Narveson's definition: "'x is A's property' means 'A has the right to determine the disposition of x.'" Note that a property right is not a right *of* property, or a right *belonging to* a piece of property, as opponents of property rights often suggest. Rather, a property right is a human right *to* property, the right of an individual to use and dispose of property that he has justly acquired. Property rights are human rights.

Indeed, as argued above, all human rights can be seen as property rights, stemming from the one fundamental right of self-ownership, our ownership of our own bodies. As Murray Rothbard put it in *Power and Market,*

> In the profoundest sense there *are* no rights but property rights. . . . There are several senses in which this is true. In the first place, each individual, as a natural fact, is the owner of *himself,* the ruler of his own person. The "human" rights of the person

that are defended in the purely free-market society are, in effect, each man's *property right* in his own being, and from *this* property right stems his right to the material goods that he has produced.

In the second place, alleged "human rights" can be boiled down to property rights . . . for example, the "human right" of free speech. Freedom of speech is supposed to mean the right of everyone to say whatever he likes. But the neglected question is: Where? Where does a man have this right? He certainly does not have it on property on which he is trespassing. In short, he has this right only either on his *own* property or on the property of someone who has agreed, as a gift or in a rental contract, to allow him on the premises. In fact, then, there is no such thing as a separate "right to free speech"; there is only a man's *property* right: the right to do as he wills with his own or to make voluntary agreements with other property owners [including those whose property may consist only of their own labor].

When we understand free speech this way, we see what's wrong with Justice Oliver Wendell Holmes's famous statement that free speech rights cannot be absolute because there is no right to falsely shout "Fire!" in a crowded theater. Who would be shouting "Fire"? Possibly the owner, or one of his agents, in which case the owner has defrauded his customers: he sold them tickets to a play or movie and then disrupted the show, not to mention endangered their lives. If not the owner, then one of the customers, who is violating the terms of his contract; his ticket entitles him to enjoy the show, not to disrupt it. The falsely-shouting-fire-in-a-crowded-theater argument is no reason to limit the right of free speech; it's an illustration of the way that property rights solve problems and of the need to protect and enforce them.

The same analysis applies to the much-debated right to privacy. In the 1965 case *Griswold v. Connecticut,* the Supreme Court struck down a Connecticut law prohibiting the use of contraceptives. Justice William O. Douglas found a right to privacy for married couples in "penumbras, formed by emanations" from various parts of the Constitution. Conservatives such as Judge Robert Bork have ridiculed such vague, rootless reasoning for thirty years. The penumbras kept on emanating to take in an unmarried couple's right to contraception and a woman's right to terminate a pregnancy, but suddenly in 1986 they were found not to emanate far enough to cover consensual homosexual acts in a private bedroom. A theory of privacy rooted in property rights wouldn't have needed penumbras and emanations—which, penumbras being imperfect shadows, are necessarily pretty vague—to find that a person has a right to purchase contraceptives from willing sellers or to engage in sexual relations with consenting partners in one's own home. "A man's home is his castle" provides a stronger foundation for privacy than "penumbras, formed by emanations."

Those who reject the libertarian principle of property rights need to do more than criticize. They need to offer an alternative system that would as effectively define who may use each particular resource and in what ways, ensure that land and other property is adequately cared for, provide a framework for economic development, and avoid the war of all against all that can ensue when control over valuable goods is not clearly defined.

## Nozick's Entitlement Theory of Justice

In his 1974 book *Anarchy, State, and Utopia,* the Harvard philosopher Robert Nozick discussed alternative conceptions of property rights in a very illuminating way. This subject is frequently called "distributive justice," but that term biases the discussion. As Nozick points out, the term as often used implies that there is some process of distribution, which may have gone awry and which we may want to correct. But in a free society there is no central distribution of resources. Milton Friedman tells of visiting China in the 1980s and being asked by a government minister, "Who in the United States is in charge of materials distribution?" Friedman was left almost speechless by the question but had to explain that in a market economy there is no person or committee "in charge of materials distribution." Millions of people produce goods—through a complex network of contracts in an advanced economy—and then exchange them. As Nozick says, "What each person gets, he gets from others who give it to him in exchange for something, or as a gift."

Nozick suggests that there are two ways of looking at the question of justice in property rights. The first is historical: if people acquired their property justly, then they are entitled to it, and it would be wrong to interfere by force to redistribute property. The other view is based on patterns or end results or what he calls "current time-slice principles." That is, "the justice of a distribution is determined by how things are distributed (who has what) as judged by some structural principle of just distribution." Advocates of a patterned distribution ask not whether property was justly acquired but whether today's pattern of distribution fits what they consider the correct pattern. There are many kinds of patterns people might prefer: whites should have more property (or money or whatever) than blacks, Christians should have more than Jews, smart people should have more, good people should have more, people should have what they need. Some of those views are abhorrent. Others may well be held by your friends and other decent people. But what they all have in common is this: They assume that a just distribution is determined by who has what, without any reference to how it was obtained. The view most likely to be held by critics of capitalism today, however, is that everyone should have equal property, or no one should have more than twice as much as anyone else, or some other variant of equality. So that is the alternative to libertarianism we'll consider.

Nozick lays out his entitlement theory of justice this way: First, people have a right to acquire unowned property. That's the principle of justice in acquisition. Second, people have a right to give their property to others, or to voluntarily exchange it with others. That's the principle of justice in transfer. Thus,

> If the world were wholly just, the following inductive definition would exhaustively cover the subject of justice in holdings:
> 1. A person who acquires a holding in accordance with the principle of justice in acquisition is entitled to that holding.
> 2. A person who acquires a holding in accordance with the principle of justice in transfer, from someone else entitled to the holding, is entitled to the holding.
> 3. No one is entitled to a holding except by (repeated) applications of 1 and 2.

The complete principle of distributive justice would say simply that a distribution is just if everyone is entitled to the holdings they possess under the distribution.

A distribution is just if it arises from another just distribution by legitimate means.

Once people have property (including the labor of their own minds and bodies, which they have inherently), they may legitimately exchange it with someone else for any property that person has legitimately acquired. They may also give it away. What people may *not* do is take another person's property without his consent.

Nozick goes on to discuss the question of equality in a famous section of his book called "How Liberty Upsets Patterns." Suppose we begin with a society in which wealth is distributed in the way that *you* think is best. It could be that all the Christians have more than all the Jews, or that the members of the Communist Party own all the property (except for our individual bodies), or whatever. But let's assume that your favorite pattern is that everyone have an equal amount of wealth, and that's what we see in our hypothetical society. Now consider just one intervening event.

Suppose that the rock group Pearl Jam goes on a concert tour. They charge people $10 to see them play. During the tour a million people come to their concerts. At the end of the tour a million people are $10 poorer than they were, and the members of Pearl Jam are $10 million richer than everyone else. Here's the question: The distribution of wealth is now unequal. Is it unjust? If so, why? We agreed that the distribution of wealth at the beginning was just, because we stipulated that it was *your* preferred distribution. Each person at the beginning was presumably entitled to the money he had, and thus entitled to spend it as he chose. Many people exercised their rights, and now the Pearl Jam musicians are richer than everybody else. Is that wrong?

All those people chose to spend their money that way. They could have bought Michael Jackson albums or granola or copies of the *New York Review of Books*. They could have given money to the Salvation Army or to Habitat for Humanity. If they were entitled to the money they had in the beginning, surely they are entitled to spend it, in which case the pattern of wealth distribution will change.

Whatever the pattern is, as different people choose to spend their money, and choose to offer goods or services to other people in order to get more money to spend, the pattern will be constantly changing. Someone will go to Pearl Jam and offer to promote their concerts in return for some of the gate receipts, or to produce albums and sell them. Someone else will start a print shop to produce the tickets for their concerts. As Nozick says, to prevent inequality in wealth, you would have to "forbid capitalist acts between consenting adults." He goes on to point out that no pattern of distribution can be maintained "without continuous interference with people's lives." Either you have to continuously stop people from spending money as they choose, or you have to continuously—or at regular intervals—take from people money that other people chose to give them.

Now it's easy to say that we don't mind rock musicians getting rich. But of course the same principle applies to capitalists, even billionaires. If Henry Ford invents a car that people want to buy, or Bill Gates a computer operating system, or Sam Walton a cheap and efficient way to distribute consumer goods, and we're allowed to spend our money as we choose, then they will get rich. To stop that, we would have to stop consenting adults from spending their money as they choose.

But what about their children? Is it fair that the mogul's children will be born to greater wealth, probably leading to better education, than you or me? The question misunderstands the nature of a complex society. In a primitive village, comprising a few people who were probably an extended family, it was appropriate to distribute the tribe's goods on the basis of "fairness." But a diverse society will never agree on a "fair" distribution of goods. What we *can* agree on is justice—that people should be able to keep what they produce. That means not that Henry Ford's son had a "right" to inherit wealth, but that Henry Ford had a right to acquire wealth and then to give it to anyone he chose, including his children. A distribution by a central authority—how your father doles out allowances, or how a teacher assigns grades—may be deemed fair or unfair. The complex process by which millions of people produce things and sell or give them to others is a different kind of process, and it makes no sense to judge it by the rules of fairness that apply to a small group under central direction.

According to the entitlement theory of justice, people have a right to exchange their justly acquired property. Some ideologies have a principle of "to each according to his ————." For Marx it was "from each according to his ability; to each according to his need." Note that Marx separates production and distribution; in between those two clauses there's some authority deciding what your ability and my need are. Nozick offers a libertarian prescription, integrating production and distribution in a just system:

> From each according to what he chooses to do, to each according to what he makes for himself (perhaps with the contracted aid of others) and what others choose to do for him and choose to give him of what they've been given previously (under this maxim) and haven't yet expended or transferred.

That lacks the vigor of a good slogan. So, to paraphrase Nozick, we can sum it up as

> *From each as he chooses, to each as he is chosen.*

## The Nonaggression Axiom

What are the limits of freedom? The corollary of the libertarian principle that "every person has the right to live his life as he chooses, so long as he does not interfere with the equal rights of others" is this:

> *No one has the right to initiate aggression against the person or property of anyone else.*

This is what libertarians call the nonaggression axiom, and it is a central principle of libertarianism. Note that the nonaggression axiom does not forbid the retaliatory use of force, that is, to regain stolen property, to punish those who have violated the rights of others, to rectify an injury, or even to prevent imminent injury from another person. What it does state is that it is wrong to use or threaten physical violence against the person or property of another who has not himself used or threatened force. Justice therefore forbids murder, rape, assault, robbery, kidnapping, and fraud. (Why fraud? Is fraud really an initiation of force? Yes, because fraud is a form of theft. If I promise to sell you a Heineken for a dollar, but I actually give you Bud Light, I have stolen your dollar.)

As noted in chapter 1, most people habitually believe in and live by this code of ethics. Libertarians believe this code should be applied consistently, to actions by governments as well as by individuals. Rights are not cumulative; you can't say that six people's rights outweigh three people's rights, so the six can take the property of the three. Nor can a million people "combine" their rights into some cumulative right to take the property of a thousand. Thus libertarians condemn government actions that take our persons or our property, or threaten us with fines or jail for the way we live our personal lives or the way we engage in voluntary interactions with others (including commercial transactions).

Freedom, in the libertarian view, is a condition in which the individual's self-ownership right and property right are not invaded or aggressed against. Philosophers sometimes call the libertarian conception of rights "negative liberty," in the sense that it imposes only negative obligations on others—the duty *not* to aggress against anyone else. But for each individual, as Ayn Rand puts it, a right is a moral claim to a positive—"his freedom to act on his own judgment, for his own goals, by his own *voluntary, uncoerced* choice."

Communitarians sometimes say that "the language of rights is morally incomplete." That's true; rights pertain only to a certain domain of morality—a narrow domain in fact—not to all of morality. Rights establish certain minimal standards for how we must treat each other: we must not kill, rape, rob, or otherwise initiate force against each other. In Ayn Rand's words, "The precondition of a civilized society is the barring of physical force from social relationships—thus establishing the principle that if men wish to deal with one another, they may do so only by means of *reason:* by discussion, persuasion and voluntary, uncoerced agreement." But the protection of rights and the establishment of a peaceful society is only a *precondition* for civilization. Most of the important questions about how we should deal with our fellow men must be answered with other moral maxims. That doesn't mean that the idea of rights is invalid or incomplete *in the domain where it applies;* it just means that most of the decisions we make every day involve choices that are only broadly circumscribed by the obligation to respect each other's rights.

## Implications of Natural Rights

The basic principles of self-ownership, the law of equal freedom, and the nonaggression axiom have infinite implications. As many ways as the state can think of to regulate and expropriate people's lives, that's how many rights libertarians can identify.

The most obvious and most outrageous attempt to violate the right of self-ownership is involuntary servitude. From time immemorial, people claimed the right to hold others as slaves. Slavery wasn't always racial; it generally began as the spoils of victory. The conquerors had the power to enslave the conquered. The greatest libertarian crusade in history was the effort to abolish chattel slavery, culminating in the nineteenth-century abolitionist movement and the heroic Underground Railroad. But despite the Thirteenth Amendment to the Constitution, which abolished involuntary servitude, we still see vestiges of it to this day. What is conscription—the military draft—if not temporary slavery (with permanent consequences, for those draftees who don't come home alive)? No issue today more clearly separates libertarians from those who put the collective ahead of the individual. The libertarian believes that people will voluntarily defend a country worth defending, and that no group of people has the right to force another group to give up a year or two of their lives—and possibly life itself—without their consent. The basic liberal principle of the dignity of the individual is violated when individuals are treated as national resources. Some conservatives (such as Senator John McCain and William F. Buckley, Jr.) and some of today's so-called liberals (such as Senator Edward M. Kennedy and Ford Foundation president Franklin Thomas) advocate a system of compulsory national service in which all young people would be required to spend a year or two working for the government. Such a system would be an abominable violation of the human right of self-ownership, and we can only hope that the Supreme Court would find it unconstitutional under the Thirteenth Amendment.

## Freedom of Conscience

It's also easy for most people to see the implications of libertarianism for freedom of conscience, free speech, and personal freedom. The modern ideas of libertarianism began in the struggle for religious toleration. What can be more inherent, more personal, to an individual than the thoughts in his mind? As religious dissidents developed their defense of toleration, the ideas of natural rights and a sphere of privacy emerged. Freedom of speech and freedom of the press are other aspects of the liberty of conscience. No one has the right to prevent another person from expressing his thoughts and trying to persuade others of his opinions. That argument today must extend to radio and television, cable, the Internet, and other forms of electronic communications. People who don't want to read books by communists (or libertarians!), or watch gory movies, or download pornographic pictures, don't have to; but they have no right to prevent others from making their own choices.

The ways that governments interfere with freedom of speech are legion. American governments have constantly tried to ban or regulate allegedly indecent, obscene, or pornographic literature and movies, despite the clear wording of the First Amendment: "Congress shall make no law . . . abridging the freedom of speech or of the press." As a headline in *Wired* magazine put it, "What part of 'no law' don't you understand?"

Libertarians see dozens of violations of free speech in American law. Information about abortion has been banned, most recently in the 1996 law regulating communication over the

Internet. The federal government has often used its monopoly post office to prevent the delivery of morally or politically offensive material. Radio and television broadcasters must get federal licenses and then comply with various federal regulations on the content of broadcasts. The Bureau of Alcohol, Tobacco, and Firearms forbids the producers of wine and other alcoholic beverages from noting on their labels that medical studies indicate that moderate consumption of alcohol reduces the risk of heart disease and increases longevity—even though the latest dietary guidelines from the Department of Health and Human Services note the benefits of moderate alcohol use. In the 1990s, more than a dozen states have passed laws making it illegal to publicly disparage the quality of perishable items—that is, fruits and vegetables—without having "sound scientific inquiry, facts, or data" to back you up.

Landlords can't advertise that an apartment is "within walking distance to synagogue"—an effective marketing point for Orthodox Jews, who aren't supposed to drive on the Sabbath—because it allegedly implies an intent to discriminate. Colleges try to ban politically incorrect speech; the University of Connecticut ordered students not to engage in "inappropriately directed laughter, inconsiderate jokes, and conspicuous exclusion [of another student] from conversation." (To be precise here, I believe that private colleges have the right to set rules for how their faculty and students will interact, including speech codes—which is not to say that such codes would be wise. But state colleges are bound by the First Amendment.)

And of course every new technology brings with it new demands for censorship from those who don't understand it, or who understand all too well that new forms of communication may shake up established orders. The 1996 telecommunications reform act, which admirably deregulated much of the industry, nevertheless included a Communications Decency Act that would prevent adults from seeing material that might be inappropriate for children. A 1996 law in France requires that at least 40 percent of the music broadcast by radio stations be French. It also requires that every second French song come from an artist who has never had a hit. "We're forcing listeners to listen to music they don't want to hear," says a radio programmer.

Most important, people who want to spend money to support the political candidates of their choice are limited to contributions of $1,000—sort of like telling the *New York Times* that it can write an editorial endorsing Bill Clinton but it can only print 1,000 copies of the paper. That's how the political establishment, while proclaiming its devotion to free speech, hobbles the kind of speech that might actually threaten its power.

There's a utilitarian argument for freedom of expression, of course: out of the clash of different opinions, truth will emerge. As John Milton put it, "Who ever knew Truth put to the worse in a free and open encounter?" But for most libertarians, the *primary* reason to defend free expression is individual rights.

The right of self-ownership certainly implies the right to decide for ourselves what food, drink, or drugs we will put into our own bodies; with whom we will make love (assuming our chosen partner agrees); and what kind of medical treatment we want (assuming a doctor agrees to provide it). These decisions are surely as personal and intimate as the choice of what to believe. We may make mistakes (at least in the eyes of others), but our ownership of our own lives means that others must confine their interference to advice and moral suasion, not coercion. And in a free society, such advice should come from private parties, not from government, which is at least potentially coercive (and in our own society is indeed quite coercive). The role of government is to protect our rights, not to poke its nose into our personal lives. Yet a few state governments as recently as 1980 banned alcohol in restaurants, and some twenty states today outlaw homosexual relations. The federal government currently prohibits the use of certain lifesaving and pain-relieving drugs that are available in Europe. It threatens us with prison if we choose to use such drugs as marijuana or cocaine. Even when it doesn't ban something, the government intrudes into our personal choices. It hectors us about smoking, nags us to eat a proper diet—all our daily foods organized into a neat pyramid chart—and advises us on how to have safe and happy sex. Libertarians don't mind advice, but we don't think the government should forcibly take our tax money and then use it to advise everyone in society on how to live.

## Freedom of Contract

The right to enter into contracts is crucially important to libertarianism and to civilization itself. The British scholar Henry Sumner Maine wrote that the history of civilization was a movement from a society of status to a society of contract—that is, from a society in which each person was born into his place and was defined by his status to one in which the relationships among individuals are determined by free consent and agreement.

Libertarianism is neither libertinism nor chaos. People in a libertarian society may be bound by many rules and restrictions. But only the most general of these is unchosen: the minimal duty to respect everyone else's natural rights. Most of the rules that bind us in a free society we assume by contract, that is, by *choice.* We may, for instance, assume an obligation by signing a rental agreement. In that case, the owner of the house assumes the obligation to allow a tenant to live in the house for, say, a year and to maintain the house in an agreed-upon condition. The tenant assumes the obligation to pay the rent every month and avoid unnecessary damage to the house. The contract may spell out other obligations assumed by either party—thirty days' notice to terminate the agreement, a guarantee of heat and hot water (probably taken for granted in modern America, but by no means assumed in America fifty years ago or in many parts of the world today), no loud parties, and so on. Once the contract is signed, both parties are bound by its terms. Both can also be said to have acquired new rights by signing the contract—not natural rights, but special rights. The owner now has a right to a payment from the tenant every month, and the tenant has a right to live in the house for an agreed-upon term. This is not a general right to an income or to housing, but a particular right created by voluntary agreement.

Other contracts, of course, can apply to virtually anything in a free society: mortgages, marriage, employment, sales, cooperative agreements, insurance, club or association membership, and so on. Why do people sign contracts? Largely to remove some of the uncertainty from life and enable us to pursue projects that require some assurance of others' continuing cooperation. You could call your employer early every morning and ask if he had work for you and what he'd be willing to pay, but both of you prefer to make a long-term agreement (even if most American employment contracts allow either party to cancel the arrangement at will). You could pay your landlady every morning for a night's lodging, but obviously you both prefer to eliminate the uncertainty of that arrangement. And for people who can't make long-term arrangements, there are short-term options as well, such as hotels for travelers, where the contract is frequently for one night's lodging.

What is the nature of a contract? Is it just a promise? No, a contract is a mutual exchange of title to property. For a contract to be valid, both parties must have legitimate title to the property that they propose to exchange. If they do, then they can agree to transfer their title to another person in return for title to some property that he owns. Remember, every object has a bundle of property rights attached to it; the owner can transfer the whole bundle of rights or only some of them. When you sell an apple or a house, you generally transfer the entire bundle of rights in return for some consideration, probably money, from the other party. But when you rent a house, you transfer only the right to live in the house for a specified period of time under specified rules. When you lend money, you transfer the title to a certain sum of money now in return for title to a certain sum at some point in the future. Since it's always better to have money now than later, the borrower generally agrees to pay back a larger sum than the one borrowed. Thus, "interest" is the inducement that persuades a lender to give up money now and get it back only later.

Failure to live up to a contract is a form of theft. If Smith borrows $1,000 from Jones, agrees to pay back $1,100 a year later, and doesn't do so, he is in effect a thief. He has stolen $1,100 that belongs to Jones. If Jones sells Smith a car, guaranteeing that it has a working radio, and it doesn't, then Jones is a thief: he has taken Smith's money and not delivered what he contracted to deliver.

Without contracts, it would be difficult for an economy to

move beyond the subsistence level. Contracts enable us to make long-term plans and to carry on business over a wide geographical area and with people we don't know.

For an extended society to work, it is essential that people meet the obligations they have assumed and that contracts be enforced. If people are not generally trustworthy, none of us will want to enter into contracts with people we don't know, and the market economy will not be able to expand and flourish. If specific individuals renege on their contracts, people won't want to do business with them and they may find limited opportunities in the market system. But when people do live up to their contracts, and especially when most people do, vast and complex networks of contracts can make possible long chains of production over time and distance, allowing us to create the amazing technological achievements and the previously unimaginable standard of living of modern capitalism.

## Do You Have to Believe in Natural Rights to Be a Libertarian?

Most intellectuals who call themselves libertarians believe in the concept of natural individual rights and agree, more or less, with the above outline. The case for rights presented here reflects the arguments of John Locke, David Hume, Thomas Jefferson, William Lloyd Garrison, and Herbert Spencer; twentieth century libertarians such as Ayn Rand, Murray Rothbard, Robert Nozick, and Roy Childs; and contemporary philosophers such as Jan Narveson, Douglas Rasmussen, Douglas Den Uyl, Tibor Machan, and David Kelley.

However, some libertarians, especially economists, do not accept the theory of natural individual rights. Jeremy Bentham, a generally libertarian British philosopher of the early nineteenth century, derided natural rights as "nonsense upon stilts." Such modern economists as Ludwig von Mises, Milton Friedman, and Milton's son David Friedman reject natural rights and argue for libertarian policy conclusions on the basis of their beneficial consequences.

Such a position is often called utilitarianism. The classic formulation of utilitarianism is to take as a standard for ethics and political philosophy "the greatest good for the greatest number." That sounds unobjectionable, but it has some problems. How do we know what is good for millions of people? And what if the overwhelming majority in some society want something truly reprehensible—to expropriate the Russian kulaks, genitally mutilate teenage girls, or murder the Jews? Surely a utilitarian faced with the claim that the greatest number thought that such a policy would do the greatest good would fall back on some other principle—probably an innate sense that certain fundamental rights are self-evident.

## Mises's Utilitarianism

The economist Ludwig von Mises was both a firm utilitarian and an uncompromising advocate of laissez-faire economics. How did he justify his rejection of all coercive interference into market processes if not by a doctrine of individual rights? He said that as an economic scientist he could demonstrate that interventionist policies would bring about results that even the advocates of those policies would consider undesirable. But, as Mises's student Murray Rothbard asks, how does Mises know what the interventionists want? Mises can demonstrate that price controls will produce shortages, but maybe the advocates of price controls are socialists who want the controls as a step toward total government control of the economy, or extreme environmentalists who deplore excessive consumption and think fewer goods are a great idea, or egalitarians who figure that at least if there are shortages the rich won't be able to buy more than the poor.

Mises explains that he "presupposes that people prefer life to death, health to sickness, nourishment to starvation, abundance to poverty." If so, the economist can demonstrate that private property and free markets are the best way to achieve that goal. He's right, as we'll discuss further in chapter 8, but he's still making a big assumption. People may well prefer *some* less abundance in exchange for more equality, or preserving the family farm, or simply hurting the rich out of envy. How can a utilitarian object to taking people's property if a majority have determined that they don't mind the reduced economic growth that such a policy will generate? Thus, most libertarians conclude that liberty is better protected by a system of individual rights than by simple utilitarianism or economic analysis.

This is not to say, Let justice be done though the heavens fall. Of course consequences matter, and few of us would be libertarians if we thought a strict adherence to individual rights would lead to a society of conflict and poverty. Because individual rights are rooted in the nature of man, it is natural that societies that respect rights are characterized by a greater degree of harmony and abundance. Laissez-faire economic policy, based on a strict respect for rights, *will* lead to the greatest prosperity for the greatest number. But the root of our social rules must be the protection of each individual's right to life, liberty, and property.

## Emergencies

In his book *The Machinery of Freedom,* after making a powerful case for the benefits of libertarian policies, David Friedman poses several objections to libertarian principles as embodied in the law of equal freedom and the nonaggression axiom. Many of them involve emergency or "lifeboat" situations. The classic lifeboat example is, suppose you're in a shipwreck, and there's only one lifeboat that will hold four people, but there are eight people trying to cling to it. How do you decide? And—directed at libertarians or other natural-rights advocates—how does your rights theory answer this question? David Friedman says, suppose only by stealing a gun or a piece of scientific equipment can you stop a madman from shooting a dozen innocent people or an asteroid from crashing into Baltimore. Would you do it, and what about property rights?

Such questions can be valuable for testing the limits of a theory of rights. In some emergencies, considerations of rights go out the window. But those questions are not the first that students of ethics should examine, and they don't tell us much about the ethical systems humans need, because such questions involve situations that humans are likely never to encounter in the course of a life. The first task of an ethical system is to enable men and women to live peaceful, productive, cooperative lives in the normal course of events. We don't live in lifeboats;

we live in a world of scarce resources in which we all seek to improve our lives and the lives of those we love.

## The Limits of Rights

We can imagine other, less outlandish, challenges to the notion that natural rights are absolute, that is, in the words of the philosophers Douglas Rasmussen and Douglas Den Uyl, that they "'trump' all other moral considerations in constitutionally determining what matters of morality will be matters of legality." Must a starving man respect the rights of others and not steal a piece of bread? Must the victims of flood or famine die of starvation or exposure while others have plenty of food and shelter?

Conditions of flood and famine are not normal. When they occur, according to Rasmussen and Den Uyl in *Liberty and Nature,* we may have to acknowledge that the conditions for social and political life no longer exist, at least temporarily. Libertarian rules enable social and political life to exist and provide a context in which people can pursue their own ends. In an emergency situation—two men fighting for one lifeboat, many people made homeless by disaster—social and political life may be impossible. Each person's moral obligation is to ensure at least the minimum conditions of his own survival. Rasmussen and Den Uyl write, "When social and political life is not possible, when it is in principle impossible for human beings to live among each other and pursue their well-being, consideration of individual rights is out of place; they do not apply."

For a man, through no fault of his own, to find himself unable to get work or assistance and on the verge of starvation is extremely rare in a functioning society. There is almost always work available at a wage sufficient to sustain life (though minimum-wage laws, taxes, and other government interventions may reduce the number of jobs). For those who really can't find work, there are relatives and friends available to help. For those without friends, there are shelters, missions, and other forms of charity. But for the sake of the theoretical analysis, let us assume that an individual has failed to find work or assistance and faces imminent starvation. He is presumably living in a world where social and political life is still possible; yet we may say that *he* is in an emergency situation and must take the action necessary for his own survival, even if that means stealing a loaf of bread. However, if his victim, on hearing his story, is unpersuaded, it may be appropriate to take the starving man to court and charge him with theft. A legal order still exists, though a judge or jury might decide to acquit the man after hearing the circumstances—without throwing out the general rules of justice and property.

Note that this analysis does not suggest that the starving man or the flood victim has a right to someone else's assistance or property; it merely says that rights cannot apply where social and political life is not possible. But have we discarded rights entirely, opening the door to redistribution of wealth to all those who find themselves in dire straits? No. We stress that these exceptions apply only in emergency situations. A key part of the situation must be that a person finds himself in a desperate situation *through no fault of his own.* It cannot be enough that he simply has less than others, or even that he has too little to survive. Rasmussen and Den Uyl write, "Poverty, ignorance, and illness are not metaphysical emergencies. Wealth and knowledge are not automatically given, like manna from heaven. The nature of human life and existence is such that every person has to use his own reason and intelligence to create wealth and knowledge."

If a person declines to get necessary education or training, refuses to work at uninteresting or poorly paid jobs, or destroys his own health, he can't claim to be in desperate straits through no fault of his own. A woman wrote to Ann Landers to ask whether she should feel obliged to give a kidney to a sister who—despite repeated warnings and offers of assistance from her family—had used alcohol and drugs to excess and ignored medical advice. Rights theory can't tell us what moral obligations we ought to feel toward family members, whatever responsibility they bear for their own condition; but it can tell us that such a person is not the moral equivalent of a shipwreck or famine victim.

We arrive at these extreme exceptions to rights protection only after several conditions have been satisfied: that one or more persons are in imminent danger of death from exposure, starvation, or illness; that they were put in such straits through no fault of their own; that there is no time or opportunity for any other solution; that despite all efforts they have been unable to find either remunerative work or private charity; and that they recognize that they have incurred an obligation to someone whose property they take, that is, that as soon as they are on their feet again they will endeavor to repay whatever property they took.

The possibility that rights may not apply to conditions where social and political life is impossible does not undermine the moral status and social benefits of rights in normal situations. We live virtually all of our lives in normal situations. Our ethics should be designed for our survival and flourishing in normal conditions.

A final word on utilitarian libertarianism: Libertarians who reject natural rights as a basis for their views nevertheless arrive at virtually the same policy conclusions as rights-based libertarians. Some even say that government should operate *as if* people had natural rights—that is, that government should protect each individual's person and property from aggression by others and otherwise leave people free to make their own decisions. The legal scholar Richard Epstein, after offering in his book *Simple Rules for a Complex World* an essentially utilitarian case for self-ownership and private property, concludes by arguing that "the consequences for human happiness and productivity" of the principle of self-ownership "are so powerful that it should be treated as a moral imperative, even though the most powerful justification for the rule is empirical, not deductive."

## What Rights Aren't

As the complaints about a proliferation of rights indicate, political debate in modern America is indeed driven by claims of rights. To some extent this reflects the overwhelming triumph of (classical) rights-based liberalism in the United States. Locke, Jefferson, Madison, and the abolitionists laid down as a fundamental rule of both law and public opinion that the function of government is to protect rights. Thus, any rights claim effectively trumps any other consideration in public policy.

Unfortunately, academic and popular understanding of natural rights has declined over the years. Too many Americans now believe that any desirable thing is a right. They fail to distinguish between a right and a value. Some claim a right to a job, others a right to be protected from the existence of pornography somewhere in town. Some claim a right not to be bothered by cigarette smoke in restaurants, others a right not to be fired if they are smokers. Gay activists claim a right not to be discriminated against; their opponents—echoing Mencken's jibe that Puritanism is "the haunting fear that someone, somewhere may be happy"—claim a right to know that no one is engaging in homosexual relationships. Thousands of lobbyists roam the halls of Congress claiming for their clients a right to welfare, housing, education, Social Security, farm subsidies, protection from imports, and so on.

As courts and legislatures recognize more and more such "rights," rights claims become ever more audacious. A woman in Boston claims "my constitutional right to work out with [the heaviest] weights I can lift," even if the heaviest weights at her gym are in the men's weight room, which is off limits to women. A man in Annapolis, Maryland, demands that the city council require pizza and other food-delivery companies to deliver to his neighborhood, which the companies say is too dangerous, and the council is receptive to his request. He says, "I want the same rights any other Annapolitan has." But no Annapolitan has the right to force anyone else to do business with him, especially when the company feels it would be putting its employees in danger. A deaf man is suing the YMCA, which won't certify him for lifeguard duty because, according to the YMCA, a lifeguard needs to be able to hear cries of distress. An unmarried couple in California claim a right to rent an apartment from a woman who says their relationship offends her religious beliefs.

How do we sort out all these rights claims? There are two basic approaches. First, we can decide on the basis of political power. Anyone who can persuade a majority of Congress, or a state legislature, or the Supreme Court, will have a "right" to whatever he desires. In that case, we will have a plethora of conflicting rights claims, and the demands on the public treasury will be limitless, but we'll have no theory to deal with them; when conflicts occur, the courts and legislatures will sort them out on an ad hoc basis. Whoever seems most sympathetic, or has the most political power, wins.

The other approach is to go back to first principles, to assess each rights claim in the light of each individual's right to life, liberty, and property. Fundamental rights *cannot* conflict. Any claim of conflicting rights must represent a misinterpretation of fundamental rights. That's one of the premises, and the virtues, of rights theory: because rights are universal, they can be enjoyed by every person at the same time in any society. Adherence to first principles may require us, in any given instance, to reject a rights claim by a sympathetic petitioner or to acknowledge someone else's right to engage in actions that most of us find offensive. What does it mean to have a right, after all, if it doesn't include the right to do wrong?

To acknowledge people's ability to take responsibility for their actions, the very essence of a rights-bearing entity, is to accept each person's right to be "irresponsible" in his exercise of those rights, subject to the minimal condition that he not violate the rights of others. David Hume recognized that justice frequently required us to make decisions that seem unfortunate in a given context: "However single acts of justice may be contrary, either to public or private interest, 'tis certain, that the whole plan or scheme is highly conducive, or indeed absolutely requisite, both to the support of society, and the well-being of every individual." Thus, he says, we may sometimes have to "restore a great fortune to a miser or a seditious bigot," but "every individual person must find himself a gainer" from the peace, order, and prosperity that a system of property rights establishes in society.

If we accept the libertarian view of individual rights, we have a standard by which to sort out all these conflicting rights claims. We can see that a person has a right to acquire property, either by homesteading unowned property or—in almost all cases in modern society—by persuading someone who owns property to give or sell it to him. The new property owner then has a right to use it as he chooses. If he wants to rent an apartment to a black person, or to a grandmother with two grandchildren, then it is a violation of property rights for zoning laws to forbid that. If a Christian landlady refuses to rent a room to unmarried couples, it would be unjust to use the power of government to force her to do so. (Of course, other people have every right to consider her prejudiced and to express their opinions, on their own property or in newspapers that choose to publish their criticisms.)

People have a right to take up any line of business for which they can find a willing employer or customers—thus the classical liberal rallying cry of *"la carrière ouverte aux talents"* ("opportunity to the talented") not protected by guilds and monopolies—but they don't have a right to force anyone to hire them or do business with them. Farmers have a right to plant crops on their own property and sell them, but they don't have "a right to a living wage." People have a right not to read information about midwifery; they have a right not to sell it in their own bookstores or allow it to be transmitted over their own on-line service; but they don't have a right to prevent other people from entering into various contracts to produce, sell, and buy such information. Here again, we see, the right to a free press comes back to freedom of property and contract.

One of the benefits of the system of private property—or several property, as Hayek and others have called it—is pluralism and the decentralization of decision making. There are 6 million businesses in the United States; rather than having one set of rules for all of them, a system of pluralism and property rights means that each business can make its own decisions. Some employers will offer higher wages and less pleasant working conditions; others will offer a different package, and potential employees can choose. Some employers will no doubt be prejudiced against blacks, or Jews, or women—or even men, as a 1995 lawsuit against the Jenny Craig Company complained —and will pay the costs associated with that, and others will profit by hiring the best workers regardless of race, gender, religion, sexual orientation, or any other non-work-related characteristic. There are 400,000 restaurants in the United States; why should they all have the same rules about smoking, as more and more governments are mandating? Why not let different restaurants experiment with different ways to attract customers? The board of directors of the Cato Institute has banned smoking in our building. That is a real imposition on one of my colleagues, who slips off to the garage for a desperate puff on the vile weed every hour or so. His attitude is, "I'd like to have an interesting job, with congenial colleagues, at a great salary, in an office that allowed smoking. But a really interesting job, with congenial colleagues, at an adequate salary, in a nonsmoking office, is better than the other alternatives available to me."

The *Wall Street Journal* reported recently that "employers will increasingly be asked to juggle the demands of workers who want to express their faith during the workday and those who don't want to hear it." Some employees are demanding the "right" to practice their religion in the workplace—with on-the-job Bible study and prayer sessions, wearing large antiabortion buttons with a color photo of a fetus, and the like—while other employees are suing to demand a "right" not to hear about religion in the workplace. Government, either through Congress or the courts, could make a rule on how employers and employees must deal with religion and other controversial ideas in the workplace. But if we relied on the system of property rights and pluralism, we would let millions of businesses make their own decisions, each owner weighing his own religious convictions, the concerns of his employees, and whatever other factors seem important to him. Potential employees could negotiate with employers, or make their own decisions about which workplace environment they preferred, while also taking into account such other considerations as salary, fringe benefits, convenience to home, hours of work, how interesting the work is, and so on. Life is full of trade-offs; better to let those trade-offs be made on a localized and decentralized basis than by a central authority.

## How the Government Complicates Rights

I've argued that conflicts over rights can be settled by relying on a consistent definition of natural rights, especially private property, on which all our rights depend. Many of the most contentious conflicts over rights in our society occur when we transfer decisions from the private sector to the government, where there is no private property. Should prayers be said in school? Should residents of an apartment complex be allowed to own guns? Should theaters present sexually explicit productions? None of these questions would be political if the schools, apartments, and theaters were private. The proper stance would be to let the owners make their own decisions, and then potential customers could decide whether they wanted to patronize the establishments.

But make these institutions public, and suddenly there is no owner with a clear property right. Some political body decides, and the whole society may get drawn into the argument. Some parents don't want the government forcing their children to listen to a prayer; but if school prayer is banned in public schools, then other parents feel that they are being denied the right to raise their children as they see fit. If Congress tells the National Endowment for the Arts not to fund allegedly obscene art, artists may feel that their liberty is restricted; but what about the liberty of the taxpayers who elected those members of Congress to spend their tax dollars wisely? Should the government be able to tell a doctor at a government-funded pregnancy clinic not to recommend abortion?

Duke University law professor Walter Dellinger, a top legal official in the Clinton administration, warned that such rules are "especially alarming in light of the growing role of government as subsidizer, landlord, employer and patron of the arts." He's right. Such rules extend the government's reach into more and more aspects of our lives. But as long as government *is* the biggest landlord and employer, we can't expect citizens and their representatives to be indifferent to how their money is spent.

Government money always comes with strings attached. And government must make rules for the property it controls, rules that will almost certainly offend some citizen-taxpayers. That's why it would be best to privatize as much property as possible, to depoliticize decision making about the use of property.

We should recognize and protect natural rights because justice demands it, and also because a system of individual rights and widely dispersed property leads to a free, tolerant, and civil society.

*Chapter 4*

# THE DIGNITY OF THE INDIVIDUAL

*N*ot long ago, on a Saturday morning in a small city in France, I walked up to an automatic teller machine set into the massive stone wall of a bank that was closed for the weekend. I stuck a piece of plastic into the machine, punched some buttons, waited a few seconds, and collected about $200, all without contact with any human being, much less anyone who knew me. I then took a taxi to the airport, where I approached a clerk at a rental-car counter, showed him a different piece of plastic, signed a form, and walked out with the keys to a $20,000 automobile, which I promised to return to someone else at a different location in a few days.

These transactions are so routine that the reader wonders why I bother to mention them. But stop for a moment and reflect on the wonders of the modern world: A man I had never seen before, who would never see me again, with whom I could barely communicate, trusted me with a car. A bank set up an automatic system that would give me cash on request thousands of miles from my home. A generation ago such things weren't possible; a couple of generations ago they would have been unimaginable; today they are the commonplace infrastructure of our economy. How did such a worldwide network of trust come about? We'll discuss the strictly economic aspects of this system in a later chapter. In this and the next few chapters, I want to explore how we get from the lone individual to the complex network of associations and connections that make up the modern world.

## Individualism

For libertarians, the basic unit of social analysis is the individual. It's hard to imagine how it could be anything else. Individuals are, in all cases, the source and foundation of creativity, activity, and society. Only individuals can think, love, pursue projects, act. Groups don't have plans or intentions. Only individuals are capable of choice, in the sense of anticipating the outcomes of alternative courses of action and weighing the consequences. Individuals, of course, often create and deliberate in groups, but it is the individual mind that ultimately makes choices. Most important, only individuals can take responsibility for their actions. As Thomas Aquinas wrote in *On the Unity of the Intellect,* the concept of a group mind or will would mean that an individual would "not be the master of his act, nor will any act of his be praiseworthy or blameworthy." Every individual is responsible for his actions; that's what gives him rights and obligates him to respect the rights of others.

But what about society? Doesn't society have rights? Isn't society responsible for lots of problems? Society is vitally important to individuals, as we'll discuss in the next few chapters. It is to achieve the benefits of interaction with others, as Locke and Hume explained, that individuals enter into society and establish a system of rights. But at the conceptual level, we must understand that society is composed of individuals. It has no independent existence. If ten people form a society, there are still ten people, not eleven. It's also hard to define the boundaries of a society; where does one "society" end and another begin? By contrast, it's easy to see where one individual ends and another begins, an important advantage for social analysis and for allocating rights and duties.

The libertarian writer Frank Chodorov wrote in *The Rise and Fall of Society* that "Society Are People":

Society is a collective concept and nothing else; it is a convenience for designating a number of people. . . . The concept of Society as a metaphysical concept falls flat when we observe that Society disappears when the component parts disperse; as in the case of a "ghost town" or of a civilization we learn about by the artifacts they left behind. When the individuals disappear so does the whole. The whole has no separate existence.

We cannot escape responsibility for our actions by blaming society. Others cannot impose obligations on us by appealing to the alleged rights of society, or of the community. In a free society we have our natural rights and our general obligation to respect the rights of other individuals. Our other obligations are those we choose to assume by contract.

Yet none of this is to defend the sort of "atomistic individualism" that philosophers and professors like to deride. We *do* live together and work in groups. How one could be an atomistic individual in our complex modern society is not clear: would that mean eating only what you grow, wearing what you make, living in a house you build for yourself, restricting yourself to natural medicines you extract from plants? Some critics of capitalism or advocates of "back to nature" might endorse such a plan, but few libertarians would want to move to a desert island and renounce the benefits of what Adam Smith called the Great Society, the complex and productive society made possible by social interaction.

Individuals benefit greatly from their interactions with other individuals, a point usually summed up by traditional philosophers as "cooperation" and by modern texts in sociology and management as "synergy." Life would indeed be nasty, brutish, and short if it were solitary.

## The Dignity of the Individual

Indeed, the dignity of the individual under libertarianism is a dignity that *enhances* social well-being. Libertarianism is good not just for individuals but for societies. The positive basis of libertarian social analysis is methodological individualism, the recognition that only individuals act. The ethical or normative basis of libertarianism is respect for the dignity and worth of every (other) individual. This is expressed in the philosopher Immanuel Kant's dictum that each person is to be treated not merely as a means but as an end in himself.

Of course, as late as Jefferson's time and beyond, the concept of the individual with full rights did not include all people. Astute observers noted that problem at the time and began to apply the ringing phrases of Locke's *Second Treatise of Government* and the Declaration of Independence more fully. The equality and individualism that underlay the emergence of capitalism naturally led people to start thinking about the rights of women and of slaves, especially African American slaves in the United States. It's no accident that feminism and abolitionism emerged out of the ferment of the Industrial Revolution and the American and French revolutions. Just as a better understanding of natural rights was developed during the American struggle against specific injustices suffered by the colonies, the feminist and abolitionist Angelina Grimké noted in an 1837 letter to Catherine E. Beecher, "I have found the Anti-Slavery cause to be the high school of morals in our land—the school in which *human rights* are more fully investigated, and better understood and taught, than in any other."

## Feminism

The liberal writer Mary Wollstonecraft (wife of William Godwin and mother of Mary Wollstonecraft Shelley, the author of *Frankenstein*) responded to Edmund Burke's *Reflections on the Revolution in France* by writing *A Vindication of the Rights of Men,* in which she argued that "the birthright of man . . . is such a degree of liberty, civil and religious, as is compatible with the liberty of every other individual with whom he is united in a social compact." Just two years later she published *A Vindication of the Rights of Woman,* which asked, "Consider . . . whether, when men contend for their freedom . . . it be not inconsistent and unjust to subjugate women?"

Women involved in the abolitionist movement also took up the feminist banner, grounding their arguments in both cases in the idea of self-ownership, the fundamental right of property in one's own person. Angelina Grimké based her work for abolition and women's rights explicitly on a Lockean libertarian foundation: "Human beings have *rights,* because they are *moral* beings: the rights of *all* men grow out of their moral nature; and as all men have the same moral nature, they have essentially the same rights. . . . If rights are founded in the nature of our moral being, then the *mere circumstance of sex* does not give to man higher rights and responsibilities, than to women." Her sister, Sarah Grimké, also a campaigner for the rights of blacks and women, criticized the Anglo-American legal principle that a wife was not responsible for a crime committed at the direction or even in the presence of her husband in a letter to the Boston Female Anti-Slavery Society: "It would be difficult to frame a law better calculated to destroy the responsibility of woman as a moral being, or a free agent." In this argument she emphasized the fundamental individualist point that every individual must, and only an individual can, take responsibility for his or her actions.

A libertarian must necessarily be a feminist, in the sense of being an advocate of equality under the law for all men and women, though unfortunately many contemporary feminists are far from being libertarians. Libertarianism is a political philosophy, not a complete guide to life. A libertarian man and woman might decide to enter into a traditional working-husband/nonworking-wife marriage, but that would be their voluntary agreement. The only thing libertarianism tells us is that they are political equals with full rights to choose the living arrangement they prefer. In their 1986 book *Gender Justice,* David L. Kirp, Mark G. Yudof, and Marlene Strong Franks endorsed this libertarian concept of feminism: "It is neither equality as sameness nor equality as differentness that adequately comprehends the issue, but instead the very different concept of equal liberty under the law, rooted in the idea of individual autonomy."

## Slavery and Racism

The abolitionist movement, too, grew logically out of the Lockean libertarianism of the American Revolution. How could

Americans proclaim that "all men are created equal . . . endowed by their Creator with certain unalienable rights," without noticing that they themselves were holding other men and women in bondage? They could not, of course, and indeed the world's first antislavery society was founded in Philadelphia the year before Jefferson wrote those words. Jefferson himself owned slaves, yet he included a passionate condemnation of slavery in his draft of the Declaration of Independence: "[King George] has waged cruel war against human nature itself, violating its most sacred rights of life and liberty in the persons of a distant people who never offended him." The Continental Congress deleted that passage, but Americans lived uneasily with the obvious contradiction between their commitment to individual rights and the institution of slavery.

Although they were intimately connected in American history, slavery and racism are not inherently bound together. In the ancient world the act of enslaving another person did not imply his moral or intellectual inferiority; it was just accepted that conquerors could enslave their captives. Greek slaves were often teachers in Roman households, their intellectual eminence acknowledged and exploited.

In any case, racism in one form or another is an age-old problem, but it clearly clashes with the universal ethics of libertarianism and the equal natural rights of all men and women. As Ayn Rand pointed out in her essay "Racism,"

> Racism is the lowest, most crudely primitive form of collectivism. It is the notion of ascribing moral, social or political significance to a man's genetic lineage . . . which means, in practice, that a man is to be judged, not by his own character and actions, but by the characters and actions of a collective of ancestors.

In her works Rand emphasized the importance of individual productive achievement to a sense of efficacy and happiness. She argued, "Like every other form of collectivism, racism is a quest for the unearned. It is a quest for automatic knowledge— for an automatic evaluation of men's characters that bypasses the responsibility of exercising rational or moral judgment— and, above all, a quest for *an automatic self-esteem* (or pseudo-self-esteem)." That is, some people want to feel good about themselves because they have the same skin color as Leonardo da Vinci or Thomas Edison, rather than because of their individual achievements; and some want to dismiss the achievements of people who are smarter, more productive, more accomplished than themselves, just by uttering a racist epithet.

## Individualism Today

How fares the individual in America today? Conservatives, liberals, and communitarians all complain at times about "excessive individualism," generally meaning that Americans seem more interested in their own jobs and families than in the schemes of social planners, pundits, and Washington interest groups. However, the real problem in America today is not an excess of individual freedom but the myriad ways in which government infringes on the rights and dignity of individuals.

Through much of Western history, racism has been wielded by whites against blacks and, to a lesser extent, people of other races. From slavery to Jim Crow to the State Sovereignty Commission of Mississippi to the comprehensive racist system of apartheid to the treatment of the native inhabitants of Australia, New Zealand, and America, some whites have used the coercive mechanisms of the state to deny both the humanity and the natural rights of people of color. Asian Americans have also been subjected to such deprivations of liberty, though never on the scale of slavery: the Chinese Exclusion Act of 1882, the nineteenth-century law forbidding Chinese Americans to testify in court, and most notoriously the incarceration of Japanese Americans (and the theft of their property) during World War II. European settlers in North America sometimes traded and lived in peace with American Indians, but too often they stole Indian lands and practiced policies of extermination, such as the notorious uprooting of Indians from the southern states and their forced march along the Trail of Tears in the 1830s.

Millions of Americans fought to overturn first slavery and more recently Jim Crow and the other trappings of state-sponsored racism. However, the civil rights movement eventually lost its moorings and undercut its libertarian goal of equal rights under the law with advocacy of a new form of state-sponsored discrimination. Instead of guaranteeing to every American equal rights to own property, make contracts, and participate in public institutions, laws today *require* racial discrimination by both governments and private businesses. The Congressional Research Service in 1995 found 160 federal programs employing explicit race and gender criteria. Throughout the early 1990s it was the policy of the University of California at Berkeley to choose half its freshman class on the basis of grades and test scores, the other half according to racial quotas. Other major colleges, despite a lot of rhetoric designed to confuse the issue, do the same.

If we hand out jobs and college admissions on the basis of race, we can expect plenty of group conflict over which groups will get how many places, just as we've seen in countries from South Africa to Malaysia where goods are handed out by racial quota. We'll get more cases like the Hispanic member of the U.S. Postal Service Board of Governors who complained that the Postal Service was hiring too many blacks and not enough Hispanics. Just as some blacks tried to "pass" as white in order to get the rights and opportunities reserved by law for whites earlier in this century, we see people today—and we can expect to see more—trying to claim membership in whatever racial group has the highest quotas. In Montgomery County, Maryland, in 1995, two half-Caucasian, half-Asian five-year-old girls were denied a place in a French-immersion school as Asian applicants but were told that they could reapply as whites. In San Francisco hundreds of parents each year change their official ethnicity to get their children into the schools they prefer, and white firefighters conduct elaborate genealogical investigations in hopes of turning up a long-lost Spanish ancestor who will qualify them as Hispanic. One California contractor won a $19 million contract from the Los Angeles rapid transit system because he was ¹/₆₄ American Indian. Soon we may need to send observers to South Africa to find out how their old Population Registration Act worked, with its racial courts deciding who was really white, black, "colored," or Asian. Hardly a happy prospect for a nation founded on the rights of the individual. How much better off we might be today if the Census Bureau had accepted the proposal of the American Civil Liberties Union to remove the "race" question from the census forms in 1960.

Of course, official race and gender discrimination is not the only way in which governments treat us as groups rather than as individuals today. We're constantly exhorted to look at public policy in terms of its effect on groups, not whether it treats individuals according to the principle of equal rights. Interest groups from the American Association of Retired Persons to the National Organization for Women to the National Gay and Lesbian Task Force to the Veterans of Foreign Wars to the National Farmers Organization to the American Federation of Government Employees encourage us to think of ourselves as members of groups, not as individuals.

First Lady Hillary Rodham Clinton epitomizes some of the problems individualism faces in contemporary America. Beginning with the sensible if often exaggerated proverb that "it takes a village to raise a child," she ends up, in her book *It Takes a Village,* calling on all 250 million Americans to raise each child. We can't possibly all take responsibility for millions of children, of course. She calls for "a consensus of values and a common vision of what we can do today, individually and collectively, to build strong families and communities." But there can be no such collective consensus. In any free society, millions of people will have different ideas about how to form families, how to rear children, and how to associate voluntarily with others. Those differences are not just a result of a lack of understanding of each other; no matter how many Harvard seminars and National Conversations funded by the National Endowment for the Humanities we have, we will never come to a national consensus on such intimate moral matters. Clinton implicitly recognizes that when she insists that there will be times when "the village itself [read: the federal government] must act in place of parents" and accept "those responsibilities in all our names through the authority we vest in government." In the end, then, she reveals her antilibertarianism: *Government* must make decisions about how we raise our children.

Even when the government doesn't step in to take children from their parents, Hillary Clinton sees it constantly advising, nagging, hectoring parents: "Videos with scenes of common-sense baby care—how to burp an infant, what to do when soap gets in his eyes, how to make a baby with an earache comfortable—could be running continuously in doctors' offices, clinics, hospitals, motor vehicle offices, or any other place where people gather and have to wait." The child-care videos could alternate with videos on the food pyramid, the evils of smoking and drugs, the need for recycling, the techniques of safe sex, the joys of physical fitness, and all the other things the responsible adult citizens of a complex modern society need to know. Sort of like the telescreen in *1984*.

When Bill Clinton announced that by his own authority he was issuing new regulations on tobacco and smoking in the name of "the young people of the United States," he said, "We're their parents, and it is up to us to protect them." And Hillary Clinton told *Newsweek* in 1996, "There is no such thing as other people's children." These are profoundly anti-individualist and antifamily ideas. Instead of recognizing individual parents as moral agents who can and must take responsibility for their own decisions and actions, the Clintons would absorb them into a giant mass of collective parenting directed by the federal government.

The growing state has increasingly treated adult citizens as children. It takes more and more money from those who produce it and doles it back to us like an allowance, through a myriad of "transfer programs" ranging from Head Start and student loans to farm subsidies, corporate welfare, unemployment programs, and Social Security. It doesn't trust us to decide for ourselves (even in consultation with our doctors) what medicines to take, or where our children should go to school, or what we can access through our computers. The state's all-encompassing embrace is particularly smothering for those who fall into its much-touted safety net, which ends up trapping people in a nightmare world of subsidy and dependence, taking away their obligation as responsible adults to support themselves and sapping them of their self-respect. A caller to a talk show on the government radio network complained recently, "You can't cut the budget without causing the total economic—and in some cases physical—annihilation of millions of us who have nowhere to turn except to the federal government." What has the government done to make millions of adult Americans afraid that they could not survive the loss of a welfare check?

Libertarians sometimes say, "Conservatives want to be your daddy, telling you what to do and what not to do. Liberals want to be your mommy, feeding you, tucking you in, and wiping your nose. Libertarians want to treat you as an adult." Libertarianism is the kind of individualism that is appropriate to a free society: treating adults as adults, letting them make their own decisions even when they make mistakes, trusting them to find the best solutions for their own lives.

## Chapter 5

# PLURALISM AND TOLERATION

One of the central facts of modern life, which any political theory must confront, is moral pluralism. Individuals have different concepts of the meaning of life, of the existence of God, of the ways to pursue happiness. One response to this reality may be termed "perfectionism," a political philosophy that seeks an institutional structure that will perfect human nature. Marx offered such an answer, claiming that socialism would allow human beings for the first time to achieve their full human potential. Theocratic religions offer a different answer, proposing to unite an entire people in a common understanding of their relationship to God. Communitarian philosophers also seek to bring about a community whose "substantive life," in the words of the Harvard University philosopher Michael Walzer, "is lived in a certain way—that is, faithful to the shared understandings of its members." Even some modern conservatives who believe, as the columnist George F. Will put it, that "statecraft is soulcraft," are trying to use the power of government to *remedy* the fact of moral pluralism.

Libertarians and individualist liberals have a different answer. Liberal theory accepts that in modern societies there will be irresolvable differences over what the good for human beings is and what their ultimate nature is. Some more Aristotelian liberals argue that human beings do indeed have one nature but that each human has an individual set of talents, needs, circumstances, and ambitions; so the good life for one person may differ from the good for another, despite their common nature. Self-directedness, the ability to choose one's own course in life, is part of the human good.

Thus, on either approach, libertarians believe the role of government is not to impose a particular morality but to establish a framework of rules that will guarantee each individual the freedom to pursue his own good in his own way—whether individually or in cooperation with others—so long as he does not infringe the freedom of others. Because no modern government can assume that its citizens share a complete and exhaustive moral code, the obligations imposed on people by force should be minimal. In the libertarian conception, the fundamental rules of the political system should be essentially negative: Don't violate the rights of others to pursue their own good in their own way. If a government tries to allocate resources and assign duties on the basis of a particular moral conception—according to need or moral desert—it will create social and political conflict. This is not to say that there is *no* substantive morality, or that all ways of life are "equally good," but merely that consensus on the best is unlikely to be reached and that when such matters are placed in the political realm, conflict is inevitable.

## Religious Toleration

One of the obvious implications of individualism, the idea that each person is an individual moral agent, is religious toleration. Libertarianism developed out of the long struggle for toleration, from the early Christians in the Roman Empire, to the Netherlands, to the Anabaptists in Central Europe, to the Dissenters from the Church of England, to the experiences of Roger Williams and Anne Hutchinson in the American colonies and beyond.

Self-ownership certainly included the concept of "a property in one's conscience," as James Madison put it. The Leveller Richard Overton wrote in 1646 that "every man by nature [is] Priest and Prophet in his own natural circuit and compass."

Locke agreed that "liberty of conscience is every man's natural right."

Beyond moral and theological arguments, though, there were strong practical arguments for religious toleration. As George H. Smith argues in his 1991 essay "Philosophies of Toleration," one group of advocates of toleration would have preferred to see uniformity of religious belief, "but they did not wish to impose uniformity in practice because of its staggering social costs—massive compulsion, civil wars, and social chaos." They recommended toleration as the best way to produce peace in society. The Jewish philosopher Baruch Spinoza, explaining the Dutch policy of toleration, wrote, "It is imperative that freedom of judgment should be granted, so that men may live together in harmony, however diverse, or even openly contradictory, their opinions may be." Spinoza pointed to the prosperity that the Dutch had achieved by allowing people of every sect to live peacefully and do business in their cities. As the English, observing the Dutch example, adopted a policy of relative toleration, Voltaire noted the same effect and recommended it to the French. Although Marx would later denounce the market for its impersonal nature, Voltaire recognized the advantages of that impersonality. As George Smith put it, "The ability to deal with others impersonally, to deal with them solely for mutual profit, means that personal characteristics, such as religious belief, become largely irrelevant."

Other advocates of toleration stressed the benefits of religious pluralism in theory. Out of argument, they said, truth will emerge. John Milton was the preeminent defender of this view, but Spinoza and Locke also endorsed it. British libertarians in the nineteenth century used terms like "free trade in religion" to oppose the establishment of the Anglican Church.

Some English Dissenters came to America to find freedom to practice religion in their own way, but not to grant it to others. They did not oppose special privileges for one religion; they just wanted it to be their own. But others among the new Americans not only supported religious toleration, they extended the argument to call for the separation of church and state, a truly radical idea at the time. After he was banished from the Massachusetts Bay Colony in 1636 for his heretical opinions, Roger

Williams wrote *The Bloudy Tenent of Persecution,* urging separation and seeking to protect Christianity from political control.
Williams's ideas, along with those of John Locke, spread
throughout the American colonies; established churches were
gradually disestablished, and the Constitution adopted in 1787
included no mention of God or religion, except for forbidding
religious tests for public office. In 1791 the First Amendment
was added, guaranteeing the free exercise of religion and forbidding any established church.

Members of the religious right today insist that America is—
or at least was—a Christian nation with a Christian government. The Dallas Baptist minister who delivered the
benediction at the Republican National Convention in 1984
says that "there is no such thing as separation of church and
state," and Christian Coalition founder Pat Robertson writes,
"The Constitution was designed to perpetuate a Christian
order." But as Isaac Kramnick and R. Laurence Moore note in
*The Godless Constitution,* Robertson's forebears understood the
Constitution better. Some Americans opposed ratification of
the Constitution because it was "coldly indifferent towards religion" and would leave "religion to shift wholly for itself." Nevertheless, the revolutionary Constitution was adopted, and
most of us believe that the experience with the separation of
church and state has been a happy one. As Roger Williams
might have predicted, churches are far stronger in the United
States, where they are left to fend for themselves, than in European countries where there is still an established church (such as
England and Sweden) or where churches are supported by gov-
ernment-collected taxes on their adherents (such as Germany).

## Separation of Conscience and State

We might reflect on *why* the separation of church and state
seems such a wise idea. First, it is wrong for the coercive authority of the state to interfere in matters of individual conscience. If we have rights, if we are individual moral agents, we
must be free to exercise our judgment and define our own relationship with God. That doesn't mean that a free, pluralistic so-

ciety won't have lots of persuasion and proselytizing—no doubt it will—but it does mean that such proselytizing must remain entirely persuasive, entirely voluntary.

Second, social harmony is enhanced by removing religion from the sphere of politics. Europe suffered through the Wars of Religion, as churches made alliances with rulers and sought to impose their theology on everyone in a region. Religious inquisitions, Roger Williams said, put towns "in an uproar." If people take their faith seriously, and if government is going to make one faith universal and compulsory, then people must contend bitterly—even to the death—to make sure that the *true* faith is established. Enshrine religion in the realm of persuasion, and there may be vigorous debate in society, but there won't be political conflict. As the experiences of Holland, England, and later the United States have shown, people can deal with one another in secular life without endorsing each other's private opinions.

Third, competition produces better results than subsidy, protection, and conformity. "Free trade in religion" is the best tool humans have to find the nearest approximation to the truth. Businesses coddled behind subsidies and tariffs will be weak and uncompetitive, and so will churches, synagogues, mosques, and temples. Religions that are protected from political interference but are otherwise on their own are likely to be stronger and more vigorous than a church that draws its support from government.

This last point reflects the humility that is an essential part of the libertarian worldview. Libertarians are sometimes criticized for being too "extreme," for having a "dogmatic" view of the role of government. In fact, their firm commitment to the full protection of individual rights and a strictly limited government reflects their fundamental humility. One reason to oppose the establishment of religion or any other morality is that we recognize the very real possibility that our own views may be wrong. Libertarians support a free market and widely dispersed property ownership because they know that the odds of a monopolist finding a great new advance for civilization are slim. Hayek stressed the crucial significance of human ignorance throughout his work. In *The Constitution of Liberty,* he wrote,

"The case for individual freedom rests chiefly on the recognition of the inevitable ignorance of all of us concerning a great many of the factors on which the achievement of our ends and welfare depends. . . . Liberty is essential in order to leave room for the unforeseeable and unpredictable." The nineteenth-century American libertarian Lillian Harman, rejecting state control of marriage and family, wrote in *Liberty* in 1895, "If I should be able to bring the entire world to live exactly as I live at present, what would that avail me in ten years, when as I hope, I shall have a broader knowledge of life, and my life therefore probably changed?" Ignorance, humility, toleration—not exactly a ringing battle cry, but an important argument for limiting the role of coercion in society.

If these themes are true, they have implications beyond religion. Religion is not the only thing that affects us personally and spiritually, and it is not the only thing that leads to cultural wars. For example, the family is the institution in which we learn most of our understanding of the world and our moral values. Despite Mario Cuomo's vision of America as a great family, or Hillary Clinton's global village, we each of us care more for our own children than for any other children, and we want to instill our own moral values and worldview in our children. That's why government interference into the family is so offensive and so controversial. We ought to establish a principle of the separation of family and state, a wall of separation as firm as that between church and state, and for the same reasons: to protect individual consciences, to reduce social conflict, and to lessen the baleful effects of subsidy and regulation on our families.

The other arena where we formally teach values to our children is education. We expect schools to give our children not only knowledge but also the moral strength to make wise decisions. Alas, in a pluralistic society we don't all agree on what those moral values should be. To begin with, some parents want reverence for God taught in the schools, and others don't. The First Amendment has correctly been interpreted to ban prayer in government schools; but to compel religious parents to pay taxes for schools and then forbid the tax-supported schools to give their children the education they want is surely unfair. In the Virginia Statute for Religious Freedom, Thomas Jefferson wrote, "To compel a man to furnish contributions of money for the propagation of opinions which he disbelieves is sinful and tyrannical." How much more offensive it is to tax a family to propagate *to their own children* opinions that they disbelieve.

The problems go well beyond religion. Should the schools require uniforms, open with the Pledge of Allegiance, allow gay teachers, separate boys and girls, teach antibusiness environmentalism, cultivate support for the Persian Gulf War, celebrate Christmas and/or Hanukkah, require drug tests? All of these decisions involve moral choices, and different parents will have different preferences. A government-run monopoly system has to make one decision for the whole community on such issues. Strict separation of education and state would respect the individual consciences of each family, reduce political conflict over highly charged issues, and strengthen each school in its sense of mission and the commitment of its students and their families. Parents could choose private schools for their children on the basis of the moral values and educational mission the schools offered, and no political conflict over what to teach would arise.

Like the church, the family, and the school, art also expresses, transmits, and challenges our deepest values. As the managing director of Baltimore's Center Stage put it, "Art has power. It has the power to sustain, to heal, to humanize . . . to change something in you. It's a frightening power, and also a beautiful power. . . . And it's essential to a civilized society." Because art—by which I include painting, sculpture, drama, literature, music, film, and more—is so powerful, dealing as it does with such basic human truths, we dare not entangle it with coercive government power. That means no censorship or regulation of art. It also means no tax-funded subsidies for arts and artists, for when government gets into the arts-funding business, we get political conflicts: Can the National Endowment for the Arts fund erotic photography? Can the Public Broadcasting System broadcast *Tales of the City,* which has gay characters? Can the Library of Congress display an exhibit on antebellum slave life? To avoid these political battles over how to spend the taxpayers' money, to keep art and its power in the realm of persuasion, we would be well advised to establish the separation of art and state.

And how about the divisive issue of race? Haven't we suffered through enough generations of government-supported racial discrimination? After the end of slavery—which was far too odious a violation of individual rights to be categorized as mere race discrimination—we added three amendments to the U.S. Constitution, each one designed to make good on the promises of the Declaration of Independence by guaranteeing every (male) American equal rights. Specifically, those amendments abolished slavery, promised equal protection of the laws to all citizens, and guaranteed that the right to vote would not be denied to anyone on the basis of race. But within a few years, state governments, with the acquiescence of the federal courts, began to limit the rights of African Americans to vote, to use public facilities, and to enter into economic life. The Jim Crow era lasted into the 1960s. Then, unfortunately, the federal government passed over the libertarian policy of equal rights for all in a blink of an eye and began to replace old forms of racial discrimination with new ones—quotas and set-asides and mandatory racial preferences. Just as the Jim Crow laws angered blacks (and all those who believed in equal rights), the new quota regime angered whites (and all those who believed in equal rights). The stage was set for more social conflict, and racial animosity seems in many ways to be increasing even as integration proceeds and incomes of African Americans rise rapidly relative to those of whites. Surely it would be better to apply the lesson of the Wars of Religion and keep government out of this sensitive area: Repeal laws that grant or deny rights or privileges on the basis of race, and establish separation of race and state.

At the same time, we should take a critical look at policies that have a disproportionately negative impact on those who have long suffered at the hands of government. Taxes and regulations that impede new businesses and job creation, for instance, especially hurt those who are not already part of the economic mainstream. Benjamin Hooks, who went on to head the NAACP, once bought a doughnut shop in Memphis from a man who had owned it for twenty-five years. "In those twenty-five years, they had passed all kinds of laws," he recalled. "You had to have separate rest rooms for men and women, you had to have ratproof walls and everything on God's earth. We were hit with all those regulations, and they cost us $30,000. We had to close the shop." He went on, "It's obvious now that nobody, but nobody, is buying into a decaying black ghetto except blacks themselves. So the effect of some regulations is almost 100 percent to exclude blacks." Occupational licensing laws also work like the medieval guilds to keep people out of good jobs. In cities like Miami, Chicago, and New York, it costs tens of thousands of dollars to buy a taxicab license, so an otherwise easy form of entrepreneurship is closed to people who don't already have capital.

One government policy whose discrimination against blacks goes largely unnoticed is the politically untouchable Social Security system. I'll say more about the overall system in chapter 10, but let me note here that like any massive, government-run, one-size-fits-all monopoly, Social Security was designed for a "typical" 1930s family. It doesn't work so well for people who don't fit the pattern. Unmarried and childless people are required to pay for survivor's insurance that they wouldn't choose to buy from a private insurer. Married working women can't get both spouse's benefits and their own, even though they must pay for them. And black people—because they have lower life expectancies than whites—pay the same taxes but receive far fewer benefits than whites. A study by the National Center for Policy Analysis found that a white male entering the labor market in 1986 could expect to receive 74 percent more in Social Security retirement benefits and 47 percent more in Medicare than a black male. A white working couple could expect about 35 percent more benefits than a black working couple. The disparity is strong at every level of income. A private, competitive retirement savings system would offer different plans to meet the needs of different people instead of one plan for everybody. As we eliminate racial preferences in the law, we should also seek to repeal laws that disproportionately harm poor people and minorities.

Now, in this as in so many areas, the libertarian solution is not a panacea. Social conflict over education, childbearing, and race will not end even with a constitutional amendment separating all of them from government interference. After all, the First Amendment has not ended legal and political battles over the government's relationship with religion. But it surely has limited and confined those battles, and the legal battles over where to draw the line in the other areas would be fought on narrower grounds than today's conflicts, where an expansive government reaches into every corner of American life. Depoliticization of our cultural disagreements would go a long way toward deescalating the cultural war.

*Chapter 6*

# LAW AND THE CONSTITUTION

$\mathcal{C}$losely tied to questions of the state's scope is the venerable libertarian principle of the rule of law. In its simplest form, this principle means that we should be governed by generally applicable laws, not by the arbitrary decisions of rulers—"a government of laws, not of men," as the Massachusetts Bill of Rights of 1780 put it.

In *The Constitution of Liberty,* Friedrich Hayek discusses the rule of law in detail. He lays out three aspects of the principle: Laws should be general and abstract, not intended to command specific actions by citizens; they should be known and certain, so that citizens can know in advance that their actions comply with the law; and they should apply equally to all persons.

These principles have important implications.

- The laws must apply to everyone, including the rulers.
- No one is above the law.
- To guard against the accumulation of arbitrary power, power should be divided.
- The laws should be made by one body and administered by another.
- An independent judiciary is necessary to ensure that the laws are administered fairly.

- Those who administer the law should have little discretion, because discretionary power is the very evil that the rule of law is intended to prevent.

## Judge-Made Law

There is a confusion in our modern language over the meaning of the word "law." We tend to think of law as something written by Congress or the state legislature. But in fact law is much older than any legislative body. As Hayek notes, "only the observance of common rules makes the peaceful existence of individuals in society possible." Those rules are the law, which originally developed through the process of deciding disputes. Laws were not laid down in advance by a lawgiver or legislative body; they were built up one by one, as each dispute was decided. Each new decision helped to delineate what rights people had, especially with regard to how they could use property and how contracts would be interpreted and enforced.

The evolution of law in this manner began before recorded history, but it is best known in the form of Roman law, especially the Justinian Code (or *Corpus Juris Civilis*), which still underlies Continental European law, and of the English common law, which continued to develop in the United States and other former English colonies. Codification of law, such as the Uniform Commercial Code, usually reflects an attempt to collect and set down in one place the decisions that judges and juries have made in myriad cases and the terms of contracts in evolving areas of the economy. The American Law Institute, a private organization, regularly recommends commercial-code revisions to legislatures. According to Hayek, even the great lawgivers of history, such as Hammurabi, Solon, and Lycurgus, "did not intend to create new law but merely to state what law was and had always been."

As English jurists such as Coke and Blackstone pointed out, the common law is part of the constitutional check on the concentration of power. A judge doesn't issue edicts; he can only rule when a dispute is brought to him. That limitation keeps the judge's power in check, and the fact that the law is made by many people involved in many disputes limits the potential for arbitrary power wielded by a lawgiver, whether a monarch or a legislature. Generally, people go to court only when their lawyers identify a problem—an unsettled area—in the law. (A lawyer's job is frequently to tell a client, "The law is clear. You have no case. You'll be wasting everybody's time and money if you go to court.") In that way, many people participate in the evolution of the law to deal with new circumstances and problems.

Legislation—which is unfortunately called law by most people—is a different process. Much legislation involves rules for running the government, in which case it is similar to the internal rules of any organization. Some other legislation, as noted above, amounts to codifying the common law. But increasingly, legislation involves commands directing how people shall act, with the purpose of effecting specific outcomes. In that way legislation moves a society away from general rules that protect rights and leave people free to pursue their own ends, toward detailed rules specifying how people should use their property and interact with others.

## The Decline of Contract Law

As legislation has superseded common law in regulating our relations with one another, legislators have taken more and more of our income in taxes and circumscribed property rights through regulations aimed at securing everything from low-cost housing to panoramic views. Judges, unfortunately, have not only upheld those legislative decisions, ignoring provisions of the U.S. Constitution that protect property rights; they have also voided contracts that they thought reflected "unequal bargaining power" or that otherwise were not in "the public interest." In any given case, if the legislator or judge thought his values would be served by transferring property from its rightful owner to a more sympathetic claimant or releasing someone from the contractual obligations he had assumed, the great benefits of a system of property and contract were dismissed.

In his book *Sweet Land of Liberty?* the legal scholar Henry Mark Holzer identifies several milestones in the government's erosion of the sanctity of contract. Before the Civil War, he points out, money in the United States consisted of gold and silver coin. To finance the Civil War, Congress authorized the issuing of inflationary paper money, which it declared to be "legal tender," meaning that it had to be accepted in payment of debts, even if the lender had expected to be repaid in gold or silver. In 1871 the Supreme Court upheld the Legal Tender Act, effectively rewriting every loan agreement—and putting people with money on notice that the government could unilaterally change the terms of future loans. Then in 1938, despite the explicit provision in the Constitution forbidding the states to enact any "law impairing the obligation of contracts," the Supreme Court upheld a Minnesota law giving borrowers more time to pay their mortgages than the contract specified, leaving lenders no choice but to wait for the money they were owed.

Around the same time, the Court delivered yet another blow to freedom of contract. One major concern of any lender is to make sure that the money repaid will be worth as much as the money lent, which may not be the case if inflation has reduced the value of money in the meantime. After the Legal Tender decision, many contracts included a "gold clause" specifying the amount of repayment in terms of gold, which holds its value better than government-issued dollars. In June 1933 the Roosevelt administration persuaded Congress to expunge the gold clause from all contracts, effectively transferring billions of dollars from creditors, who had lent money in good faith, to borrowers, who would be able to repay the money in inflationary dollars. In each of these cases legislators and judges said that in their opinion the apparent need of one group of contracting parties should outweigh the obligations those parties had voluntarily assumed. Such decisions have progressively undermined economic progress, which depends on security in one's property and confidence that contractual obligations will be carried out.

## Special-Interest Law

In broad measure, the United States is a nation governed by the rule of law. But one can point to laws—Hayek would call them legislation, not true laws—that seem to conflict with the rule of law. There are outright, up-front subsidies and bailouts for specific companies, such as Congress's 1979 guarantee of $1.5 billion in loans to the Chrysler Corporation. Somewhat less obviously, there are clauses in many bills along the lines of "but this requirement shall not apply to any corporation incorporated in the state of Illinois on August 14, 1967"—that is, one firm is being exempted from a requirement imposed on its competitors. There are large incentives in the tax code for particular products such as ethanol, a corn-based gasoline substitute, 65 percent of which is produced by one company, the generous political contributor Archer-Daniels-Midland. There are valuable parts of the broadcast frequency spectrum set aside for minority-owned businesses, and there are government contracts reserved for small businesses.

The Fifth Amendment states that if private property is taken for public use, the owner must be compensated. Yet regulations take the value of property all the time, and governments have resisted paying owners for their loss. Property-rights advocates say, "If the government wants to preserve the coastline by forbidding me to build a house on my property, or wants to create a bicycle path through my land, fine—pay me for the value of my property that is taken." But courts have generally allowed the government to get away with such takings, and they are often imposed arbitrarily, after an owner has bought a piece of property with a particular plan in mind. Even if property is being taken for a public purpose, the owner ought to be compensated; but often the purpose is clearly private, not public—as when the city of Detroit condemned the homes and businesses in a Polish-American neighborhood called Poletown so that General Motors could build a plant there. To add insult to injury, after people were forced to move from the neighborhood where they had lived all their lives, GM decided not to build the plant after all.

Occupational licensing laws often conflict with the spirit of the rule of law. Requiring individuals to comply with specific state regulations in order to offer their services to the public as lawyers, cabdrivers, cosmetologists, or some 800 other occupations may not run afoul of the rule of law, though it is surely a violation of economic liberty. But requiring a hairdresser who is licensed in Tennessee to live in Kentucky for a year before she can practice her trade there clearly seems to treat citizens differently under the law and is obviously intended to create the equivalent of a protective tariff for the benefit of hairdressers already residing in Kentucky.

Perhaps the most serious way that current American law violates the rule of law is in the delegation of legislative and judicial power to unelected and invisible administrators. In 1948 Winston Churchill complained, "I am told that 300 officials have the power to make new regulations, apart altogether from Parliament, carrying with them the penalty of imprisonment for crimes hitherto unknown to the law." We should be so lucky today as to have only 300 officials with the power to make laws. Until Franklin Roosevelt's New Deal, it was understood that the U.S. Constitution gave the exclusive power of lawmaking to Congress. In conformity with the rule of law, it gave the president the power to execute the laws and the judiciary the power to interpret and enforce them. In the 1930s, however, Congress started passing broad laws and leaving the details up to administrative agencies. Such agencies—the Agriculture Department, the Federal Trade Commission, the Food and Drug Administration, the Environmental Protection Agency, and countless more—now churn out rules and regulations that clearly have the force of law but were never passed by the constitutional lawmaking authority. Sometimes Congress didn't know how to make its broad promises real, sometimes it didn't want to vote on the actual trade-offs involved in giving some people what they wanted at the expense of other people, sometimes it just couldn't be bothered with the details. The result is tens of thousands of bureaucrats churning out laws—60,000 pages of them in a typical year—for which Congress takes no responsibility.

Compounding the insult to the rule of law is that these agencies then interpret and enforce their own rules, deciding how they will apply in each individual case. They are legislator, prosecutor, judge, jury, and executioner, all in one—as clear a violation of the rule of law as one could imagine. A particular problem is the federalization and criminalization of environmental law over the past three decades. In its zeal to protect the environment, the federal government has created a web of regulations so dense that compliance with the law is, essentially, unachievable. Prosecutors and courts have stripped environmental criminal suspects of such traditional legal defenses as good faith, fair warning, and double jeopardy, while effectively requiring potential suspects to incriminate themselves. It is when pursuing a goal as public-spirited as environmental protection that we must remind ourselves to be most careful in following rules and abiding by constitutional protections, lest the worth of the goal lead us to erode the principles that allow us to achieve all our goals.

## Constitutional Limits on Government

Perhaps the most remarkable American contribution to protecting individual rights and the rule of law was our written Constitution. The purpose of government was made clear in the Declaration of Independence: "to secure these rights, governments are instituted among men." Having concluded that government was necessary, the Americans sought to devise a constitution that would limit the government to just that purpose.

The power to protect rights is naturally held by each individual, and it is *delegated* to government in the Constitution. To make it clear that the Constitution was not a general grant of power to government, the specific powers granted to the federal government are *enumerated* in Article I, Section 8. Because they are delegated and enumerated, the powers of the federal government are *limited*. A government of delegated, enumerated, and limited powers—that is the great American contribution to the development of liberty under law.

The legal scholar Roger Pilon lays out the meaning of the

Constitution in his 1995 essay "Restoring Constitutional Government":

> Congress may act in any given area or on any given subject, therefore, only if it has authority under the Constitution to do so. If not, that area or subject must be addressed by state, local, or private action.
>
> The doctrine of enumerated powers, as just stated, was meant by the Framers to be the centerpiece of the Constitution. As such, it serves two basic functions. First, it explains and justifies federal power: flowing from the people to the government, power is legitimate insofar as it has been thus delegated. But second, the very doctrine that justifies federal power serves also to limit it, for the government has only those powers that the people have given it. Indeed, it was the enumeration of powers, not the enumeration of rights in the Bill of Rights, that was meant by the Framers to be the principal limitation on government power. For the Framers could hardly have enumerated all of our rights, whereas they could enumerate federal powers. By implication, where there is no power, there is a right belonging to the states or the people.

Today, when a new federal law is proposed, many libertarian-minded people on both the right and the left look to the Bill of Rights to see whether the law will violate any constitutional rights. But we should look first to the enumerated powers to see if the federal government has been granted the power to undertake the proposed action. Only if it has such a power should we move on to ask whether its proposed action would violate any protected right.

Much—perhaps most—of what the federal government does today is not authorized in Article I, Section 8. That is to say, the federal government has assumed many powers that were not delegated by the people and not enumerated in the Constitution. It would be hard to find in the Constitution any authorization for economic planning, aid to education, a government-run retirement program, farm subsidies, art subsidies, corporate welfare, energy production, public housing, or most of the rest of the panoply of federal undertakings.

For much of our history the limits on federal powers were

taken for granted. As early as 1794, James Madison, the principal author of the Constitution, rose in the House of Representatives to oppose a bill because he could not "undertake to lay his finger on that article of the Federal Constitution which granted a right to Congress of expending, on objects of benevolence, the money of their constituents." As late as 1887, President Grover Cleveland vetoed a bill to provide seeds for drought-stricken farmers because he could "find no warrant for such an appropriation in the Constitution." Things had changed by 1935, when Franklin Roosevelt wrote to the chairman of the House Ways and Means Committee, "I hope your committee will not permit doubts as to constitutionality, however reasonable, to block the suggested legislation." Thirty-three years later, Rexford Tugwell, one of Roosevelt's principal advisers, admitted, "To the extent that these [New Deal policies] developed, they were tortured interpretations of a document intended to prevent them."

Today, it seems, we do not even ask where Congress finds the constitutional authority to pass the laws it does. It's hard to remember when a member of Congress rose to ask, "Where in the Constitution do we find this power?" Should an outside critic do so, he will likely be referred to the Constitution's preamble:

> We, the people of the United States, in order to form a more perfect Union, establish justice, insure domestic tranquility, provide for the common defence, promote the general welfare, and secure the blessings of liberty to ourselves and our posterity, do ordain and establish this Constitution of the United States.

The mention of "general welfare," it will be said, authorizes virtually anything Congress wants to do. But that is a misreading of the general welfare clause. Of course, as Locke and Hume argued, we create government to enhance our welfare in the broadest sense. But what will enhance our welfare is the opportunity to live in a civil society, where our life, liberty, and property are protected and we are left free to pursue happiness in our own way. Our welfare is decidedly not enhanced by a limitless government, arrogating to itself the power to decide that anything from a Chrysler bailout to a V-chip to a job-training program would be good for us. A narrower criticism of this expansive reading of the general welfare clause is that by "general welfare" the Framers were making clear that the government must act in the interest of all, not on behalf of any particular person or group—but virtually everything Congress does today involves taking money from some people to give it to others.

The value of a written constitution is that is lays out precisely what the government's powers are and, at least by omission, indicates what they are not. It sets up orderly procedures for the operation of government and, more important, systems for checking any attempt to exceed constitutional authority. But the real check on any government's power is the eternal vigilance of the people. The U.S. Constitution was a brilliant design not just because its Framers were geniuses but because the American people in the founding era were well aware of the dangers of tyranny and steeped in the rights theory of Locke and the experience with British constitutionalism. A friend of mine told me around 1990 that he had been engaged by people in the newly liberated Bulgaria to help them write a constitution that would protect liberty. "I'm sure you'll write a great constitution," I told him, "even better than the U.S. Constitution, but it's not just a matter of writing a good document and handing it to the popular assembly. It took 500 years to write the U.S. Constitution—from Magna Carta in 1215 to the Constitutional Convention in 1787." The question is whether the people of Bulgaria appreciate the importance to liberty and prosperity of guaranteeing individual rights through a government of delegated, enumerated, and limited powers. Here in the United States, the question is whether Americans *still* appreciate the Constitution and the thinking that underlies it.

How could the U.S. Constitution be improved? Hayek warns us to be cautious in our attempts to improve long-standing institutions, and any of us would be well advised to approach with humility the task of improving upon the work of Washington, Adams, Madison, Hamilton, Mason, Randolph, Franklin, and their colleagues. But with 200 years of experience, we can perhaps suggest some minor improvements. The general framework of delegated, enumerated, and thus limited powers is obviously in keeping with libertarian values. A libertarian would enthusiastically endorse the separation of powers and would have no obvious criticism of the structure of a legislative body with two houses apportioned differently, a president with a veto, a reasonably difficult amendment process, and so on.

Someone has suggested that on top of the safeguards against excessive government already in the Constitution—the structure of enumerated and limited powers, the Bill of Rights, the Ninth Amendment clarifying that all other rights are retained by the people, the Tenth Amendment reserving unenumerated powers to the states or the people—one more layer be added: an amendment reading, "And we mean it." In that spirit, were one revising the U.S. Constitution either for Americans or for some other country, one might add a clause clarifying that the powers granted in Article I, Section 8, are indeed *all* the powers of the federal government. And in case that, too, was insufficient, one might expand the Bill of Rights to guarantee not just separation of church and state but separation of family and state, school and state, race and state, art and state, even economy and state. One might also want to amend the Constitution to

- require a balanced budget, as Thomas Jefferson recommended and as almost all state constitutions do;
- forbid Congress to delegate its lawmaking authority to administrative agencies;
- revive the colonial principle of rotation in office by limiting the terms of members of Congress as well as the president; and
- give the president a line-item veto so he could veto individual parts of a bill, or clarify that when Article I refers to a "bill," it means a single piece of legislation dealing with a single subject, not a massive amalgamation of subjects and appropriations.

The Framers of the Constitution and the Bill of Rights wrote their limits on government and their guarantees of specific rights based on their experience with the depredations of liberty by the British government. With 200 more years' experience with the ways governments seek to break the bounds we place on them, we see new rights to enumerate and new limits to place on power.

For now, however, enforcing the Constitution as it stands would be a big step in the libertarian direction, that is, in the direction of protecting every American's liberty and keeping the coercive power of the state out of civil society.

*Chapter 7*

# CIVIL SOCIETY

*I*n the libertarian view, the role of government is to protect people's rights—that is all. But that is quite enough of a task, and a government that does a good job of it deserves our respect and congratulations. The protection of rights, however, is only a minimal condition for the pursuit of happiness. As Locke and Hume argued, we establish government so that we may be secure in our lives, liberties, and property as we go about the business of surviving and flourishing.

We can barely survive, and hardly flourish, without interacting with other people. We want to associate with others to achieve instrumental ends—producing more food, exchanging goods, developing new technology—but also because we feel a deep need for connectedness, for love and friendship and community. The associations we form with others make up what we call civil society. Those associations can take an amazing variety of forms—families, churches, schools, clubs, fraternal societies, condominium associations, neighborhood groups, and the myriad forms of commercial society, such as partnerships, corporations, labor unions, and trade associations. All of these associations serve human needs in different ways. Civil society may be broadly defined as all the natural and voluntary associations in society. Some analysts distinguish between commercial and nonprofit organizations, arguing that businesses are part of the market, not of civil society; but I follow the tradition that the real distinction is between associations that are coercive (the state) and those that are natural or voluntary (everything else). Whether a particular association is established to make a profit or to achieve some other purpose, the key characteristic is that our participation in it is voluntary. The associations within civil society are created to achieve particular purposes, but civil society as a whole has no purpose; it is the undesigned, spontaneously emerging result of all those purposive associations.

Some people don't really like civil society. Karl Marx, for instance. Commenting on political freedom in an early essay, "On the Jewish Question," Marx wrote that "the so-called rights of man . . . are nothing but the rights of the member of civil society, i.e., egoistic man, man separated from other men and the community." He argued that "man as he is in civil society" is "an individual withdrawn behind his private interests and whims and separated from the community." Recall that Thomas Paine distinguished society from government, civil society from political society. Marx revives that distinction, but with a twist: He wants political society to squeeze out civil society. When people are truly free, he says, they will see themselves as citizens of the whole political community, not "decomposed" into different, nonuniversal roles as a trader, a laborer, a Jew, a Protestant. Each person will be "a communal being" united with all other citizens, and the state will no longer be seen as an instrument to protect rights so that individuals can pursue their selfish ends but as the entity through which everyone will achieve "the human essence [which] is the true collectivity of man." It was never made clear just how this liberation would arrive, and the actual experience of Marxist regimes was hardly liberating, but the hostility to civil society is clear enough.

Marxism is a bad word these days (as it should be), but Marx's powerful hold on so many people for so long indicates that he was on to something when he wrote about people feeling alienated and atomized. People do want to feel at least some connection to other people. In traditional, precapitalist communities they didn't have much choice about it; in a village, people you had known all your life were all around you. Like it or not, you couldn't avoid having a sense of community. As liberalism and the Industrial Revolution brought freedom, affluence, and mobility to more people, more and more of them chose to leave the villages of their birth, often even the countries of their birth, and go off to make a better life elsewhere. The decision to leave indicated that people expected to find a better life; and continuing mobility and emigration, generation after generation in modern society, would seem to indicate that people *do* find better opportunities in new places. But even a person who is glad he left the village or the old country may feel a loss of that sense of community, just as one's departure from the family to become an adult may generate a profound sense of loss even as one enjoys autonomy and independence. That's the longing to which Marxism seemed, to many people, to provide an answer.

Ironically, Marxism promised freedom and community but delivered tyranny and atomization. The tyranny of the Marxist countries is well known, but it may not be so well understood that Marxism created a society far more atomized than anything in the capitalist world. The Marxist rulers in the Soviet empire, in the first place, believed theoretically that men under conditions of "true freedom" would have no need for organizations catering to their individual interests, and in the second place, understood practically that independent associations would threaten the power of the state. Thus, they not only eliminated private economic activity, they sought to stamp out churches, independent schools, political organizations, neighborhood associations, and everything else, down to the garden clubs. After all, the theory went, such nonuniversal organizations contributed to atomization. What happened, of course, was that people deprived of any form of community and connectedness between the family and the all-powerful state became atomistic individuals with a vengeance. As the philosopher and anthropologist Ernest Gellner wrote, "The system created isolated, amoral, cynical individualists-without-opportunity, skilled at double-talk and trimming." The normal ways in which people were tied to their neighbors, their fellow parishioners, the people with whom they did business were destroyed, leaving them suspicious and distrustful of one another, seeing no reason to cooperate with others or even to treat them with respect.

The even greater irony, perhaps, was that Marxism eventually produced a renewed appreciation for civil society. As the corruption of the Brezhnev years faded into liberalization under Gorbachev, people began to look for an alternative to socialism, and they found it in the concepts of civil society, pluralism, and freedom of association. The billionaire investor George Soros, eager to liberate the land of his birth (Hungary) and its neighbors, began by making large contributions not to bring about political revolution but to rebuild civil society. He sought to subsidize everything from chess clubs to independent newspapers, to get people once again working together in nonstate institutions. The burgeoning of civil society was not the only factor in the restoration of freedom to Central and Eastern Europe, but a stronger civil society will help to protect the new freedom, as well as supply all the other benefits that people can achieve only in association.

Even people who aren't Marxists share some of Marx's concerns about community and atomization. Communitarian philosophers, who believe individuals must necessarily be seen as part of a community, worry that people in the West, especially in the United States, overemphasize claims to individual rights at the expense of the community. Their view of our relationship to others could be represented as a series of concentric circles: an individual is part of a family, a neighborhood, a city, a metropolitan area, a state, a nation. The implication of these arguments is that we sometimes forget to focus on all the circles and that we should somehow be encouraged to do so.

But are the circles merely concentric? A better way to understand community in the modern world is as a series of *intersecting* circles, with myriad complex connections among them. Each of us has many ways of relating to other people—precisely what Marx complained of and libertarians celebrate. One person may be a wife, mother, daughter, sister, cousin; an employee of one business, an owner of another, a stockholder in others; a renter and a landlord; an officer in a condominium association; active in the Little League and the Girl Scouts; a member of the Presbyterian Church; a precinct worker for the Democratic Party; a member of a professional association; a member of a bridge club, a Jane Austen fan club, a feminist consciousness-raising group, a neighborhood crimewatch, and more. (True, this particular person probably feels pretty frazzled, but at least in principle, one can have an indefinite number of associations and connections.) Most of these associations serve a particular purpose—to make money, to reduce crime, to help one's children—but they also give people connections with other people. No one of them, however, exhausts one's personality and defines one completely. (One *can* approximate such exhaustive definition by joining an all-embracing religious community, say, a Roman Catholic order of contemplative nuns, but such choices are voluntary and—because one can't alienate one's right to make choices—reversible.)

In this libertarian conception we connect to different people in different ways by free and voluntary consent. Ernest Gellner says that modern civil society requires "modular man." Instead of being entirely the product of, and absorbed by, a particular culture, modular man "can combine into specific-purpose, *ad hoc,* limited associations, without binding himself by some blood ritual." He can form links with others, "which are effective even though they are flexible, specific, instrumental."

As individuals combine in countless ways, community emerges: not the close community of the village, or the messianic community promised by Marxism, national socialism, and all-fulfilling religions, but a community of free individuals in voluntarily chosen associations. Individuals do not emerge from community; community emerges from individuals. It emerges not because anyone plans it, certainly not because the state creates it, but because it must. To fulfill their needs and desires, individuals must combine with others. Society is an association of individuals governed by legal rules, or perhaps an association of associations, but not one large community, or one family, in Mario Cuomo's and Pat Buchanan's utterly misguided conception. The rules of the family or small group are not—cannot be—the rules of the extended society.

The distinction between individual and community can be misleading. Some critics say that community involves a surrender of one's individuality. But membership in a group need not diminish people's individuality; it can amplify it, by freeing people from the limits they face as lone individuals and increasing their opportunities to achieve their own goals. Such a view of community requires that membership be chosen, not compulsory.

## Cooperation

Because humans can't achieve much of what they want on their own, they cooperate with other people in a variety of ways. The government's protection of rights and freedom of action creates an environment in which individuals can pursue their goals, secure in their person and property. The result is a complex network of free association in which people voluntarily assume and fulfill obligations and contracts.

Freedom of association helps to reduce social conflict. It allows members of society to link themselves together and build intertwining networks of personal relationships. Many of these relationships cross religious, political, and ethnic boundaries. (Others, of course, such as religious and ethnic associations, unite people within a particular group.) The result is that diverse and unfamiliar people come together in fellowship. Tensions that might otherwise divide people are countered by these aspects of connectedness. A Catholic and a Protestant, who might otherwise find themselves in conflict, meet as buyer and seller in the marketplace, as members of the same parent-teacher association, or as participants in a softball league, where they also meet and associate with Muslims, Jews, Hindus, Taoists, and nonbelievers. They may disagree about religion, may even believe one another engaged in mortal error, but civil society provides spaces where they may cooperate peacefully. A *Washington Post* story on the growing popularity of noontime worship services begins, "On the street, these men and women are clerks and lawyers, Democrats and Republicans, city dwellers and suburbanites. Here, they are Catholics." A different story might begin, "Outside, these men and women are Catholics and Baptists, black and white, gay and straight, married and single. Here, they are employees of America Online." Or "here, they are tutors for underprivileged children." In each circumstance, people who may not see themselves as comfortable members of a tight community with the others in the group can come together for a specific purpose, in the process learning to coexist if not to embrace.

No one person made the complex order that emerges. No one designed it. It is the product of many human actions but of no design.

## Personal Responsibility and Trust

In a previous chapter I recounted the remarkable network of trust that allows me to get cash and automobiles halfway around the world. If critics of libertarianism were right, wouldn't the "atomistic" commercial society tend to *reduce* the levels of trust and cooperation that allow bank machines to dispense cash to strangers? This common criticism is belied by the evidence around us.

If we are going to pursue happiness by entering into agreements with others, it's important that we be able to rely on each other. Other than the minimal obligation not to violate the rights of others, in a free society we have only the obligations we voluntarily assume. But when we do assume obligations by entering into contracts or joining associations, we are both morally and legally bound to live up to our agreements. Several factors help to ensure that we do: our own sense of right and wrong; our desire to have the approval of others; moral exhortation; and, when necessary, various ways of enforcing those obligations, including the refusal of others to do business with people who default on their obligations.

As society develops and people want to take on larger tasks, it becomes necessary to be able to trust more people. At first, people may have trusted only their own family or the people in their village or tribe. The extension of the circle of trust is one of the great advances in civilization. Contracts and associations play a major role in enabling us to trust each other.

Like the hero celebrated in a country song, my father was a man "who could borrow money at the bank simply on his word." That kind of honor and trustworthiness is essential to markets and to civilization. But it isn't enough in an extended society. My father's good reputation didn't extend much beyond the small town where we lived, and he would have had trouble borrowing money in a hurry even a few towns over, much less across the country or around the world. But as I noted above, I have instant access to cash and credit virtually anywhere in the world—not because I have a better reputation than my father, but because the free market has developed credit institutions that extend around the world. As long as I pay my bills, the complex financial networks of American Express and Visa and MOST allow me to get goods, services, or cash wherever I go. These systems work so well that we take them for granted, but they are truly a marvel. They work on a much larger scale than my personal cash withdrawals and car rentals, of course. The combination of institutions that vouch for an individual's creditworthiness and legal institutions to punish contract violations when necessary makes possible vast economic undertakings, from the design and construction of airplanes to building a tunnel under the English Channel to worldwide computer networks such as CompuServe and America Online.

As credit becomes so widespread and readily available, some people come to think of it as a right. They get morally exercised when people are denied credit. They demand regulation of credit bureaus, suppression of bad credit information, limits on interest rates, and so on. Such people don't understand the crucial importance of trust. They seem not to realize that people don't want to lend their hard-earned money to unreliable credit risks. If reliable credit information is unavailable, interest rates will go up to cover the increased risk. If information is unreliable enough, the extension of credit will grind to a halt, or credit will be available only through personal and family connections, surely the opposite of what critics of credit bureaus want.

The network of trust and credit relies on all the institutions of a free society: individual rights and responsibility, secure property rights, freedom of contract, free markets, and the rule of law. A complex order rests on a simple but secure foundation. As in chaos theory, a simple nonlinear equation can produce endless mathematical complexity, so the simple rules of a free society can produce infinitely complex social, economic, and legal relationships.

## The Dimensions of Civil Society

It would be difficult to describe all the forms that civil society takes in a complex world. More than 100 years ago, Alexis de Tocqueville wrote in *Democracy in America,* "Americans of all ages, all conditions, and all dispositions constantly form associations . . . to give entertainments, to found seminaries, to build inns, to construct churches, to diffuse books, to send missionaries to the antipodes; in this manner they found hospitals, prisons, and schools." Today you can pick up any daily newspaper and take a look at the kinds of organizations described there—businesess, trade associations, ethnic and religious associations, neighborhood groups, music and theater groups, museums, charities, schools, and more. On the day I started writing this chapter, I picked up the *Washington Post.* Besides all the usual groups that form the background to each day's news, I found three stories that stood out for me as examples of the diversity of civil society.

On the front page was a story about three double-income suburban families who have created a supper club in which each family cooks one meal a week that the other two families pick up and take home. That way the busy families get more home-cooked family meals than any of them could produce on their own, in the hectic world of the two-career family. Not quite as much community, perhaps, as if the three families sat down and ate together, but the participants say they do feel a sense of extended family: "We stand in each other's kitchens and talk about each other's children." Another story discussed a devout Baptist family who "try to shelter their [six children] from the temptations and trials of the secular world, creating a life populated largely by people with similar values and beliefs." The mother schools her children at home, tries to provide wholesome books, videos, and games for them, and gets them involved with other children at their church, in their home-schooling network, and through the oldest son's interest in piano. In some ways it might seem that this family is withdrawing from civil society, but I believe we should see the story as an example of the diversity that civil society allows, even for those who want to pursue a way of life different from that desired by most people in the larger society. Finally, another story told of a children's play group that has connected five families for ten years. Not only did the group provide playmates for the children, but by taking turns babysitting, the mothers could give each other "a few precious moments of independence." The author concluded, "[My daughter] can't remember a time when she didn't know her play group friends, and I can barely remember when I didn't know mine. Bonds between friends can be like that. In the absence of nearby kin they can be the most sustaining ones of all."

## Charity and Mutual Aid

Charitable institutions are an important aspect of civil society. They are the focus of the quotation above from Tocqueville. People have a natural desire to help the less fortunate, and they form associations with others to do so, ranging from local soup kitchens and church charity bazaars to complex national and international enterprises like United Way, the Salvation Army, Doctors without Borders, and Save the Children. Americans spend some $150 billion on charity every year.

Critics of libertarianism say, "You want to abolish essential government programs and put nothing in their place." But the absence of coercive government programs is most decidedly not nothing. It's a growing economy, the individual initiative and creativity of millions of people, and thousands of associations set up to achieve common purposes. What kind of social analysis is it that looks at a complex society like the United States and sees "nothing" except what government does?

Charity plays an important role in a free society. But it is not *the* answer to the question of how a free society will help the poor. The first answer to that question is that by dramatically increasing and spreading wealth, a free economy eases and even eliminates poverty. By the standards of history, even poor people in the United States and Europe are enormously wealthy. The fabulous palace of Versailles had no plumbing facilities; the orange trees on the grounds were an attempt to cover up the stench. Gorman Beauchamp of the University of Michigan wrote in the *American Scholar* in 1995 about the abundance that free markets and modern technology have produced:

> [A film] on the life of Empress Wu, China's equivalent of Catherine the Great . . . opened with a scene of a mounted courier riding furiously to pass some obviously precious packet to another courier who tears off to the next station to pass the packet on to another courier—and so on across North China to Peking and ultimately to the Imperial Palace. The content of the packet, brought so effortfully from the distant mountain peaks, was then revealed to be—ice. Ice to chill the emperor's drinks.
>
> What struck me so forcefully about this scene, I remember, was the realization that I could have, any time I chose, all the ice I wanted simply by opening my refrigerator door. In this respect, as in countless others, the material level of my life—a young person of no consequence, living on a modest stipend—was markedly superior to that of a powerful emperor of China. . . .
>
> I am warmer in the winter (central heating) and cooler in the summer (air conditioning) than he was; I get more and better information faster and more reliably than he did; I can get to any destination more quickly and comfortably; I am (most likely) in less pain less of the time and get better medical care; I see better longer (bifocals) and have better teeth (fluoride) and a dentist who uses Novocain; and while he may have had a golden bird to sing for him—okay, okay, that was the Byzantine emperor—I have Rosa Ponselle or Ezio Pinza or Billie Holiday or Edith Piaf [for younger readers, we might add, or the Rolling Stones, or the Grateful Dead, or Alanis Morrisette] or any one of literally hundreds of performers whose voices I have on my shelves and can summon up with the flick of a couple of switches.

We should not lose sight of the universal poverty and backbreaking labor that free markets have eliminated. But by contemporary standards, of course, millions of Americans do live in a poverty that is less material than spiritually deadening—marked by a feeling of hopelessness. So the second answer to the question is that government should stop trapping people in poverty and making it difficult for them to escape. Taxes and regulations eliminate jobs, especially for the least skilled, and the welfare system makes possible unwed motherhood and long-term dependency. A third answer is mutual aid: people banding together not to help the less fortunate but to help themselves through times of trouble. I will deal with economic growth, welfare, and charity in subsequent chapters, but here I want to focus on mutual aid.

Mutual aid has a long history—and not just in the West, by any means. The early craft guilds, before they became the stultified monopolies known to every student of medieval history, were mutual-aid associations of people in the same trade. In the African custom of *susu,* people would contribute a certain amount into a pot, and when the fund reached a certain amount, members took turns collecting it. As the Ghanaian economist George Ayittey writes, "Were the 'primitive' *susu* system introduced in America it would be called a *credit union.*" Or if introduced by Korean Americans it might be called the *keh,* a group of people who get together once a month for dinner, socializing, advice, and the contribution of money to a common pot to be given each month to one participant.

The historian Judith M. Bennett wrote in the February 1992 issue of *Past and Present* about the "ales" of medieval and early modern England at which people would gather for drinking, dancing, and games, paying above-market prices to help out a neighbor: church-ales, to raise money for the parish; bride-ales, to get a marrying couple started; and help-ales, to assist those who had fallen on hard times. Bennett calls the ales an example of how ordinary people "looked not only to the 'better sort' for relief, but also to each other," a "social institution through which neighbours and friends assisted each other in times of crisis or need." The ales reaffirmed social solidarity among working people. They usually required the active efforts of the person in need, and contributions depended on the degree to which the person was judged deserving. Unlike charity, ales involved a relationship among equals: "By merging alms-giving with both conviviality and commerce, charity-ales minimized the potential social divisiveness of poverty and charity." There was also a sense of reciprocity among "people who could reasonably expect that they would both contribute to and benefit from charity ales during the course of their lives."

A more modern example of mutual aid—which until recently has gone virtually unnoticed by historians who study poverty, charity, and welfare—is the role of fraternal and friendly societies. David Green of London's Institute of Economic Affairs describes the ways that British manual workers formed "friendly societies," which were self-governing mutual-benefit associations. Individuals joined and contributed to the group, pledging to help each other in times of trouble. Because they were mutual associations, the payments received—sick pay, medical care, burial expenses, and survivor's benefits—were "not a matter of largesse but entitlement, earned by the regular contributions paid into the common fund by every member and justified by the obligation to do the same for other members." Some societies were just neighborhood clubs, but others evolved into national federations with hundreds of thousands of members and extensive investments. By 1801 it is estimated that there were 7,200 societies in Britain with 648,000 adult male members, out of a total population of 9 million. By 1911 there were 9 million people covered by voluntary insurance associations, more than two-thirds of them in friendly societies. They had names such as the Manchester Unity of Oddfellows, the Ancient Order of Foresters, and the Workingmen's Conservative Friendly Society.

The friendly societies had an important economic purpose—to jointly insure against sickness, old age, and death. But they served other purposes as well, such as fellowship, entertainment, and enlargement of one's network of contacts. More important, members of the society felt bound together by common ideals. A central purpose was the promotion of good character. They understood that developing good habits is not easy; many of us find it helpful to have external support for our good intentions. Churches and synagogues provide that for many people; Alcoholics Anonymous provides it for a particular aspect of good character, sobriety. Another benefit of the friendly societies was that working people got experience in running an organization, a rare opportunity in Britain's class-based society.

The historian David Beito has done similar pioneering research on American fraternal societies such as the Masons, Elks, Odd Fellows, and Knights of Pythias. Beito writes, "Only churches rivaled fraternal societies as institutional providers of social welfare before the advent of the welfare state. In 1920, about eighteen million Americans belonged to fraternal societies, i.e. nearly 30 percent of all adults." A 1910 article in *Everybody's Magazine* explained, "Rich men insure in the big companies to create an estate, poor men insure in the fraternal orders to create bread and meat. It is an insurance against want, the poorhouse, charity and degradation." Note the aversion to charity: people joined fraternal societies so that they could mutually provide for their own needs in time of misfortune and not be forced to the indignity of taking charity from others.

At first, fraternal insurance protection centered around the death benefit. By the early twentieth century, many orders were also offering sickness or accident insurance. An interesting aspect of fraternal insurance is how it overcomes the problem of moral hazard, the risk that people will take advantage of the insurance system. When dealing with a government agency or distant insurance company, an individual may be tempted to malinger, to claim exaggerated benefits for minor or nonexistent problems. But the feeling of community with other members of the fraternal order and the desire to have the approval of one's peers reduce the temptation to cheat. Beito suggests that that is why fraternal societies "continued to dominate the sickness insurance market long after they had lost their competitive edge in life insurance"—where malingering is a bit more problematic. By 1910 fraternal health insurance often included treatment by a "lodge doctor," who contracted to provide medical care to all the members for a fixed price.

Immigrants formed many fraternal societies, such as the National Slovak Society, the Croatian Fraternal Union, the Polish Falcons of America, and the United Societies of the U.S.A. for Russian Slovaks. Jewish groups included the Arbeiter Ring (Workmen's Circle), the American-Hebrew Alliance, the National Council of Jewish Women, the Hebrew Immigrants Aid Society, and more. By 1918 there were more than 150,000 members in the largest Czech-American associations. Springfield, Illinois, with a total Italian population of 3,000 in 1910, had a dozen Italian societies.

In his landmark 1944 study *An American Dilemma,* the Swedish economist Gunnar Myrdal asserted that African Americans of all classes were even more likely than whites to join fraternal orders such as the Prince Hall Masons, the True Reformers, the Grand United Order of Galilean Fishermen, and parallel versions of the Elks, the Odd Fellows, and the Knights of Pythias. He estimated that over 4,000 associations in Chicago were formed by the city's 275,000 blacks. In 1910 the sociologist Howard W. Odum estimated that in the South, the "total membership of the negro societies, paying and nonpaying, is nearly equal to the total church membership." Fraternal societies, he said, were "a vital part" of black "community life, often its center."

Like the British societies, American fraternal societies emphasized a code of ethics and each member's mutual obligations to the other members. The historian Don H. Doyle, in *The Social Order of a Frontier Community,* found that the small town of Jacksonville, Illinois, had "dozens . . . of fraternal lodges, reform societies, literary clubs, and fire companies" and that the lodges enforced "a broad moral discipline affecting personal behavior in general and temperance in particular, matters closely tied to the all-important problem of obtaining credit."

Fellowship and solidarity discouraged members from claiming benefits without good cause, but the societies also had rules and practices to ensure adherence to them. The rules of the socialist-oriented Western Miners' Federation denied benefits to members when "the sickness or accident was caused by intemperance, imprudence or immoral conduct." The Sojourna Lodge of the House of Ruth, the largest black women's voluntary organization in the early part of the century, required members to present a notarized medical certificate from a doctor in order to claim sickness benefits and also had a committee on sickness to both support and investigate sick members.

Fraternal associations also helped people cope with the increasing mobility of society. Some of the multibranch British societies provided members with places to stay when they went to other towns to look for work. Doyle found that "for the transient member, a transfer card from the Odd Fellows or Masons was more than a ticket of readmission to another lodge. It was also portable certification of the status and reputation he had established in his former community, and it gave him access to a whole new network of business and social contacts."

Critics frequently assert that libertarian solutions to social problems are fantastical. "Eliminate the government's safety net, and just *hope* that churches, charities, and mutual-aid groups will expand to fill the gap?" The answer is twofold. Yes, these groups will step up to the plate; they always have. But more important, the *existence* of the government's safety net and the massive taxes that support it have squeezed out those efforts. The forms that mutual aid takes are countless, from play groups and supper clubs to trade associations to neighborhood crime watches. They have declined dramatically not because of women entering the workforce, or because of television's hold on our free time, but because of government's expansion.

## Government and Civil Society

Government's protection of individual rights is vital for creating a space in which people can pursue their many and varied interests in voluntary association with others. When government expands beyond that role, however, it pushes into the realm of civil society. As government borrowing "crowds out" private borrowing, government activity in any field crowds out voluntary (including commercial) activity.

From the Progressive Era on, the state has increasingly disrupted natural communities and mediating institutions in America. Public schools replaced private community schools, and large, distant, unmanageable school districts replaced smaller districts. Social Security not only took away the need to save for one's own retirement but weakened family bonds by reducing parents' reliance on their children. Zoning laws reduced the availability of affordable housing, limited opportunities for extended families to live together, and removed retail stores from residential neighborhoods, reducing community interaction. Day-care regulations limited home day care. In all these ways, civil society was crowded out by the state.

What happens to communities as the state expands? The welfare state takes over the responsibilities of individuals and communities and in the process takes away much of what brings satisfaction to life: If government is supposed to feed the poor, then local charities aren't needed. If a central bureaucracy downtown manages the schools, then parents' organizations are less important. If government agencies manage the community center, teach children about sex, and care for the elderly, then families and neighborhood associations feel less needed.

## From Charity and Mutual Aid to Welfare State

Charity and mutual aid have particularly been squeezed by the expansion of the state. Judith Bennett notes that as early as the thirteenth century, "ecclesiastical and royal officials had ordered the elimination of scot-ales." By the seventeenth century, the opposition was more serious because of a general campaign against traditional culture, a move toward more centralized control of charity, and the development of tax-funded support for the poor.

During the above discussion on fraternal societies, readers may have wondered: if they were so great, where are they now? Many of them are still around, of course, but they have fewer members and less stature in society, at least partly because the state took over their functions. David Green writes, "It was at the height of their expansion that the state intervened and transformed the friendly societies by introducing compulsory national [health] insurance." Their major function nationalized, the societies atrophied. Beito found that American fraternal insurance was impeded by medical licensing laws that undermined the lodge-doctor arrangement, by legal prohibitions on certain forms of insurance, and by the rise of the welfare state. As the states and the federal government created workers' compensation, mothers' pensions, and Social Security, the need for mutual aid societies diminished. Some of that impact may have been unintentional, but President Theodore Roosevelt objected to the immigrant fraternal societies, saying, "The American people should itself [note the collective pronoun] do these things for the immigrants." Even the historian Michael Katz, a supporter of the welfare state, concedes that federal welfare initiatives "may have weakened [these] networks of support within inner cities, transforming the experience of poverty and fueling the rise of homelessness."

The government is still squeezing out charitable institutions. The Salvation Army operates twenty homeless shelters in Detroit, but in 1995 the city of Detroit passed a law to license and regulate homeless shelters. The law required that all staffers be trained, that all menus be approved by a registered dietitian, that all medication be kept in a locked storage area, that the shelter ascertain the ages of the people in the shelter and make sure that the children attend school. All fine ideas, but the Salvation Army official in charge of the shelters says, "All these requirements cost money, and our budget is $10 a day per person." What will happen? Some shelters will probably close, and either the homeless will live in abandoned buildings and cardboard boxes or there will be pressure for Detroit to spend even more money to build city-run shelters. And Salvation Army volunteers will have one less opportunity to help.

Texas bureaucrats demand that a successful drug-treatment program called Teen Challenge comply with state regulations on record keeping, shelter-maintenance standards, and especially the use of licensed counselors instead of its religiously based program, often run by ex-alcoholics and reformed addicts. Teen Challenge does not take government grants, and a Department of Health and Human Services study found it to be both the best and the cheapest of drug-treatment programs examined. But in 1995 the state of Texas ordered the South Texas program to shut down or pay a fine of $4,000 a day. Teen Challenge took the bureaucrats to court, at the very least diverting some of its scarce time and money to fighting for permission to stay open.

What is the cost to our society of having government take over more and more roles that individuals and communities used to serve? Tocqueville warned us of what might happen:

After having thus successively taken each member of the community in its powerful grasp and fashioned them at will, the supreme power then extends its arm over the whole community. It covers the surface of society with a network of small complicated rules, minute and uniform, through which the most original minds and the most energetic characters cannot penetrate, to rise above the crowd. The will of man is not shattered, but softened, bent, and guided: men are seldom forced by it to act, but they are constantly restrained from acting: such a power does not destroy, but it prevents existence; it does not tyrannize, but it compresses, enervates, extinguishes, and stupefies a people, till each nation is reduced to nothing better than a flock of timid and industrious animals, of which the government is the shepherd.

As Charles Murray puts it, "When the government takes away a core function [of communities], it depletes not only the source of vitality pertaining to that particular function, but also the vitality of a much larger family of responses." The attitude of "let the government take care of it" becomes a habit.

In his book *In Pursuit: Of Happiness and Good Government,* Murray reported some evidence that relying on government does indeed substitute for private action. He found that from the 1940s to 1964, the percentage of American income given to philanthropic causes rose—as we might expect, given that incomes were rising and people probably felt able to do more for others. "Then, suddenly, sometime during 1964–65, in the middle of an economic boom, this consistent trend was reversed." Although incomes continued to grow (the great slowdown in economic growth didn't begin until about 1973), the percentage of income given to philanthropy fell. Then in 1981, during a recession, the trend suddenly reversed itself, and contributions as a percentage of income rose sharply. What happened? Murray suggests that when the Great Society began in 1964–65, with President Lyndon Johnson proclaiming that the federal government would launch a War on Poverty, maybe people figured their own contributions weren't needed so much. Then in 1981 President Ronald Reagan came into office, promising to cut back government spending; maybe then people figured that if the government wasn't going to help the poor, they'd better.

## The Formation of Character

Expansive government destroys more than institutions and charitable contributions; it also undermines the moral character necessary to both civil society and liberty under law. The "bourgeois virtues" of work, thrift, sobriety, prudence, fidelity, self-reliance, and a concern for one's reputation developed and endured because they are the virtues necessary for advancement in a world where food and shelter must be produced and people are responsible for their own flourishing. Government can't do much to instill those virtues in people, but it can do much to undermine them. As David Frum writes in *Dead Right,*

> Why be thrifty when your old age and health care are provided for, no matter how profligately you acted in your youth? Why be prudent when the state insures your bank deposits, replaces your flooded-out house, buys all the wheat you can grow, and rescues you when you stray into a foreign battle zone? Why be diligent when half your earnings are taken from you and given to the idle? Why be sober when the taxpayers run clinics to cure you of your drug habit as soon as it no longer amuses you?

Frum sums up government's impact on individual character as "the emancipation of the individual from the restrictions imposed on it by limited resources, or religious dread, or community disapproval, or the risk of disease or personal catastrophe." Now one might suppose that the very aim of libertarianism is the emancipation of the individual, and so it is—but the emancipation of the individual from artificial, coercive restraints on his actions. Libertarians never suggested that people be "emancipated" from the reality of the world, from the obligation to pay one's own way and to take responsibility for the consequences of one's own actions. As a moral matter, individuals must be free to make their own decisions and to succeed or fail according to their own choices. As a practical matter, as Frum points out, when we shield people from the consequences of their actions, we get a society characterized not by thrift, sobriety, diligence, self-reliance, and prudence but by profligacy, intemperance, indolence, dependency, and indifference to consequences.

To return to the image with which we began chapter 4—being able to get cash and rent cars around the world—the human need for cooperation has helped to create vast and complex networks of trust, credit, and exchange. For such networks to function, we need several things: a willingness on the part of most people to cooperate with others and to keep their promises, the freedom to refuse to do business with those who refuse to live up to their commitments, a legal system that enforces the fulfillment of contracts, and a market economy that allows us to produce and exchange goods and services on the basis of secure property rights and individual consent. Such a framework lets people develop a diverse and complicated civil society that serves an incredible variety of needs.

## Chapter 8

# THE MARKET PROCESS

$\mathcal{W}$hen I go to the supermarket, I encounter a veritable cornucopia of food—from milk and bread to Wolfgang Puck's Spago Pizza and fresh kiwis from New Zealand. The average supermarket today has 30,000 items, double the number just ten years ago. Like most shoppers, I take this abundance for granted. I stand in the middle of this culinary festival and say something like, "I can't believe this crummy store doesn't have Diet Caffeine-free Cherry Coke in 12-ounce cans!"

But how does this marvelous feat happen? How is it that I, who couldn't find a farm with a map, can go to a store at any time of day or night and expect to find all the food I want, in convenient packages and ready for purchase, with extra quantities of turkey in November and lemonade in June? Who plans this complex undertaking?

The secret, of course, is precisely that no one plans it—no one *could* plan it. The modern supermarket is a commonplace but ultimately astounding example of the infinitely complex spontaneous order known as the free market.

The market arises from the fact that humans can accomplish more in cooperation with others than we can individually, and the fact that we can recognize this. If we were a species for whom cooperation was not more productive than isolated work, or if we were unable to discern the benefits of cooperation, then we would not only remain isolated and atomistic, but, as Ludwig von Mises explains, "Each man would have been forced to view all other men as his enemies; his craving for the satisfaction of his own appetites would have brought him into an implacable conflict with all his neighbors." Without the possibility of mutual benefit from cooperation and the division of labor, neither feelings of sympathy and friendship nor the market order itself could arise. Those who say that humans "are made for cooperation, not competition" fail to recognize that the market *is* cooperation. (Indeed, it is people competing to cooperate better!)

The economist Paul Heyne compares planning with spontaneous order this way: There are three major airports in the San Francisco Bay area. Every day thousands of airplanes take off from those airports, each one bound for a different destination. Getting them all in the air and back on the ground on time and without colliding with each other is an incredibly complex task, and the air traffic control system is a marvel of sophisticated organization. But also every day in the Bay area people make thousands of times as many trips in automobiles, with far more individuated points of origin, destinations, and "flight plans." *That* system, the coordination of millions of automobile trips, is far too complex for any traffic control system to manage, so we have to let it operate spontaneously within a few specific rules: drive on the right, stop at lights, yield when making a left turn. There are accidents, to be sure, and traffic congestion—much of which could be alleviated if the roads themselves were built and operated according to market principles—but the point is that it would be simply impossible to *plan* and consciously coordinate all those automobile trips. Contrary to our initial impression, then, it is precisely the *less* complex systems that can be planned and the *more* complex systems that must develop spontaneously.

Many people accept that markets are necessary but still feel that there is something vaguely immoral about them. They fear that markets lead to inequality, or they dislike the self-interest reflected in markets. Markets are often called "brutal" or "dog-eat-dog." But as this chapter will demonstrate, markets are not just essential to economic progress, they are more consensual and lead to more virtue and equality than government coercion.

## Information and Coordination

Markets are based on consent. No business sends an invoice for a product you haven't ordered, like an income tax form. No business can force you to trade. Businesses try to find out what you want and offer it to you. People who are trying to make money by selling groceries, or cars, or computers, or machines that make cars and computers need to know what consumers want and how much they would be willing to pay. Where do businesses get the information? It's not in a massive book. In a market economy, it isn't embodied in orders from a planning agency (though of course, theoretically, in socialist economies producers *do* act on orders from above).

### Prices

This vitally important information about other people's wants is embodied in prices. Prices don't just tell us how much something costs at the store. The price system pulls together all the information available in the economy about what each person wants, how much he values it, and how it can best be produced. Prices make that information *usable* to both producer and consumer. Each price contains within it information about consumer demands and costs of production, ranging from the amount of labor needed to produce the item to the cost of labor to the bad weather on the other side of the world that is raising the price of the raw materials needed to produce the good. Instead of having to know all the details, one is presented with a simple number: the price.

Market prices tell producers when something can't be produced at a cost less than what consumers will pay for it. The real cost of anything is not the price in dollars; it is whatever could have been done instead with the resources used. Your cost of reading this book is whatever you would have done with your time otherwise: gone to a movie, slept late, read a different book, cleaned the house. The cost of a $15 CD is whatever you would have done with that $15 otherwise. Every use of time or other resources to produce one good incurs a cost, which economists call the *opportunity cost*. That resource can't be used to produce anything else.

The information that prices deliver allows people to work together to produce more. The point of an economy is not just to produce more things; it's to produce more things *that people want*. Prices tell all of us what other people want. When prices for certain goods rise, we tend to reduce our consumption of those goods. Some of us calculate whether we could make money by starting to produce those goods. When prices (that is, wages or salaries) for some kinds of labor rise, we consider whether we ought to move into that field. Young people think about training for jobs that are starting to pay more, and they move away from training that prepares them for jobs for which wages are declining.

In any economy more complex than a village—maybe even more complex than a nuclear family—it's difficult to know just what everyone wants, what everyone can do, and what everyone is willing to do at what price. In the family, we love one another, and we have an intimate knowledge of each person's abilities, needs, and preferences, so we don't need prices to determine what each person will contribute and receive. Beyond the family, it is good that we act benevolently toward other people. But no matter how much preachers and teachers exhort us to love one another, we will never love everyone in society as much, or know their needs as well, as the people in our family. The price system reflects the choices of millions of producers, consumers, and resource owners who may never meet and coordinates their efforts. Although we can never feel affection for—or even meet—everyone in the economy, market prices help us to work together to produce more of what everyone wants.

Unlike government, which at best takes the will of the majority (and more often acts according to pressure from a small group) and imposes it on everyone, markets use prices to let buyers and sellers freely decide what they want to do with their money. Nobody can afford everything, and some people can afford much more than others, but each person is free to spend his money as he chooses. And if 51 percent of the people like black cars, or Barry Manilow, dissenters are free to buy something else; they don't have to organize a political movement to get the whole country to switch to blue cars or Willie Nelson.

## Competition

All this talk about the marvel of coordination shouldn't leave the impression that the market process isn't competitive. Our individual plans are always in conflict with those of other people; we plan to sell our services or our goods to customers, but other people are also hoping to sell to the same customers. It is precisely through competition that we find out how things can be produced at the least cost, by discovering who will sell us raw materials or labor services for the lowest price.

The basic economic question is how to combine all the resources in society, including human effort, to produce the greatest possible output—not the most pounds of steel, or the most computers, or the most exciting movies, but the *combination* of output that will satisfy people most. We want to produce as much as we can of each good that people want, but not so much that it would be better to produce something else instead. The prices we're willing to pay for a good or service, and the prices we're willing to accept for our labor or for what we've produced, guide entrepreneurs toward the right solution.

When we make decisions in the market, each decision is made incrementally, or "on the margin": do I want *this* steak, one more magazine, a three-bedroom house? Our willingness to pay, and the point at which we're not willing to buy another unit, tells producers how much they can afford to spend on producing the product. If they can't produce another one for less than the "market-clearing" price, they know not to devote more resources to production of that product. When consumers show rising interest in computers and declining interest in televisions, firms will pay more for raw materials and labor to produce computers. When the cost of hiring more labor and materials reaches the limit of what consumers are willing to pay for the finished product, firms stop drawing more resources in. As these decisions are repeated thousands, millions, billions, of times, a complex system of coordination develops that brings to consumers everything from kiwis to Pentium chips.

It is the competition of all firms to attract new customers that produces this coordination. If one firm senses that consumer demand for computers is increasing, and it is the first to produce more computers, it will be rewarded. Conversely, its television-producing competitor may find its sales declining. In practice, tens of thousands of firms do well, and thousands go out of business, every year. This is the "creative destruction" of the market. Harsh as the consumers' judgment may feel to someone who loses a job or an investment, the market works on a principle of equality. In a free market no firm gets special privileges from government, and each must constantly satisfy consumers to stay in business.

Far from *inducing* self-interest, as critics charge, in the marketplace the *fact* of self-interest induces people to serve others. Markets reward honesty because people are more willing to do business with those who have a reputation for honesty. Markets reward civility because people prefer to deal with courteous partners and suppliers.

## Socialism

It is the absence of market prices that makes socialism unworkable, as Ludwig von Mises pointed out in the 1920s. Socialists have often considered the question of production an engineering question: Just do some calculations to figure out what would be most efficient. It's true that an engineer can answer a specific question about the production process, such as, What's the most efficient way to use tin to make a 10-ounce soup can, that is, what shape of can would contain 10 ounces with the smallest surface area? But the economic question—the efficient use of all relevant resources—can't be answered by the engineer. Should the can be made of aluminum, or of platinum? Everyone knows that a platinum soup can would be ridiculous, but we know it *because* the price system tells us so. An engineer would tell you that silver or platinum wire would conduct electricity better than copper. Why do we use copper? Because it delivers the best results for the cost. That's an economic problem, not an engineering problem.

Without prices, how would the socialist planner know what to produce? He could take a poll and find that people want bread, meat, shoes, refrigerators, televisions. But how much bread and how many shoes? And what resources should be used to make which goods? "Enough," one might answer. But, beyond absolute subsistence, how much bread is enough? At what point would people prefer a new pair of shoes to more food? If there's a limited amount of steel available, how much of it should be used for cars and how much for ovens? And most important, what combination of resources is the least expensive way to produce each good? The problem is impossible to solve in a theoretical model; without the information conveyed by prices, planners are "planning" blind.

In practice, Soviet factory managers had to establish markets illegally among themselves. They were not allowed to use money prices, so marvelously complex systems of indirect exchange—or barter—emerged. Soviet economists identified at least eighty different media of exchange, from vodka to ball bearings to motor oil to tractor tires. The closest analogy to such a clumsy market that Americans have ever encountered was probably the bargaining skill of Radar O'Reilly on the television show *M*A*S*H*. Radar was also operating in a centrally planned economy—the U.S. Army—and his unit had no money with which to purchase supplies, so he would get on the phone, call other M*A*S*H units, and arrange elaborate trades of surgical gloves for C rations for penicillin for bourbon, each unit trading something it had been overallocated for what it had been underallocated. Imagine running an entire economy like that.

## Property and Exchange

One major reason that economic calculation is impossible under socialism is that there is no private property, so there are no owners to indicate through prices what they would be willing to accept in exchange for some of their property. In chapter 3 we examined the right to hold private property. Here we look at the economic importance of the institution of private property. Property is at the root of the prosperity produced by a free market. When people have secure title to property—whether it is land, buildings, equipment, or anything else—they can use that property to achieve their ends.

All property must be owned by someone. There are several

reasons to prefer diverse private ownership to government ownership. Private owners tend to take better care of their property because they will reap the benefits of any increase in its value, or suffer if its value declines. If you let the condition of your house deteriorate, you will not be able to sell it for as much as if you had kept it in good condition—which serves as a strong incentive to maintain it well. Owners generally take better care of property than renters do; that is, they maintain the capital value rather than, in effect, using up its value. That's why many rental agreements require the renter to put down a deposit, to ensure that he, too, will have an incentive to maintain the property value. Privately owned rental apartments are much better maintained than public housing. The reason is that no one really owns "public" property; no individual will lose his investment if the value of public property declines.

Private ownership allows people to profit from improving their property, by building on it or otherwise making it more valuable. People can also profit by improving themselves, of course, through education and the development of good habits, as long as they are allowed to reap the profits that come from such improvement. There's not much point in improving your skills, for instance, if regulations will keep you from entering your chosen occupation or high taxes will take most of your higher income.

The economic value of an asset reflects the income it will produce in the future. Thus private owners, who have the right to that income, have an incentive to maintain the asset. When land is scarce and privately owned, owners will seek to extract value from it now and also to ensure that they will be able to continue receiving value from it in the future. That's why timber companies don't cut all the trees on their land and instead continually plant more trees to replace the ones cut down. They may be moved by a concern for the environment, but the future income from the property is probably a more powerful incentive. In the socialist countries of Eastern Europe, where the government controlled all property, there was no real owner to worry about the future value of property; and pollution and environmental destruction were far worse than in the West. Václav Klaus, the prime minister of the Czech Republic, said in

1995, "The worst environmental damage occurs in countries without private property, markets, or prices."

Another benefit of private property, not so clearly economic, is that it diffuses power. When one entity, such as the government, owns all property, individuals have little protection from the will of the government. The institution of private property gives many individuals a place to call their own, a place where they are safe from depredation by others and by the state. This aspect of private property is captured in the axiom, "A man's home is his castle." Private property is essential for privacy and for freedom of the press. Try to imagine "freedom of the press" in a country where the government owned all the presses and all the paper.

## Division of Labor

Because people have different abilities and preferences, and natural resources are distributed unevenly around the world, we can produce more if we work at different tasks. Through the *division of labor,* we all seek to produce what we're best at, so we'll have more to trade with others. In *The Wealth of Nations,* Adam Smith described a pin factory where the production of pins was broken into "about eighteen different operations," each performed by specific workers. With such specialization, the workers could produce 4,800 pins per worker per day; without the division of labor, Smith doubted that one pinmaker could make 20 pins in a day. Note that there are gains to be had from specialization even if one person is better at everything. Economists call this the principle of *comparative advantage.* If Friday can catch twice as many fish as Crusoe but can find three times as many ripe fruits in a day, then both of them will be better off if Crusoe specializes in fishing and Friday specializes in foraging. As they do specialize, of course, each is likely to improve by repetition and experimentation.

People engage in exchange because they expect to become better off. As Adam Smith put it in a famous passage quoted earlier but relevant here as well,

> It is not from the benevolence of the butcher, the brewer, or the baker that we expect our dinner, but from their regard to their

own interest. We address ourselves, not to their humanity but to their self-love, and never talk to them of our own necessities but of their advantages.

That doesn't mean that people are always selfish and unconcerned about their fellow man. As noted earlier, the fact that the butcher must persuade you to buy his meat encourages him to pay attention to your wants and needs. Store clerks in the West are famously more pleasant than were their Soviet-era counterparts.

Still, it makes sense that social institutions operate effectively when people *do* act in their self-interest. In fact, when people act in their own interest in a free market, they improve the well-being of the whole society. Because people trade things they value less for things they value more, every trade increases the value of both goods. I will only trade my book for your CD if I value the CD more than the book, and if you value the book more than the CD. We're both better off. Similarly, if I trade my labor for a paycheck from Microsoft, it's because I value the money more than the time, and the shareholders of Microsoft value my labor more than the money they give up. Through millions of such transactions, goods and services move to people who value them most, and the whole society is made better off.

Capitalism encourages people to serve others in order to achieve their own ends. Under any system, talented and ambitious people are likely to acquire more wealth than others. In a statist system, whether the old precapitalist regimes or a "modern" socialist country, the way to get ahead is to get your hands on the levers of power and force other people to do your bidding. In a free market, you have to *persuade* others to do what you want. How do you do that? By offering them something *they* want. So the most talented and ambitious people have an incentive to find out what others want and try to supply it.

Private ownership under the rule of law *prevents* the kind of selfishness that involves taking what you want from those who own it. It also encourages people who want to get rich to produce goods and services that other people want. And so they do—Henry Ford with his cheap, efficient automobiles; Bill Cosby with his popular television show; Sam Walton with his discount stores; Bill Gates with his computer operating system; and many obscure people in a complex economy like ours, such as Philip Zaffere, who cleared $200 million when he sold the company he had founded, which made Stove Top stuffing and Mrs. Paul's fish sticks. Leona Helmsley may not *be* a nice person, but to get rich in the hotel business, she has to provide a comfortable room and clerks who *seem* nice.

## Profits, Losses, and Entrepreneurs

Everyone can see what roles consumers and producers—whether farmers, laborers, craftsmen, or factory owners—play in a market system, but sometimes the role of the entrepreneur or middleman is not so well understood. Historically, there has been a lot of hostility directed at middlemen. (Often this has taken the form of racial or ethnic prejudice, against Jewish entrepreneurs in Europe and the United States, Indians and Lebanese in Africa, Chinese in much of Asia, and Koreans in today's inner cities, as Thomas Sowell points out in *Race and Culture.* Economic ignorance is obviously not the only source of such attitudes, but a better understanding of economics would help to alleviate it.) The feeling seems to be, the farmer grows the wheat, the miller grinds it, the baker makes bread, but what value is added by the traders and distributors who move the wheat along the path to the consumer? Of what value is the Wall Street trader who spends his time exploiting price discrepancies between markets?

In a complex economy the role of the entrepreneur is vitally important. He might even be viewed as the person who actually performs the coordination that is the market process, the person who directs resources to where they're most needed. In a sense, we are all entrepreneurs. Every person tries to forecast the future and allocate his own resources wisely. Even Robinson Crusoe had to predict whether future weather conditions meant that he had better spend more time building a shelter at the expense of eating better today. Each of us forecasts where our skills will be most in demand, what potential customers will be willing to pay for our products, whether products we want will cost more or less next week, where we should invest our retirement savings. Of course, no one is really the much-derided "economic man," making calculations only on the basis of monetary return. We may take a less remunerative job because it involves interesting work or is near our home; we may start a photography business because we *like* photography, even though we could make more money selling business equipment; we may be willing to pay more for products sold by friends or by environmentally sensitive companies. We make most of our economic decisions on the basis of a combination of factors, including price, convenience, enjoyment, personal relationships, and so on. The only thing economic analysis assumes is that we all make choices that are in our own interest, *however we define our interest.*

But economists use the term "entrepreneur" to denote a specific participant in the market process, one who is neither producer nor consumer but someone who sees and acts on an opportunity to move resources from where they are less valuable to where they are more valuable. He may see that kiwis sell for 30¢ on the West Coast and 50¢ on the East Coast, and that he can transport them for 10¢ each, so he can make 10¢ a kiwi by buying them in the West and shipping them east. He may discover that one company wants to buy an office building for up to $10 million, and that another company has an appropriate office building that it would sell for $8 million. By buying and reselling it (or simply by bringing buyer and seller together for a fee), he can make a tidy profit. He may see that radios could be produced very cheaply in Malaysia and sold in the United States for less than they currently cost, so he contracts with a manufacturer to produce radios and ship them here. He or another entrepreneur may then see that American firms could supply insurance in Malaysia cheaper than any Malaysian firm, so another profitable exchange can be made.

In each case the entrepreneur's role is to see a situation in which resources could be used in a way more valuable than they are now being used. His reward for seeing that is a portion of the value that he adds to both sides. If, to satisfy some people's skepticism about middlemen, we outlawed entrepreneurial activity, what would happen? Easterners would be deprived of kiwis they would gladly pay for, Americans would pay more for radios, one company wouldn't get an office building it could use, and another wouldn't get cash that it would value more than a building. But these are just the surface manifestations. What would really happen is that our complex modern economy would grind to a halt. Middlemen exist for a reason, because their services are worth something to the people they trade with. Farmers could bring their own goods to market, but most of them find it more efficient to concentrate on farming and sell their produce to middlemen. Consumers could go to farm states and buy produce from farmers there, but it's clearly more efficient to go to the grocery.

The role of entrepreneurs in allocating capital goods—the resources that are used to produce consumer goods—is even more necessary. As an economy gets wealthier and more complex, its structure of production lengthens. That is, there are more steps between raw materials and consumer goods. The first capital goods were probably nets for catching fish. By Adam Smith's time, there were several more steps involved in producing the machines that would help workers make pins in a factory. Today, just imagine the steps involved in getting a computer to the consumer: the store, which someone has to invest in; the transportation system; the firm that produces the computer; the software engineers, who had to be educated; the chips, which had to be designed and produced; the metal, glass, and plastic, which had to be produced, refined, and molded, and so on and so on. As the structure of production lengthens, requiring investments in production processes long before consumers will decide whether to purchase a product, it becomes ever more essential to have people constantly looking for opportunities to use resources more efficiently.

People engage in economic activity to get something they want—more goods and services, ultimately, but in the immediate situation, a paycheck or a purchase. Workers get paid for their labor, farmers sell their products. The reward an entrepreneur gets is profit. The word "profit" can mean different things. To an accountant it just means the money left over after a period of economic activity. Often that money is really the salary paid to the business owner for his labor, or interest earned on money lent to borrowers. Pure entrepreneurial profit comes out of the gap between the lower-valued and higher-valued use of a resource that the entrepreneur has spotted and acted on. It reflects his correct forecast about what consumers would prefer. The flip side is that entrepreneurs sometimes estimate wrongly, in which case they sustain entrepreneurial losses.

Sometimes people get upset about high profits. They want to limit profits or tax them away, especially those notorious "windfall profits." (You rarely hear people saying that society should chip in to help those businessmen who make "windfall losses.") In fact, we should be grateful to those who make profits. As the economist Murray Rothbard put it, "profits are an index that maladjustments [that is, less efficient uses of resources] are being met and combatted by the profit-making entrepreneurs." Or, as Israel Kirzner of New York University explains, "The entrepreneurial search for profits implies a *search for situations where resources are misallocated.*" The higher the profit an entrepreneur makes, the bigger the gap he discovered between how resources were being used and how they *could* be used, and thus the more he has benefited society. When critics complain that drug companies' profits are too high, they imply that high profits on such essential products are immoral. In fact, high profits signal the need for more investment in making drugs and curing disease. The drug companies that were making the highest profits were filling the *greatest* gap between what consumers needed and what the market was hitherto producing. A limit on drug company profits would discourage investment just where it was most needed.

It's not the profit maker we should criticize, but the loss maker. But we don't need any windfall-loss tax. The market punishes entrepreneurs who make wrong predictions in the form of losses, and enough losses will remove him from the role of entrepreneur and encourage him to go to work for somebody who is better at allocating resources.

Through this immensely complex process—which looks so simple on the surface, with an endless stream of consumer products flowing into stores—free-market prices help us all to coordinate our efforts and raise our standard of living.

Enthusiasts for the market process sometimes refer to "the

magic of the marketplace." But there's no magic involved, just the spontaneous order of peaceful, productive people freely interacting, each seeking his own gain but led to cooperate with others in order to achieve it. It doesn't happen overnight, but through years and centuries the market process has brought us from a society characterized by backbreaking labor to achieve bare subsistence and an average life expectancy of twenty-five years to today's truly amazing level of abundance, health, and technology.

## Economic Growth

How does economic growth happen? How did we get from a world in which people had only their own labor, land, and readily apparent natural resources to today's complex economic structure supporting an unprecedented standard of living?

In their highly readable little book, *What Everyone Should Know about Economics and Prosperity,* the economists James D. Gwartney and Richard L. Stroup offer a concise guide to the sources of prosperity. A first point to note is that to consume more, we must produce more. Scarcity is a basic part of the human condition; that is, our wants always exceed the resources available to satisfy them. To satisfy more of our wants, we must learn to use resources more efficiently.

We should also note that our goal is not to increase "growth of the economy," much less gross national product, national income, or any other statistical aggregate. There are many problems with such statistics (even though I will occasionally use them in this book), and they can lead people to make gross errors in economic observation, such as the notorious estimates that the Soviet economy was much larger than it was or the ridiculous statistics showing that the East German economy was half the size of West Germany's per capita. The goal of economic activity is to increase the supply of consumer goods for people, which will entail also increasing the supply of capital goods with which to produce consumer goods. It may be hard to measure that accurately, but we should remember that our concern is real goods, not statistics.

One way to produce real economic growth is through saving and investment. By consuming less today, we can produce and consume more tomorrow. There are two basic benefits of saving. The first is to set something aside "for a rainy day," a metaphor that recalls a primitive, even Robinson Crusoe economy. Crusoe sets aside some of the fish and berries he gathers today in case he is sick tomorrow or the weather prevents him from gathering more food. The second benefit is even more important. We save and invest so we can *produce* more in the future. If Crusoe saves food for a few days, he can take a day to produce a net, which would allow him to catch many more fish. In a complex economy, savings allow us to open a business or to invent or purchase equipment to make us more productive. The higher our level of saving (either as individuals or as a society), the more investments we can make in future production, and the higher our future standard of living—and that of our children—can be.

A complex economy needs an efficient capital market to attract savings and channel them into investments that will produce new wealth. The capital market includes markets for stocks, real estate, and businesses, and financial institutions such as banks, insurance companies, mutual funds, and investment firms. As Gwartney and Stroup write, "The capital market coordinates the actions of savers who supply funds to the market and investors seeking funds to finance various business activities. Private investors have a strong incentive to evaluate potential projects carefully and search for profitable projects." Investors are rewarded for making the right decisions—for channeling capital to projects that serve consumers' needs—and penalized with losses for channeling scarce capital to the wrong projects. We often hear disparaging references to "paper entrepreneurs," with a sort of macho disdain for people who don't "make things" like steel and automobiles. But in an increasingly complex economy, no task is more important than allocating capital to the right projects, and it is entirely appropriate that the market rewards people handsomely for making the *right* investment decisions.

Another source of economic growth is improvements in human capital, that is, the skills of workers. People who improve their skills—by learning to read and write, or learning carpentry or computer programming, or going to medical school—will usually be rewarded with higher earnings.

Improvements in technology also contribute to economic growth. Beginning with the Industrial Revolution about 250 years ago, technological changes have transformed our world. The steam engine, internal combustion, electricity, and nuclear power have replaced human and animal power as our principal sources of energy. Transportation has been revolutionized by the railroad, the automobile, and the airplane. Labor-saving devices such as washing machines, stoves, microwave ovens, computers, and a whole panoply of industrial machines have allowed us to produce more in less time. Entertainment has been changed beyond recognition by records, tapes, compact disks, movies, and television. In the eighteenth century only the Austro-Hungarian emperor and his court could hear Mozart; today anyone can hear Mozart, Mancini, or Madonna for a few dollars. Hollywood may produce plenty of trash (though we should remember that it's trash that people choose to watch), but more people have seen Shakespeare's *Richard III* performed in movies featuring Laurence Olivier and Ian McKellen than saw all the stage performances in history.

An often-overlooked source of growth is improvements in economic organization. A system of property rights, the rule of law, and minimal government allows maximum scope for people to experiment with new forms of cooperation. The development of the corporation allowed larger economic tasks to be undertaken than individuals or partnerships could achieve. Organizations such as condominium associations, mutual funds, insurance companies, banks, worker-owned cooperatives, and others are attempts to solve particular economic problems by new forms of association. Some of these forms turn out to be inefficient; many of the corporate conglomerates of the 1960s, for instance, proved to be unmanageable, and shareholders lost money. The rapid feedback of the market process ensures that successful forms of organization will be copied and unsuccessful forms will be discouraged.

All these sources of growth—saving, investment, improvements in human capital, technology, and economic organization—reflect the choices of individuals spurred by their own interest in a free market. The market in the United States and Western Europe is hardly as free as it could be, but its relative freedom has produced huge increases in output. As Gwartney and Stroup point out, "Workers in North America, Europe, and Japan produce about five times more output per capita than their ancestors did 50 years ago." So, not surprisingly, "their inflation-adjusted per capita income—what economists call real income—is approximately five times higher."

## Government's Discoordination

What is the role of government in the economy? To begin with, it plays a very important role: protecting property rights and freedom of exchange, so that market prices can bring about coordination of individual plans. When it goes beyond this role, trying to supply particular goods or services or encourage particular outcomes, it not only doesn't help the process of coordination, it actually does the opposite—it *discoordinates*. Prices convey information. If prices are controlled or interfered with by the government, then they won't convey *accurate information*. The more interference, the more inaccurate the information, the less economic coordination, and the less satisfaction of wants. Interference in the information conveyed by prices is just as destructive to economic progress as interference in language would be to having a conversation.

### Preserving Jobs

Whenever a better way is found to satisfy any human need (or when demand for any product falls), some of the resources previously employed in satisfying it will no longer be needed. Those no-longer-needed resources may be machines or factories or labor services. Individuals may lose their investments or their jobs when a competitor comes along with a cheaper way of meeting consumers' needs. We should be sympathetic to those who find themselves unemployed or faced with a loss of their investment in such a situation, but we should not lose sight of the *benefits* of competition and creative destruction. People in such a situation often want the government to step in, to maintain demand for their product, or bar a competitor from the market, or somehow preserve their jobs.

In the long run, however, it makes no sense to try to preserve unnecessary jobs or investments. Imagine if we had tried to preserve the jobs in the buggy industry when the automobile came along. We would have been keeping resources—land, labor, and capital—in an industry that could no longer satisfy consumers as well as other uses of those resources. To take a more recent example—one that should be familiar to those who entered school in the 1960s, though perhaps entirely unfamiliar to younger people—the slide rule was completely replaced by the calculator in a matter of just a few years in the 1970s. Should we have preserved the jobs of those making slide rules? For what purpose? Who would have bought slide rules once calculators became available and inexpensive? If we did that every time a firm or an industry became uneconomical, we would soon have a standard of living comparable to that of the Soviet Union.

It's often said that the point of an economy, or at least of economic policy, is to create jobs. That's backward. The point of an economy is to produce things that people want. If we really wanted to create lots and lots of jobs, the economist Richard McKenzie points out, we could do it with a three-word federal policy: Outlaw farm machinery. That would create about 60 million jobs, but it would mean withdrawing workers from where they are most productive and using them to produce food that could be produced much more efficiently by fewer workers and more machinery. We would all be much worse off.

Norman Macrae, long-time deputy editor of the *Economist,* has pointed out that in England, since the Industrial Revolution, about two-thirds of all the jobs that existed at the beginning of each century have been eliminated by the end of the century, yet there have been three times as many people employed at the end of the century. He notes that "in the late 1880s, about 60 percent of the work force in both the United States and Britain were in agriculture, domestic service, and jobs related to horse transport. Today, only 3 percent of the work force are in those occupations." During the twentieth century most workers moved from those jobs to manufacturing and then service jobs. During the twenty-first century it's likely that many, perhaps most, workers will move from hands-on production work to information work. Along the way many people will lose their jobs and their investments, but the result will be a higher standard of living for everyone. If we're lucky, fifty years from now we will be producing five times as much output per person as we do today—unless government distorts price signals, impedes coordination, and holds resources in unproductive uses.

In other words, the best way to "preserve" jobs is to unleash the economy. Jobs will *change,* but there will always be more new jobs created than old ones lost. This is true even in cases of technological progress; people get replaced by machines in one field, but the higher level of capital investment in the economy means a rising level of wages for other jobs.

## Price Controls

Controls on prices—including wages, the price of labor—are perhaps the most direct way in which government distorts price signals. Sometimes governments try to set minimum prices, but more often they want to limit maximum prices. Price controls are usually implemented in response to rising prices. Prices rise for several reasons. In a free market, a rising price usually indicates either rising demand for the product or a reduction in supply. In either case, there will be a tendency for resources to move into that market to take advantage of the rising price, which will tend to reduce or even reverse the price increase. (We might note that, over the long run, in real terms, the only price that consistently seems to rise is the price of human labor. Looking back a hundred years or so, we see that prices of goods—from wheat to oil to computers—have fallen, while the real wage rate has quintupled in fifty years. The only thing getting more scarce in economic terms, that is, relative to all other factors, is people.)

*Rent control* is a particularly pervasive example of price control. Every economist understands that rent controls produce shortages of rental housing. If the controls are set so as to hold rents below their market value, then people will demand more rental housing than they would otherwise. That is, the price set by the state is not the market-clearing price: more people will come to the city, or look for bigger apartments than they would be willing to pay a market price for, or stay in large apartments after the children move out, or seek to rent even though they could afford to buy a house. But since rents are being held below market value, investors prefer to invest in something on which they can get a full market return, so the supply of housing won't increase to meet the demand.

In fact, if rent control remains in effect, the supply may shrink, as owners decide to live in their property rather than rent it out, or deteriorating housing is not maintained or replaced. If landlords can't rent apartments to the highest bidder, they will find other ways to choose among potential tenants; they may take under-the-table bribes, known in New York City as "key money," or they may discriminate on the basis of race, sexual favors, or some other nonprice factor. In extreme circumstances, which may be seen in some neighborhoods of the South Bronx, owners of apartment buildings that don't bring in enough rent to cover the property taxes and thus can't even be sold simply abandon them and try to disappear.

As with so many kinds of government intervention, the problems created by rent control lead to more intervention. Landlords try to convert their unprofitable apartment buildings to condominiums, so city councils pass laws restricting condo conversions. In the market, tenants and landlords have good reason to try to keep one another happy, but rent control means that tenants are just a burden on the landlord, so landlords and tenants end up fighting, and governments create landlord-tenant commissions to regulate every aspect of their interaction. Bribery and inside information become the best way to find an apartment. The city council in Washington, D.C., once passed an ordinance that would repeal rent control as soon as the vacancy rate rose above a certain level—indicating a sufficient supply of available housing—but of course the supply of housing won't increase as long as rent controls are in place. It's no wonder that the Swedish economist Assar Lindbeck wrote, "Next to bombing, rent control seems in many cases to be the most efficient technique so far known for destroying cities."

Controls aren't always designed to keep prices down. Sometimes government tries to set minimum prices, such as the *minimum wage law.* Perhaps no issue better illustrates the sometimes counterintuitive nature of spontaneous order, the market process, and the coordination function of prices. Eighty percent of Americans consistently support an increase in the minimum wage, and why not? The idea sounds good: it's hard to make a living on, say, $4 an hour, so why not set a minimum wage of $5? But just as maximum prices create shortages, minimum prices produce surpluses. Workers whose productivity to an employer is less than the legal minimum won't be hired at all. Again, the price signal is distorted, and coordination can't occur. We noted earlier that the market process produces a job for everyone who wants one—except when the process isn't allowed to work. As economists William Baumol and Alan Blinder (later a member of the Clinton administration) wrote in their textbook *Economics: Principles and Policies,* "The primary consequence of the minimum wage law is *not* an increase in the incomes of the least skilled workers but a restriction of their employment opportunities." Employers will hire a skilled worker instead of two unskilled workers, or invest in machinery, or just let some jobs go undone. Older people say there used to be ushers in movie theaters; maybe there still would be, if theaters could offer less than the minimum wage to people looking for a first job. Instead, the teenage unemployment rate is several times as high as it was in the 1950s. The way to raise wages is not to outlaw work for less than a certain wage but to increase the accumulation of capital so that each employee can produce more, and to increase the skills of each employee so he can produce more with the same tools.

*Farm price supports* are another example of minimum prices. In any growing, noninflationary economy, we would expect prices to fall gently; more production means that the real price of everything, in terms of labor, is falling. Agricultural produce, being the "first" products in any economy, would be the clearest example of this. Indeed, over the past 200 years supplies of grain and other basic farm produce have been rising, and prices have been falling (when measured by hours of labor needed to buy units of produce). With food more plentiful, we need fewer people working on farms. Falling prices send that signal to farmers. That's why 53 percent of Americans were farmers in 1870, and only about 2.5 percent are today. That's good news; it means all those people can produce something else, making themselves and all the rest of us richer.

But starting in the 1920s the federal government decided to keep farm prices high, to keep farmers happy. That is, it decided to block the price signals that were telling farmers to move to more profitable endeavors. It set minimum prices for farm produce and promised to buy enough of each product to keep the price at that level. In return, farmers took some of their land out of production. That's where we get the popular jibe that the farm program "pays farmers not to farm." Of course, farmers aren't dumb. They put their worst land in the "soil bank" and farmed their best land. Then, since the government would pay an above-market price on anything they could produce on the land in production, farmers improved their technology, fertilizer, and seeds to increase production. The government ended up buying more crops than it had intended, piling up billions of dollars in surplus produce. (Perhaps the only consolation to American consumers and taxpayers is that the European Community has pursued similar but even more uneconomic programs, producing what European critics call "wine lakes" and "butter mountains.") Some of the surplus food was sent to poor countries such as India—which sounds nice, except that it *lowered* prices there and discouraged local farmers from producing, thus helping to keep the countries poor and in need of the surpluses that American farmers kept producing and selling to the U.S. government.

Farm programs have changed over the years, but the goal has typically been to keep prices high and thus distort the price signals that would otherwise encourage farmers to go into more productive lines of work.

Wage and price controls are the clumsiest possible intervention into the market's coordination process. They're the economic equivalent of Michael Jordan standing between you and a friend, waving his arms, as you try to toss a basketball back and forth.

## Taxation

The clumsy interventions described above should sound patently unfair and inegalitarian. Now let's consider an ever-popular form of coercion by which governments extract money directly from those who earn it: taxation. Taxes reduce the return each individual gets from economic activity. Since one of the important functions of income—including profits and losses—is to direct resources toward their most highly valued uses, an artificial reduction in the return has a distorting effect on economic calculation. Defenders of taxation may argue that a tax levied equally on all economic activity would be neutral in its effects. The diverse and uncountable array of taxes levied by contemporary governments—sales taxes, property taxes, inheritance taxes, luxury taxes, sin taxes, business-incorporation taxes, corporate income taxes, Social Security taxes, and income taxes levied at different rates on different people—would suggest that governments are not trying very hard to achieve a neutral system of taxation. But even if they did try, they would fail. Taxes always have different effects on different economic actors. They drive the marginal supplier or the marginal purchaser out of the market. Since taxation is always coupled with government expenditure, the combination can only have the effect of diverting resources from where consumers wanted them used to some other use chosen by political officials.

Taxes inhibit the vital function of entrepreneurship by reducing the return the entrepreneur can earn by noticing and remedying a misallocation of resources. If you tax something, you get less of it; taxing the rewards of entrepreneurship means that we will get less entrepreneurship, less alertness to ways that resources could be shifted to serve consumers' needs better.

Taxes create a wedge between buyers and sellers, including employers and employees, that can prevent productive exchanges from being made. If I'm willing to pay up to $200 for a suit, and you're willing to sell it for any price above $190, we have an obvious opportunity for an exchange that will benefit both of us. But add on a 10 percent sales tax, and there will be no price that we can agree on. If I'm willing to work for as little as $30,000, and you value my services at $35,000, then we should be able work out a deal somewhere between those two figures. But add on a Social Security tax of 15.3 percent, and a federal income tax of 28 percent, and a state income tax, and maybe a city income tax, and we won't be able to agree on a price. If taxes were lower, there would be more money in the private sector being directed to the satisfaction of consumer demand, and more demand for workers and thus less unemployment.

High tax rates discourage work effort. Why work overtime if the government will take half of what you earn? Why invest in a risky business opportunity when the government promises to take half of any profit but to let you bear the losses? In all these ways, taxes reduce the productive effort directed toward serving human needs.

High taxes may also encourage investors to put their money into tax-sheltered investments rather than into projects whose real return is greater in the absence of the tax differential. They also induce people to spend money on wasteful but tax-deductible purchases like offices fancier than their business really requires, vacations disguised as business travel, company automobiles, and so on. Such expenditures may be worthwhile to the people who make them; we know that when they spend their own money on them. But the tax laws may encourage overinvestment in things for which people wouldn't spend their own money. Finally, compliance with tax laws diverts resources from producing other goods. Businesses and individuals spend 5.5 billion worker-hours each year on tax paperwork—the equivalent of 2,750,000 workers who could be producing goods and services that consumers want.

## Regulation

A book could easily be written on the effects of government regulation on the market process. Here we can look only at a few basic points. We should begin by noting that some rules, commonly known as "regulations," are an inherent part of the market process in a system of property rights and the rule of law. Prohibitions on polluting other people's air, water, and land, for instance, are an acknowledgment of their property rights (chapter 10 will discuss in slightly more detail the kinds of rules that are effective and appropriate). Rules requiring people to live up to the terms of contracts, such as prohibitions on fraud, are also part of the common-law framework of the market process.

Unfortunately, most of the regulations promulgated by legislative bodies and administrative agencies these days don't fall into those categories. The regulations that concern us here are explicitly designed to bring about an economic outcome different from what the market process would have produced. Sometimes we can point to specific problems generated by such regulations: rent controls reduce the supply of housing; airline regulation raises the cost of air travel; a lengthy drug-approval process keeps lifesaving and pain-relieving drugs out of the hands of consumers. Often, however, it is more difficult to assess the effect of a regulation, which is to say, to figure out what *would* have happened if the market's coordination process had been allowed to work. It is precisely the *least* obvious absences of coordination that regulation may invisibly prevent market participants from discovering and remedying. If we are persuaded that the market process works to satisfy consumer demands—that is, to allocate resources in the way that will produce the most value for a given level of resources—then we will conclude that there are always costs to regulations that prevent voluntary exchanges from being made.

Robert Samuelson wrote in *Newsweek* in 1994:

> The totality of federal regulations now comes to 202 volumes numbering 131,803 pages. This is 14 times greater than in 1950 and nearly four times greater than in 1965. There are 16 volumes of environmental regulations, 19 volumes of agricultural regulations and 2 volumes of employment regulations.

If you run a business, you'd better know what's in all those regulations—and the 60,000 or so pages of new regulations (some of which replace or alter old regulations) published each year in the *Federal Register*. About 130,000 people work in federal regulatory agencies, and the economist Thomas D. Hopkins, writing in the *Journal of Regulation and Social Costs,* estimates that regulation costs our economy some $600 billion a year in lost output—resources that could have gone to satisfying consumer needs. Clifford Winston of the Brookings Institution estimates that "society has gained at least $36–$46 billion (1990 dollars) annually from deregulation," which suggests that for all the recent deregulation of transportation, communications, energy, and financial services, the regulatory burden has barely been reduced.

Winston also writes that "economists found it difficult to predict, or even consider, changes in firms' operations and technology, and consumers' responses to these changes, that developed in response to regulatory reform." That is, the discoordinations produced by interference with the market process are so great and so complex that it is very difficult to assess them and predict the improvements in coordination that would occur under deregulation. To take just one example, economists recognized that the regulation of trucking prices and routes by the Interstate Commerce Commission was producing major inefficiencies. They predicted that deregulation could save consumers and businesses $5 billion to $8 billion a year by making trucking more efficient. They were right; in fact, a 1990 study for the U.S. Department of Transportation estimated annual savings from the 1980 deregulation at about $10 billion. What the economists did not predict was a far more important outcome: cheaper, more reliable trucking allowed firms to reduce their inventory, knowing that they would be able to get their products to buyers when they were needed. The inventory savings, which amounted to some $56 billion to $90 billion a year by the mid-1980s, dwarfed the direct savings in trucking costs.

The real motivation for regulation is often self-interest in the worst sense, an attempt to get something through government coercion that you couldn't get through the actions of consumers. There are all kinds of such so-called transfer-seeking, many of which are discussed in chapter 9. You can get a higher tax imposed on a competitive industry than on your own. If you're a big company, you can support regulations that will cost large and small companies similar amounts of money, hurting the small companies proportionally more. You can get a tariff to protect your product from foreign competition. You can get a regulation that makes it cheaper for customers to buy your product than your competitor's. You can get a licensing law to limit the number of people in your industry, and on and on. All these regulations distort the market process and move resources away from their highest-valued use.

But these days many regulations are advanced by people who generally believe them to be in the public interest, people who may even believe firmly in the market process except when regulation seems really necessary. Regulations are enacted to guarantee safety in consumer products; to forbid discrimination on the basis of race, sex, religion, national origin, marital status, sexual orientation, personal appearance, or Appalachian origin; to reduce inconveniences faced by disabled people; to ensure the efficacy of pharmaceutical drugs; to guarantee access to health insurance; to discourage corporate layoffs; and for myriad other noble causes. It's hard to argue with the goals of any of these regulations. We all want a society of safe and effective products, free from discrimination, where everyone has health insurance and a secure job.

But the attempt to realize such goals by regulation is self-defeating. It substitutes the judgment of a small group of fallible politicians for the results of a market process that coordinates the needs and preferences of millions of people. It sets up static, backward-looking rules that can never deal with changing circumstances as well as voluntary exchange and contract. No one regulation will destroy the market process. But each one acts like a termite, eating away at the structure of a system that is rugged but not indestructible. And if regulation does indeed cost our economy anywhere near $600 billion, then it is costing lives. A 1994 study from Harvard University's Center for Risk Analysis found that our command-and-control regulatory system may be costing as many as 60,000 lives a year, by spending resources on negligible risks, leaving less money for people to spend on protecting themselves from bigger but less dramatic risks. As Aaron Wildavsky of the University of California at Berkeley wrote, wealthier is healthier and richer is safer. As people get richer, they purchase more health and safety—not just medical care, but better nutrition, better sanitation, shorter work hours, safer workplaces and kitchens. The cost of every regulation proposed to improve health or safety should be weighed against the health costs that will be incurred by individuals' having less wealth. Also, Wildavsky argued, competitive institutions and processes produce better results over time than centralized systems, so the competitive market process is more likely to develop advances in health and safety than are more heavily regulatory or bureaucratic systems.

## *International Trade*

One of the important applications of the principle of comparative advantage is international trade. To an economist there is nothing really special about international trade; individuals make trades when both of them expect to benefit, whether they live across the street, in different states, or in different countries.

Since 1776, when Adam Smith demonstrated the benefits of free trade, there has been little *intellectual* debate on the subject. More than most economic topics, the debate over trade has been spurred by special interests seeking advantages from government that they could not gain in the marketplace.

Whenever two individuals make a trade, both expect to benefit; and both theory and observation tell us that more often than not both parties do benefit, and the level of wealth in society is enhanced. The division of labor allows people to specialize in what they're best at and to exchange with those who specialize in something else. As Smith wrote, "It is the maxim of every prudent . . . family, never to attempt to make at home what it will cost . . . more to make than to buy. . . . What is prudence in the conduct of every private family can scarce be folly in that of a great kingdom."

That is, it's usually best to sell where you can get the highest price and buy where you can get the lowest price. But somehow, the drawing of national boundaries confuses people's thinking on the benefits of trade. Maybe it's because "balance of trade" statistics are calculated on a national basis. We could just as well calculate the balance of trade between New York and New Jersey, or between Massachusetts and California. For that matter, you could calculate your own balance of trade between yourself and everyone you deal with. If I did that, I would have huge trade deficits with my grocer, my dentist, and my department store, because I buy a great deal from them and they never buy anything from me. My only trade surpluses would be with my employer and the publisher of this book, because I buy almost nothing from them. What would be the sense of such calculations? I expected to benefit from each transaction, and the only balance I care about is that my income exceed my expenditures. The best way to make that happen is to concentrate on doing what I do best and let others do what they do best.

The very notion of a "balance of trade" is misguided. Trade has to balance. Just as an individual cannot long consume more than he produces (except if he is a thief or the beneficiary of gifts, charity, or government transfer payments), all the individuals in a country cannot consume more than they produce, or import more than they export. As pleasant as it would be to imagine, producers in other countries will not give us their products for free or in return for dollars that are never exchanged for our goods and services. A national "balance of trade" is just a composite of all the trades made by individuals in the nation; if each of those trades makes economic sense, the aggregate cannot be a problem.

Frederic Bastiat pointed out that a nation could improve its balance of trade by loading a ship with exports, recording the departure of the ship, and then sinking it outside the three-mile boundary. Goods were exported, none were imported, and the balance of trade is favorable. Clearly that would not be a sensible policy.

The real problem may be a fundamental economic mistake: regarding exports as good and imports as bad. We see this fallacy in every discussion of trade negotiations. Newspapers always report that the United States "gave up" some of its restrictions on imports in return for similar "concessions" from other countries. But we're not giving up anything when the U.S. government lets American consumers buy from foreign suppliers. The point of economic activity is consumption. We produce in order that we may consume. We sell in order to buy. And we export to pay for our imports. For each participant in international trade, the goal is to acquire consumption goods as cheaply as possible. The benefit of trade is the import; the cost is the export.

During his 1996 presidential campaign, Pat Buchanan stood at the port of Baltimore and said, "This harbor in Baltimore is one of the biggest and busiest in the nation. There needs to be more American goods going out." That's fundamentally mistaken. We don't want to send any more of our wealth overseas than we have to in order to acquire goods from overseas. If Saudi Arabia would give us oil for free, or if Japan would give us televisions for free, Americans would be better off. The people and capital that used to produce televisions—or used to produce things that were traded for televisions—could then shift to producing other goods. Unfortunately for us, we don't get those goods from other countries for free. But if we can get them cheaper than it would cost us to produce them ourselves, we're better off.

Sometimes international trade is seen in terms of competition between nations. We should view it, instead, like domestic trade, as a form of cooperation. By trading, people in both countries can prosper. And we should remember that goods are produced by individuals and businesses, not by nation-states. "Japan" doesn't produce televisions; "the United States" doesn't produce the world's most popular entertainment. *Individuals,* organized into partnerships and corporations in each country, produce and exchange. In any case, today's economy is so globally integrated that it's not clear even what a "Japanese" or "Dutch" company is. If Ford Motor Company owns a controlling interest in Mazda, which produces cars in Malaysia and sells them in Europe, which "country" is racking up points on the international scoreboard? The immediate winners would seem to be investors in the United States and Japan, workers in Malaysia, and consumers in Europe; but of course the broader benefits of international trade will accrue to investors, workers, and consumers in all those areas.

The benefit of international trade to consumers is clear: we can buy goods produced in other countries if we find them better or cheaper. There are other benefits as well. First, it allows the division of labor to work on a broader scale, enabling the people in each country to produce the goods at which they have a comparative advantage. As Mises put it, "The inhabitants of [Switzerland] prefer to manufacture watches instead of growing wheat. Watchmaking is for them the cheapest way to acquire wheat. On the other hand the growing of wheat is the cheapest way for the Canadian farmer to acquire watches."

A great advantage of the price system is that it gives us one standard by which to determine what goods any of us should produce. Should we produce coffee, corn, radios, movies, or flange-making machines? The answer is, whichever one will give us the greatest profit. The economist Michael Boskin of Stanford University got in hot water when he was chairman of President George Bush's Council of Economic Advisers for reportedly saying something that was absolutely true: A dollar's worth of potato chips is worth just as much as a dollar's worth of computer chips, and it doesn't matter which one you produce. A country as technologically advanced as the United States is going to produce a lot of high-tech products, though in many cases we produce the designs here—which is where we get the most profit—and then have the actual computer chips, televisions, and so on produced where production wages are cheaper. We also seem to have a huge comparative advantage in producing popular culture: movies, television, music, computer games, and so on. And despite our technological advancement, we have vast amounts of rich farmland and highly productive farmers, so we also produce many agricultural products more cheaply than anyone else. Contrary to mercantilist notions, a number of economies have prospered through the export mainly of relatively unprocessed materials such as timber, meat, grain, wool, and minerals. Just think of Canada, the United States, Australia, and New Zealand. Others have prospered as traders and manufacturers, despite a decided lack of natural resources. Think of Holland, Switzerland, Britain, Japan, and Hong Kong. The key is free markets, not specific resources or products.

Remember, it's not necessary that every country have an *absolute* advantage at producing something; it will always have a *comparative* advantage in something. Even if Liz Claiborne is the best typist in her company, she's still going to design clothes and hire someone else to type. Even if Americans can produce every conceivable product more cheaply than Mexicans, both countries will still gain from trading, because Mexican firms will make the goods they are *relatively*—even if not absolutely—more efficient at producing.

International trade also makes possible economies of scale (that is, the efficiencies that companies can achieve by producing in large quantities), which couldn't be achieved in smaller national economies. That's less important for American companies, which already have the world's largest market, than for companies in Switzerland, Hong Kong, Taiwan, and other small nations. But even American companies, especially if they produce something for a narrow market, can reduce their unit costs by selling internationally.

Free international trade is an important competitive spur to domestic companies. American cars are better than they were twenty years ago because of the competition from Japanese and other foreign companies. According to Brink Lindsey, a trade lawyer, integrated steel manufacturers have also improved their efficiency in response to foreign competition, and "American semiconductor manufacturers, faced with brutal Japanese competition in high-volume memory chips, have improved their manufacturing efficiency and concentrated resources on their own strengths in design-intensive logic chips."

When governments restrict international trade at the behest of domestic interest groups, they impede the information and coordination process of the market. They "protect" some industries and jobs, but only at the expense of the whole economy. Protectionism prevents capital and labor from moving to uses that would better satisfy consumer demand. Like laborsaving machinery, imports reduce employment in one part of the economy, allowing those workers to move to more productive jobs.

The nineteenth-century economist Henry George pointed out in *Protection or Free Trade* that nations try to embargo their enemies to restrict their foreign trade in time of war, which is much like protectionism: "Blockading squadrons are a means whereby nations seek to prevent their enemies from trading; protective tariffs are a means whereby nations attempt to prevent their own people from trading. What protectionism teaches us, is to do to ourselves in time of peace what enemies seek to do to us in time of war."

Finally, a great benefit of international trade is to reduce the chances of war. Nineteenth-century liberals said, "When goods cannot cross borders, armies will." Trade creates people on both sides of national borders with an interest in peace and increases international contacts and understanding. That doesn't mean there will never be a war between countries practicing free trade, but commercial relations do seem to improve the prospects for peace.

## Government and the Productive Process

In all these ways and more, government interferes with the co-operation and coordination that are the market process. Introducing government intervention into the market is like introducing a monkey wrench into a complex machine. It can only reduce its efficiency. Fortunately, the market process is more like a computer network than a machine; instead of coming to a complete stop, the market process routes information around the destructive intervention. Its efficiency is reduced but not halted. Each intervention into the market may cost a great economy only a little. Adam Smith once encountered a young man who bemoaned some new policy, saying, "This will be the ruin of Great Britain," to which Smith replied, "Young man, there is a deal of ruin in a nation." Similarly, the great British historian Thomas Babington Macaulay wrote, "It has often been found that that profuse expenditure, heavy taxation, absurd commercial restriction, corrupt tribunals [etc.] have not been able to destroy capital so fast as the exertions of private citizens have been able to create it."

It is our great good fortune that the market process is so resilient, that it can continue to progress and produce despite the burden of so much taxation and regulation. But there are real costs. If we look only at the slowdown in U.S. productivity per worker, and thus in economic growth, that began in the early 1970s—largely because of a dramatic growth in taxes and regulation in the 1960s and 1970s—the average American could be 40 percent richer today, if productivity had continued to increase as fast as it did during the preceding twenty-five years. Prosperous people may think that a 40 percent increase in wealth and income wouldn't be all that important (though I would certainly like to see the new technologies and products that would make up part of that increase), but lower-income Americans would undoubtedly have their lives improved by that kind of growth.

Each new tax, each new regulation, makes property a little less secure, gives each individual a little less incentive to create wealth, makes our society a little less adaptable to change, concentrates power a little more. There is a deal of ruin in a nation, but civil society is not infinitely resilient.

## What Is Seen and What Is Not Seen

Every proposal for government intervention in the economy involves a sleight of hand. Like a magician, the politician who proposes a tax, a subsidy, or a program wants the voters to look only at his right hand and to be diverted from observing his left hand.

In the early nineteenth century, Frederic Bastiat wrote a brilliant essay that inspired Henry Hazlitt's bestselling book *Economics in One Lesson.* As Hazlitt put it, "The whole of economics can be reduced to a single lesson . . .: *The art of economics consists in looking not merely at the immediate but at the longer effects of any act or policy; it consists in tracing the consequences of that policy not merely for one group but for all groups*" (emphasis in original).

Bastiat and Hazlitt both began with the story of the broken window. In a small town a teenager breaks a shop window. At first everyone gathers out front and calls him a vandal. But then someone says that, after all, someone will have to replace the window. The money that the shopkeeper pays him will allow the window installer to buy a new suit. The tailor then will be able to buy a new desk. As the money circulates, everyone in town may come to benefit from the boy's vandalism. *What is seen* is the money circulating from replacing the window; *what is not seen* is what would have been done with the money if no window had been broken. Either the shopkeeper would have saved it, adding to investment capital and producing a higher standard of living later, or he would have spent it. Perhaps *he* would have bought a new suit or a new desk. The town is not better off; people in the town have had to spend some money replacing something rather than producing new wealth.

In such simple form, the fallacy may sound obviously absurd. Who would claim that a broken window could benefit society? But as Bastiat and Hazlitt pointed out, the same fallacy can be found in the newspapers every day. The clearest example is the story that always appears two days after a natural disaster. Yes, Hurricane Andrew was awful, people reflect on the second day, but think of all the construction jobs that will be created as we rebuild our homes and factories. Indeed, a Florida newspaper headline read, "Hurricane Andrew Good News for S. Florida Economy." The *Washington Post* reported that Japan is considering building a new capital somewhere other than Tokyo. There may be good arguments for the idea, but not this one: "Supporters argue a new capital would boost Japan's sluggish economy. The massive construction project would create many jobs, and the ripples would be felt throughout the nation's economy." They would indeed, but in both these cases we must look at what is not seen. A hurricane destroys real wealth in society—houses, factories, churches, equipment. The capital and labor that go into rebuilding them are not being used to produce *additional* wealth. As for building a new capital, it would create as many jobs as constructing the pyramids; but if there's no good reason for a new capital, then capital and labor are being diverted from more productive uses.

A related fallacy is the claim that West Germany and Japan grew so fast after World War II not because they had lower taxes and freer markets than some of the war's winners, but because their factories were destroyed and they built newer, more modern factories. To my knowledge, the people making such claims never actually urged bombing the factories of, say, France and Great Britain in order to boost their economic growth.

The broken-window fallacy has far broader application:

• Every time local politicians propose to tax people in order to build a stadium for a centimillionaire major-league owner, they hold out in their right hand the promise that the increased business activity will more than replace the money spent. But they don't want you to look at the left hand—the jobs and wealth created by the money that people would have spent if it hadn't been taxed away for the stadium.

• After the federal government gave the Chrysler Corporation $1.5 billion in loan guarantees, newspapers reported that the effort was a success because Chrysler stayed in business. What they didn't report—what they couldn't report—was *what was not seen*: the homes that weren't built, the businesses that weren't expanded, with the money that other people couldn't borrow because the government directed scarce savings to Chrysler.

• In every generation since the Industrial Revolution, people have worried that automation was going to eliminate jobs. In 1945 First Lady Eleanor Roosevelt wrote, "We have reached a point today where labor-saving devices are good only when they do not throw the worker out of his job." It would seem they couldn't save much labor in that case. Gunnar Myrdal, who actually received a Nobel Prize in economics, wrote in 1970 in *The Challenge of World Poverty,* that laborsaving machines should not be introduced in underdeveloped countries because they "decrease the demand for labor." Of course automation reduces the demand for particular labor, but that means it frees up labor to do something else. If things can be produced with fewer resources, then more things can be produced—more clothes, more houses, more vaccinations to keep children from dying, more food for malnourished people, more water-treatment plants to combat cholera and dysentery.

Every scheme to create jobs through government spending means that people will be taxed to pay for the project. The money spent by government is then not spent by the people who earned it, on projects *they* would have chosen. Television stations can send cameras to film the people who got jobs or services from the program; they can't find the people who *didn't* get a job because a little bit of money was diverted from everyone in society to pay for the visible program.

## Capitalism and Freedom

In his pathbreaking essay, "The Use of Knowledge in Society," Friedrich Hayek wrote,

> We often take the working of [the price system] for granted. I am convinced that if it were the result of deliberate human design, and if the people guided by the price changes understood that their decisions have significance far beyond their immediate aim, this mechanism would have been acclaimed as one of the greatest triumphs of the human mind.

But as I stress throughout this book, the great spontaneous institutions of society—law, language, and markets—were not designed by anyone. We all participate, unwittingly, in making them work, and we do indeed take them for granted. That's fine. They do evolve spontaneously, after all. We need simply to remember to *let* the market process work its apparent magic and not let the government clumsily intervene in it so deeply that it grinds to a halt.

## Chapter 9

# WHAT BIG GOVERNMENT IS ALL ABOUT

*G*overnment has an important role to play in a free society. It is supposed to protect our rights, creating a society in which people can live their lives and undertake projects reasonably secure from the threat of murder, assault, theft, or foreign invasion. By the standards of most governments in history, this is an extremely modest role. That's what made the American Revolution so revolutionary. The Declaration of Independence proclaimed, "To secure these rights, governments are instituted among men." Not "to make men moral." Not "to boost economic growth." Not "to ensure everyone a decent standard of living." Just the simple, revolutionary idea that government's role was limited to securing our rights. But imagine how much better off we would all be if our government did an adequate job at this simple, limited task.

Unfortunately, most governments fail to live up to Thomas Jefferson's vision in two ways. First, they don't do a good job of swiftly and surely apprehending and punishing those who violate our rights. Second, they seek to aggrandize themselves by taking on more and more power, intruding themselves into more aspects of our lives, demanding more of our money, and depriving us of our liberty.

The most revolutionary aspect of the American Revolution was that it sought to create from scratch a national government limited to very little more than protecting individual rights. During the Middle Ages, in England and other European countries, the idea of limits on government had grown. Cities had written their own constitutional charters, and representative assemblies had sought to control kings through documents such as Magna Carta and the Golden Bull of Hungary. Many of the American colonists—and some of their British supporters such as Edmund Burke—saw the Revolution as a reclaiming of their rights as Englishmen. But the soaring words of the Declaration and the strict rules of the Constitution went further than any previous effort in declaring the natural rights of life, liberty, and property and delegating to the new government only the powers necessary to protect those rights.

We should distinguish at this point between "government" and "state." Those two terms are sometimes used interchangeably, especially in American English, but they actually refer to two very important but easily confused kinds of institutions. A government is the consensual organization by which we adjudicate disputes, defend our rights, and provide for certain common needs. A condominium association, for example, has a government to adjudicate disputes among owners, regulate the use of common areas, make the residents secure from outside intruders, and provide for other common needs. We can readily see why people seek to have a government in this sense. In every case, the residents agree to the terms of the government (its constitution or charter or bylaws) and give their consent to be governed by it. A state, on the other hand, is a coercive organization asserting or enjoying a monopoly over the use of physical force in some geographic area and exercising power over its subjects. The audacity and the genius of the American Founders was to attempt to create a government that would not be a state.

Historically, the real origins of the state lie in conquest and economic exploitation. The sociologist Franz Oppenheimer pointed out that there are two basic ways to acquire the means to satisfy our human needs. "These are work and robbery, one's own labor and the forcible appropriation of the labor of others." He called work and free exchange the "economic means" of acquiring wealth, and the appropriation of the work of others the "political means."

From this basic insight, Oppenheimer said, we can discern the origins of the state. Banditry and robbery and fraud are the usual ways in which people seek to forcibly appropriate what others have produced. But how much more efficient it would be to organize and regularize robbery! According to Oppenheimer, "The State is the organization of the political means." States arose when one group conquered another and settled in to rule them. Instead of looting the conquered group and moving on, the conquerors settled down and switched from looting to taxing. This regularization had some advantages for the conquered society, which is one reason it endured: rather than planting crops or building houses and then being subject to unpredictable looting by marauders, the peaceful and productive people may prefer simply to be forced to give up, say, 25 percent of their crop to their rulers, secure in the knowledge that that will—usually—be the full extent of the depredation and that they will be protected from marauders.

This basic understanding of the distinction between society and the state, between the people and the rulers, has deep roots in Western civilization, going back to Samuel's warning to the people of Israel that a king would "take your sons, and your daughters, and your fields" and to the Christian concept that the state is conceived in sin. The Levellers, the great fighters for English liberty in the time of Charles I and Cromwell, understood that the origins of the English state lay in the conquest of England by the Normans, who imposed on free Englishmen a "Norman yoke." A century later, when Thomas Paine sought to undermine the legitimacy of the British monarchy, he pointed out, "A French bastard, landing with an armed banditti, and establishing himself king of England against the consent of the natives, is in plain terms a very paltry rascally original."

In a 1925 essay, "More of the Same," the journalist H. L. Mencken agreed:

> The average man . . . sees clearly that government is something lying outside him and outside the generality of his fellow men— that it is a separate, independent, and hostile power, only partly under his control, and capable of doing him great harm. . . . [Government] is apprehended, not as a committee of citizens

chosen to carry on the communal business of the whole population, but as a separate and autonomous corporation, mainly devoted to exploiting the population for the benefit of its own members. . . . When a private citizen is robbed, a worthy man is deprived of the fruits of his industry and thrift; when the government is robbed, the worst that happens is that certain rogues and loafers have less money to play with than they had before.

## The Democratic State

It is usually argued in the United States that all this may have been true in ancient times, or even in the countries our forefathers fled, but that in a democratic country "*we* are the government." The Founders themselves hoped that a democratic—or, as they would have said, a republican—form of government would never violate people's rights or do anything against the interests of the people. The unfortunate reality is that we can't all be the government. Most of us are too busy working, producing wealth, taking care of our families to watch what the rulers are doing. What normal, productive person can read a single one of the 1,000-page budget bills that Congress passes each year to find out what's really in it? Not one American in a hundred knows how much he really pays in taxes, given the many ways that politicians hide the real costs.

Yes, we have the power every four years or so to turn the rascals out and put in a new set of rascals. But many factors limit the value of that power:

• There aren't many fundamentally different alternatives on the ballot. The choice between Bush and Clinton, or Clinton and Dole, is hardly worth getting excited about. Even the supposedly revolutionary Congress of 1994 barely slowed the rate at which the federal government got bigger.

• We have to choose a package deal. *Sesame Street* recently gave us an example of what that means. In an election special, the Muppets and their human friends have $3 to spend, and they learn about voting by deciding whether to buy crayons or juice.

*Rosita:* You count the people who want crayons. Then you count
    the people who want juice. If more people want juice, it's juice
    for everyone. If more people want crayons, it's crayons.
*Telly:* Sounds crazy but it might just work!

But why not let each child buy what *he* wants? Who needs
democracy for such decisions? There *may* be some public goods,
but surely juice and crayons don't count. In the real world, one
candidate offers higher taxes, legalized abortion, and getting
out of the War in Vietnam; another promises a balanced budget, school prayer, and escalation of the war. What if you want
a balanced budget *and* withdrawal from Vietnam? In the marketplace, you get lots of choices; politics forces you to choose
among only a few.

• People employ what economists call "rational ignorance."
That is, we all spend our time learning about things we can actually do something about, not political issues that we can't really affect. That's why more than half of us can't name either of
our U.S. senators. (I'm sure the readers of this book can, but 54
percent of those polled by the *Washington Post* couldn't.) And
why most of us have no clue about how much of the federal
budget goes to Medicare, foreign aid, or any other program. As
an Alabama businessman told the *Post,* "Politics doesn't interest
me. I don't follow it. . . . Always had to make a living." Ellen
Goodman, a sensitive, good-government liberal columnist,
complains about a friend who has spent months researching
new cars, and of her own efforts to study the sugar, fiber, fat,
and price of various cereals. "Would my car-buying friend use
the hours he spent comparing fuel-injection systems to compare
national health plans?" Goodman asked. "Maybe not. Will the
moments I spend studying cereals be devoted to studying the
greenhouse effect on grain? Maybe not." *Certainly* not—and
why should they? Goodman and her friend will get the cars and
the cereal they want, but what good would it do to study national health plans? After a great deal of research on medicine,
economics, and bureaucracy, her friend may decide which
health-care plan he prefers. He then turns to studying the presidential candidates, only to discover that they offer only vague
indications of which health-care plan they would implement.

But after diligent investigation, our well-informed voter chooses a candidate. Unfortunately, the voter doesn't like that candidate's stand on anything else—the package-deal problem—but he decides to vote on the issue of health care. He has a one in a hundred million chance of influencing the outcome of the presidential election, after which, if his candidate is successful, he faces a Congress with different ideas, and in any case, it turns out the candidate was dissembling in the first place. Instinctively realizing all this, most voters don't spend much time studying public policy. Give that same man three health insurance plans that *he* can choose from, though, and chances are that he *will* spend some time studying them.

• Finally, as noted above, the candidates are likely to be kidding themselves or the voters anyway. One could argue that in every presidential election since 1968, the American people have tried to vote for smaller government, but in that time the federal budget has risen from $178 billion to $1.6 trillion. George Bush made *one* promise that every voter noticed in the 1992 campaign: "Read my lips, no new taxes." Then he raised them. If we are the government, why do we get so many policies we don't want, from school busing and the war in Vietnam to huge deficits, tax rates higher than almost any American approves, and the war in Bosnia?

No, even in a democracy there is a fundamental difference between the rulers and the ruled. Mark Twain once said, "It could probably be shown by facts and figures that there is no distinctly native American criminal class except Congress." Of course, Congress is no worse than its counterparts in other countries.

One of the most charming and honest descriptions of politics ever penned came from a letter written by Lord Bolingbroke, an English Tory leader in the eighteenth century.

I am afraid that we came to Court in the same dispositions as all parties have done; that the principal spring of our actions was to have the government of the state in our hands; that our principal views were the conservation of this power, great employments to ourselves, and great opportunities of rewarding those who had helped to raise us and of hurting those who stood in opposition to us.

Libertarians recognize that power tends to corrupt its holders. How many politicians, no matter how well intentioned, can avoid abusing the considerable power of today's expansive governments? Look at Senator Robert Byrd's constant exertions to move the entire federal payroll to West Virginia, or Senator Bob Dole's long record of generous contributions from the Archer-Daniels-Midland Corporation and his championing of huge federal subsidies for ADM. Or note the clear echo of Bolingbroke's letter in a White House aide's notes about Hillary Clinton's instructions to fire the career civil servants at the White House Travel Office: "We need those people out—We need our people in—We need the slots."

A particularly striking illustration of what we might call Bolingbroke's Law is the record of Maryland governor Parris Glendening. Elected in 1994, Glendening seemed a clean, honest, moderate, technocratic former professor. He might give Maryland big government, but at least it would be clean government. So what did he do when he took office? Well, here's how the *Washington Post* described his first budget: "In his first major act as Maryland governor, Parris N. Glendening unveiled a no-new-taxes budget that unabashedly steers the biggest share of spending to the three areas that voted most strongly for him: Montgomery and Prince George's counties and Baltimore." Lord Bolingbroke, call your office. A few days later it turned out that Glendening and his top aide were collecting tens of thousands of dollars in early pension payments from Prince George's County—where Glendening had served as county executive until his election as governor—thanks to his creative interpretation of rules that gave early pension benefits to government employees who suffered "involuntary separation" from their jobs. Glendening decided that he had been "involuntarily separated" because of the two-term limit on the county executive. And he "demanded" the resignations of his top aides a month before he left his county job—making them also victims of "involuntary separation"—whereupon he hired them as his top aides in the governor's mansion.

Like the Energizer bunny, the Glendening money train just kept on going. In May 1995, the governor asked the legislature to spend $1.5 million in taxpayer funds to rescue a struggling high-tech firm in Prince George's County headed by one of his political supporters. Then in August, Frank W. Stegman, the state secretary of labor, licensing, and regulation, hired the wife of Theodore J. Knapp, the state personnel secretary and a colleague of Stegman's from the Prince George's government, for a job in his agency. No ingrate, Knapp then returned the favor by recommending a $10,000 raise in Stegman's meager $100,542 salary.

If this is what the apparently honest politicians do, just imagine what the others are up to.


## Why Government Gets Too Big

Thomas Jefferson wrote, "The natural progress of things is for liberty to yield and government to gain ground." Two hundred years later, James M. Buchanan won a Nobel Prize in economics for a lifetime of scholarly research confirming Jefferson's insights. Buchanan's theory, developed along with Gordon Tullock, is called Public Choice. It's based on one fundamental point: Bureaucrats and politicians are just as self-interested as the rest of us. But lots of scholars did—and do—believe otherwise, and that's why textbooks tell us that people in the private economy are self-interested but the government acts in the public interest. Notice the little sleight of hand in that last sentence? I said "people in the private economy," but then I said "government acts." Switching from the individual to the collective confuses the issue. Because actually, the *government* doesn't act. *Some people in the government* act. And why should the guy who graduates from college and goes to work for Microsoft be self-interested, while his roommate who goes to work for the Department of Housing and Urban Development is suddenly inspired by altruism and starts acting in the public interest?

As it turns out, making the simple economic assumption that politicians and bureaucrats act just like everyone else, namely, in their own interest, has enormous explanatory power.

Far better than the simplistic civics-book model that assumes public officials act in the public interest, the Public Choice model explains voting patterns, lobbying efforts, deficit spending, corruption, the expansion of government, and the opposition of lobbyists and members of Congress to term limits. In addition, the Public Choice model explains why self-interested behavior has positive effects in a competitive marketplace but does such harm in the political process.

Of course politicians and bureaucrats act in their own interest. One of the key concepts of Public Choice is *concentrated benefits and diffuse costs.* That means that the benefits of any government program are concentrated on a few people, while the costs are diffused among many people. Take ADM's ethanol subsidy, for instance. If ADM makes $200 million a year from it, it costs each American about a dollar. Did you know about it? Probably not. Now that you do, are you going to write your congressman and complain? Probably not. Are you going to fly to Washington, take your senator out to dinner, give him a $1,000 contribution, and ask him not to vote for the ethanol subsidy? Of course not. But you can bet that ADM chairman Dwayne Andreas is doing all that and more. Think about it: How much would you spend to get a $200 million subsidy from the federal government? About $199 million if you had to, I'll bet. So who will members of Congress listen to? The average Americans who don't know that they're paying a dollar each for Dwayne Andreas's profits? Or Andreas, who's making a list and checking it twice to see who's voting for his subsidy?

If it were just ethanol, of course, it wouldn't matter very much. But most federal programs work the same way. Take the farm program. A few billion dollars for subsidized farmers, who make up about 1 percent of the U.S. population; a few dollars a year for each taxpayer. The farm program is even more tricky than that. Many of its costs involve raising food prices, so consumers are paying for it without realizing it.

Billions of dollars are spent every year in Washington to get a piece of the trillion dollars of taxpayers' money that Congress spends every year. Consider this ad from the *Washington Post:*

*InfraStructure* . . . is a new Washington buzzword for: A. America's crumbling physical plant? $3 trillion is needed to repair highways, bridges, sewers, etc. B. Billions of federal reconstruction dollars? The 5¢ per gallon gasoline tax is only the beginning. C. *Your bible for infrastructure spending—where the money is going and how to get your share*—in a concise biweekly newsletter? ANSWER: All of the above. Subscribe today.

Countless such newsletters tell people what kind of money the government is handing out and how to get their hands on it.

In 1987 an advertisement in the Durango, Colorado, *Herald* touting the Animas-La Plata dam and irrigation project made explicit the usual hidden calculations of those trying to get their hands on federal dollars: "Why we should support the Animas-La Plata Project: Because someone else is paying the tab! We get the water. We get the reservoir. They get the bill."

Economists call this process rent-seeking, or transfer-seeking. It's another illustration of Oppenheimer's distinction between the economic and the political means. Some individuals and businesses produce wealth. They grow food or build things people want to buy or perform useful services. Others find it easier to go to Washington, a state capital, or a city hall and get a subsidy, tariff, quota, or restriction on their competitors. That's the political means to wealth, and, sadly, it's been growing faster than the economic means.

Of course, in the modern world of trillion-dollar governments handing out favors like Santa Claus, it becomes harder to distinguish between the producers and the transfer-seekers, the predators and the prey. The state tries to confuse us, like the three-card monte dealer, by taking our money as quietly as possible and then handing some of it back to us with great ceremony. We all end up railing against taxes but then demanding our Medicare, our subsidized mass transit, our farm programs, our free national parks, and on and on and on. Frederic Bastiat explained it in the nineteenth century: "The State is that great fiction by which everyone tries to live at the expense of everyone else." In the aggregate, we all lose, but it's hard to know who is a net loser and who is a net winner in the immediate circumstance.

In his book *Demosclerosis,* the journalist Jonathan Rauch described the process of transfer-seeking:

> In America, only a few classes of people have the power to take your money if you don't fend them off. One is the criminal class. People who break into your car or rob your house (or punch holes in your roof) are members of the parasite economy in the classic sense: they take your wealth if you don't actively fight them off. Such people are costly to society, not only for what they take, but for the high cost of fending them off. They make us buy locks, alarms, iron gates, security guards, policemen, insurance, and on and on. . . .
>
> Criminals, however, aren't the only ones who play the distributive game. Legal, noncriminal transfer-seeking is perfectly possible—on one condition. You need the law's help. That is, you need to persuade politicians or courts to intervene on your behalf.

Thus, he goes on, every group in society comes up with a way for the government to help it or penalize its competitors: businesses seek tariffs, unions call for minimum-wage laws (which make high-priced skilled workers more economical than cheaper, low-skilled workers), postal workers get Congress to outlaw private competition, businesses seek subtle twists in regulations that hurt their competitors more than themselves. And because the benefits of every such rule are concentrated on a few people, while the costs are spread out over many consumers or taxpayers, the few profit at the expense of the many, and they reward the politicians who made it happen.

Another reason that government grows too big is what Milton and Rose Friedman have called "the tyranny of the status quo." That is, when a new government program is proposed, it's the subject of heated debate. (At least if we're talking about big programs like farm subsidies or Medicare. Plenty of smaller programs get slipped into the budget with little or no debate, and some of them get pretty big after a few years.) But once it has passed, debate over the program virtually ceases. After that, Congress just considers every year how much to increase its budget. There's no longer any debate about whether the program should exist. Reforms like zero-based budgeting and sunset laws are supposed to counter this problem, but they haven't had much effect. When the federal government moved to shut down the Civil Aeronautics Board in 1979, they found that there were no guidelines for terminating a government agency—it just never happens. Even President Clinton's own National Performance Review—the much-touted "reinventing government" project—said, "The federal government seems unable to abandon the obsolete. It knows how to add, but not to subtract." But you could search a Clinton budget for a long time and not find a proposal to eliminate a program.

One element of the tyranny of the status quo is what Washingtonians call the iron triangle, which protects every agency and program. The Iron Triangle consists of the congressional committee or subcommittee that oversees the program, the bureaucrats who administer it, and the special interests that benefit from it. There's a revolving door between these groups: a congressional staffer writes a regulation, then she goes over to the executive branch to administer it, then she moves to the private sector and makes big bucks lobbying her former colleagues on behalf of the regulated interest group. Or a corporate lobbyist makes contributions to members of Congress in order to get a new regulatory agency created, after which he's appointed to the board of the agency—because who else understands the problem so well?

If bureaucrats and politicians are self-interested, like the rest of us, how will they act in government? Well, no doubt they will sometimes seek to serve the public interest. Most people believe in trying to do the right thing. But the incentives in government are not good. To make more money in the private economy, you have to offer people something they want. If you do, you'll attract customers; if you don't, you may go out of business, or lose your job, or lose your investment. That keeps businesses on their toes, trying to find ways to better serve consumers. But bureaucrats don't have customers. They don't make more money by satisfying more consumers. Instead, they amass money and power by enlarging their agencies. What do bureaucrats "maximize"? Bureaucrats! Their incentive, then, is to find ways to hire more people, expand their authority, and spend more taxpayers' dollars. Discover a new problem that your agency could work on, and Congress may give you another billion dollars, another deputy, and another whole bureau under your control. Even if you don't discover a new problem, just advertise that the problem you were commissioned to handle is getting a lot worse, and you may get more money and power. Solve a problem, on the other hand—improve children's test scores or get all the welfare recipients into jobs—and Congress or your state legislature is likely to decide you don't need more money. (It could even decide to shut your agency down, though this is largely an idle threat.) What an incentive system! How many problems are likely to get solved when the system punishes problem solving?

The obvious answer would seem to be to change the incentive system. But that's easier said than done. Government doesn't have customers, who can use its products or try a competitor instead, so it's difficult to decide when government *is* doing a good job. If more people send letters every year, is the U.S. Postal Service doing a good job of serving its customers? Not necessarily, because its customers are captive. If they want to mail a letter, they have to do it through the Postal Service (unless they're willing to pay at least ten times as much money for overnight service). As long as any institution gets its money coercively, through legally required payments, it is difficult if not impossible to measure its success at serving customers. Meanwhile, special interests within the system—politicians, administrators, unions—fight over the spoils and resist any attempts to measure their productivity or efficiency.

To see the self-interested nature of those in the state, just look at any day's newspapers. Check out how much better the federal employees' pension system is than Social Security. Look at the $2 million pensions that will be collected by retiring members of Congress. Note that when Congress and the president temporarily shut down the federal government, they kept on getting *their* paychecks while rank-and-file employees had to wait.

Political scientist James L. Payne examined the record of 14 separate appropriations hearings, committee meetings where members of Congress decide which programs to fund and by how much. He found that a total of 1,060 witnesses testified, of which 1,014 testified in favor of the proposed spending and only 7 against (the remainder were not clearly for or against). In other words, in only half the hearings was there even *one* witness against the program. Congressional staff members confirmed that the same was true in each member's office: The ratio of people coming in to ask the congressman to spend money versus those who opposed any particular program was "several thousand to one."

No matter how opposed to spending a new legislator may be, the constant, day-in-and-day-out, year-in-and-year-out requests for money have an effect. He would increasingly say, We've got to get spending down, but *this* program is necessary. Studies indeed show that the longer a person stays in Congress, the more spending he votes for. That's why Payne called Washington a Culture of Spending, in which it takes almost superhuman effort to remember the general interest and vote against programs that will benefit some particular person who visited your office or testified before your committee.

About a century ago a group of brilliant Italian scholars set out to study the nature of the state and its monetary affairs. One of them, Amilcare Puviani, tried to answer this question: If a government were trying to squeeze as much money as possible out of its population, what would it do? He came up with eleven strategies that such a government would employ. They're worth examining:

1. The use of indirect rather than direct taxes, so that the tax is hidden in the price of goods
2. Inflation, by which the state reduces the value of everyone else's currency
3. Borrowing, so as to postpone the necessary taxation
4. Gift and luxury taxes, where the tax accompanies the receipt or purchase of something special, lessening the annoyance of the tax
5. "Temporary" taxes, which somehow never get repealed when the emergency passes
6. Taxes that exploit social conflict, by placing higher taxes on unpopular groups (such as the rich, or cigarette smokers, or windfall profit makers)
7. The threat of social collapse or withholding monopoly government services if taxes are reduced

8. Collection of the total tax burden in relatively small increments (a sales tax, or income tax withholding) over time, rather than in a yearly lump sum

9. Taxes whose exact incidence cannot be predicted in advance, thus keeping the taxpayer unaware of just how much he is paying

10. Extraordinary budget complexity to hide the budget process from public understanding

11. The use of generalized expenditure categories, such as "education" or "defense," to make it difficult for outsiders to assess the individual components of the budget

Notice anything about this list? The United States government uses every one of those strategies—and so do most foreign governments. That just might lead a cynical observer to conclude that the government was actually *trying* to soak the taxpayers for as much money as it could get, rather than, say, raising just enough for its essential functions.

In all these ways, government's constant instinct is to grow, to take on more tasks, to arrogate more power to itself, to extract more money from the citizenry. It seems that Jefferson was right: "The natural progress of things is for liberty to yield and government to gain ground."

## Big Government and Its Court Intellectuals

The power of the state has always rested on more than just laws and the might to back them up, of course. It's much more efficient to persuade than to force people to accept their rulers. Rulers have always employed priests, magicians, and intellectuals to keep the people content. In ancient times, priests assured the people that the king was himself divine; as recently as World War II the Japanese people were told that their emperor was directly descended from the sun.

Rulers have often given money and privilege to intellectuals who would contribute to their rule. Sometimes these court intellectuals actually lived at court, participating in the luxurious life that was otherwise denied to commoners. Others were appointed to high office, ensconced at state universities, or funded by the National Endowment for the Humanities.

In the post-Enlightenment world, ruling classes have realized that divine ordinance would not be sufficient to maintain their hold on popular loyalty. They have thus tried to ally themselves with secular intellectuals from painters and scriptwriters to historians, sociologists, city planners, economists, and technocrats. Sometimes the intellectuals had to be wooed; sometimes they were positively eager to glorify the state, as did the professors at the University of Berlin in the nineteenth century, who proclaimed themselves "the intellectual bodyguard of the House of Hohenzollern" (that is, the rulers of Prussia).

In modern America, for at least two generations, the majority of intellectuals have told the populace that an ever bigger state was needed—to deal with the complexity of modern life, and to help the poor, and to stabilize the business cycle, and to enhance economic growth, and to bring about racial justice, and to protect the environment, and to build mass transit, and for numerous other purposes. Coincidentally, that ever bigger state has meant ever more jobs for intellectuals. A minimal government, one that would, in Jefferson's words, "restrain men from injuring one another [and] leave them otherwise free to regulate their own pursuits of industry and improvement," would have little use for planners and model builders; and a free society might not evidence much demand for sociologists and urban planners. Thus, many intellectuals are simply acting in their class interest when they churn out books and studies and movies and newspaper articles on the need for bigger government.

Don't be fooled, by the way, by the supposedly "irreverent" and "antiestablishment" and even "antigovernment" stances of many modern intellectuals, even some of those funded by the state itself. Look closely, and you'll see that the "establishment" they oppose is the capitalist system of productive enterprise, not the leviathan in Washington. And in their brave criticisms of government, they generally chide the state for doing too *little* or mock the elected officials who are trying halfheartedly to respond to public demand for less government. The provocative documentaries on the State (oops, "Public") Broadcasting System's *Frontline* and *P.O.V.* usually indict the American state for its inaction. What ruling class wouldn't be glad to subsidize dissident intellectuals who constantly demand that the ruling class expand its scope and power?

Court intellectuals are not simply corrupt, of course. Many of them genuinely believe that a permanently growing state is in the public interest. Why is that? Why did European and American intellectuals turn from the courageous and visionary libertarianism of Milton and Locke and Smith and Mill to a crabbed and reactionary statism—of Marx, of course, but also of T. H. Green, John Maynard Keynes, John Rawls, and Catharine MacKinnon? One answer we've already examined: The state moved to co-opt them and make them its handmaidens, with access to some of the perks of power. But that's not the whole answer. Many distinguished scholars have tried to fathom the great attraction statism and planning holds for intellectuals.

Let me suggest at least a few reasons. First, the idea of planning has great appeal for intellectuals because they like to analyze and to put things in order. They are enthusiastic builders of systems and models, models by which the builder can measure reality against an ideal system. And if an individual or a business profits by planning a course of action, shouldn't the same be true for a whole society? Planning, the intellectual believes, is the application of human intelligence and rationality to the social system. What could be more appealing to an intellectual, whose stock in trade is his intelligence and rationality?

Intellectuals have devised all sorts of planning systems for states, especially in the twentieth century, with its explosion in knowledge and in demand for intellectuals. Marxism was the great comprehensive plan for all of society, but its very comprehensiveness frightened many people. A close cousin was fascism, a system that proposed to leave productive resources in private hands but to coordinate them according to a central plan. In his book *Fascism: Doctrine and Institutions,* Benito Mussolini, who ruled Italy from 1922 until 1943, presented fascism as a direct response to individualist liberalism:

> It is opposed to classical liberalism, which arose as a reaction to absolutism and exhausted its historical function when the State became the expression of the conscience and will of the people. Liberalism denied the State in the name of the individual; Fas-

cism reasserts the rights of the State as expressing the real essence of the individual.

In the 1930s fascism was much admired by some American intellectuals, who despaired of bringing such a rational system to the still individualist United States. The *Nation,* by then a socialist magazine, found "the New Deal in the United States, the new forms of economic organization in Germany and Italy, and the planned economy of the Soviet Union" all signs of a tendency "for nations and groups, capital as well as labor, [to] demand a larger measure of security than can be provided by a system of free competition." After fascism was discredited by its association with Hitler and Mussolini, statist intellectuals came up with new names for central planning in a system of officially private property: the French "indicative planning" of the 1960s, the "national economic planning" proposed by economist Wassily Leontief and labor leader Leonard Woodcock in the 1970s, the "economic democracy" of Tom Hayden and Derek Shearer, the reindustrialization policy of Felix Rohatyn and Robert Reich, and the "competitiveness" policy also touted by Reich. As each variant was discredited, intellectuals moved on to another name and a superficially different plan. But each one involved the state hiring intellectuals, who would rationally determine what society needed and direct everyone's economic activities accordingly.

Despite the growing disillusionment with big government, the Holy Grail of planning dies hard among intellectuals. What was the Clinton health-care proposal but a central plan for one-seventh of the American economy? And that wasn't the only example of President Clinton's fascination with planning. In a little-noted comment during the 1992 campaign, Clinton offered a breathtaking view of the ability and obligation of government to plan the economy:

> We ought to say right now, we ought to have a national inventory of the capacity of every . . . manufacturing plant in the United States: every airplane plant, every small business subcontractor, everybody working in defense.
>
> We ought to know what the inventory is, what the skills of the work force are and match it against the kind of things we have to

produce in the next 20 years and then we have to decide how to get from here to there. From what we have to what we need to do.

After the election, a White House aide named Ira Magaziner fleshed out this sweeping vision: Defense conversion would require a twenty-year plan developed by government committees, "a detailed organizational plan . . . to lay out how, in specific, a proposal like this could be implemented." Five-year plans, you see, had failed in the Soviet Union; maybe a twenty-year plan would be sufficient to the task.

A second reason that intellectuals are attracted to state power is what Thomas Sowell calls their unconstrained view of man, the view that there are no natural limits to building a utopia on earth. This perspective is understandable in the late twentieth century, after two centuries of the most rapid advances in knowledge, life expectancy, and standard of living ever witnessed on earth. The attitude is summed up in the popular catchphrase, "If we can put a man on the moon, why can't we . . . cure cancer, end racism, pay teachers more than movie stars, stop pollution?" After all, human ingenuity over the past 200 years has moved us from a life that was "nasty, brutish, and short" to a society that has conquered many age-old diseases, dramatically reduced the barriers to travel, and vastly increased the store of knowledge. But these achievements were not just willed into being; they took effort, physical and intellectual, and they occurred in a social system largely based on the rule of law, private property, and individual freedom.

The vulgar version of the unconstrained view of man can be seen in a bumper sticker I spied in my Washington neighborhood: "Demand a cure for AIDS." Well, of course; how cruel of . . . corporations or society or the government or whomever . . . not to give us the cure for AIDS. Let's demand it. If we can put a man on the moon, we can find a cure for AIDS.

The more sophisticated exponents of the unconstrained view would laugh at such a naive version; they *are* intellectuals, after all. But they, too, fail to understand the limits on human knowledge that prevent us from solving all problems at once, the trade-offs that are ignored in the sweeping plans they promulgate.

Finally, the libertarian vision of a free society seems, to many people, essentially irrational because society is supposed to be left to its own devices. Karl Marx, a brilliant if profoundly wrong scholar, complained about "the anarchy of capitalist production." Indeed, it seems that way. In a great society, millions of people go about their daily routines according to no central plan. Every day some businesses start and others fail, people are hired and others are fired. At this very moment several different companies are developing similar or even identical products to offer to consumers: Internet web-browsers, perhaps, or roast-chicken restaurants, or drugs to relieve stress on the heart. Wouldn't it make more sense to have a central authority pick one company to do each project, and to make sure all companies are putting resources into truly important tasks rather than Rap Star Barbie or new colors for Chevrolets? No, it wouldn't— and that's what is so hard for intellectuals to see. The market process coordinates economic activity much better than any plan ever could. In fact, that sentence dramatically understates the comparison. *No* plan could give us the standard of living we have today. *Only* the apparently chaotic market process can coordinate the desires and abilities of thousands, millions, billions of people in order to produce a continually higher living standard for the whole society.

The inability to see this results in what F. A. Hayek called the Fatal Conceit—the idea that smart people could plan an economic system that would be better than the unplanned, anarchic market. It is a remarkably persistent notion.

## The State and War

The apotheosis of state power is war. In war the state's force is not hidden or implicit; it is vividly on display. War creates a hell on earth, a nightmare of destruction on an otherwise unimaginable scale. No matter how much hatred people may sometimes feel for other groups of people, it's difficult to conceive why nations have chosen so often to go to war. The calculation of the ruling class may be different from that of the people, however. War often brings the state more power, by drawing more people under its control. But war can enhance state power even in the absence of conquest. (Losing a war, of course, can topple a ruling class, so making war is a gamble, but the payoff is good enough to attract gamblers.)

Classical liberals have long understood the connection between war and state power. Thomas Paine wrote that an observer of the British government would conclude "that taxes were not raised to carry on wars, but that wars were raised to carry on taxes." That is, the English and other European governments gave the impression of quarreling *in order* "to fleece their countries by taxes." The early twentieth-century liberal Randolph Bourne wrote simply, "War is the health of the State"—the only way to create a herd instinct in a free people and the best way to extend the powers of government.

U.S. history provides ample evidence of that. The great leaps in federal spending, taxation, and regulation have occurred during wartime—first, notably, the Civil War, then World War I and World War II. War threatens the survival of the society, so even naturally libertarian Americans are more willing to put up with state demands at such a time—and courts agree to sanction unconstitutional extensions of federal power. Then, after the emergency passes, the government neglects to give up the power it has seized, the courts agree that a precedent has been set, and the state settles comfortably into its new, larger domain. During major American wars, the federal budget has gone up ten- or twenty-fold, then fallen after the war, but never to as low a level as it was before. Take World War I, for example: Federal spending was $713 million in 1916 but rose to nearly $19 billion in 1919. It never again fell below $2.9 billion.

It isn't just money, of course. Wartime has occasioned such extensions of state power as conscription, the income tax, tax withholding, wage and price controls, rent control, censorship, crackdowns on dissent, and Prohibition, which really began with a 1917 statute. World War I was one of the great disasters of history: In Europe it ended ninety-nine years of relative peace and unprecedented economic progress and led to the rise of communism in Russia and Nazism in Germany and to the even greater destruction of World War II. In the United States the consequences were far less dramatic but still noteworthy; in two short years President Woodrow Wilson and Congress created the Council of National Defense, the United States Food Administration, the United States Fuel Administration, the War Industries Board, the Emergency Fleet Corporation, the United States Grain Corporation, the United States Housing Corporation, and the War Finance Corporation. Wilson also nationalized the railroads. It was a dramatic leap toward the megastate we now struggle under, and it could not have been done in the absence of the war.

Statists have always been fascinated by war and its possibilities, even if they sometimes shrink from the implications. The rulers and the court intellectuals understand that free people have their own concerns—family and work and recreation—and it's not easy to get them enrolled voluntarily in the rulers' crusades and schemes. Court intellectuals are constantly calling for a "national effort" to undertake some task or other, and most people blithely ignore them and go on about the business of providing for their families and trying to build a better mousetrap. But in time of war—*then* you can organize society and get everyone dancing to the same tune. As early as 1910, William James came up with the idea of "The Moral Equivalent of War," in an essay proposing that young Americans be conscripted into "an army enlisted against Nature" that would cause them to "get the childishness knocked out of them, and to come back into society with healthier sympathies and soberer ideas."

The fascination of collectivists with war and its "moral equivalent" is undying. In 1977 President Carter revived James's phrase to describe his energy policy, with its emphasis on government direction and reduced living standards. It was to be his peacetime substitute for the sacrifice and despotism of war. In 1988 the Democratic Leadership Council proposed an almost-compulsory national service program, which would entail "sacrifice" and "self-denial" and revive "the American tradition of civic obligation." Nowhere in the DLC paper on the subject was there any mention of the American tradition of individual rights. The proposal was described as a way to "broaden the political base of support for new public initiatives that otherwise would not be possible in the current era of budgetary restraint." In other words, it would be a way for government to hand out benefits by enlisting cheap, quasi-conscript labor. The last chapter of the paper was, inevitably, titled "The Moral Equivalent of War."

Then, in 1993 DLC chairman Bill Clinton became president and proposed his own national service plan, and darned if it didn't sound a lot like "the moral equivalent of war." He wanted to "rekindle the excitement of being Americans" and "bring together men and women of every age and race and lift up our nation's spirit" to "attack the problems of our time." Eventually, perhaps, every young person would be enlisted. For the moment, however, the president envisioned "an army of 100,000 young people . . . to serve here at home . . . to serve our country."

In 1982 British Labour Party leader Michael Foot, a distinguished leftist intellectual, was asked for an example of socialism in practice that could "serve as a model of the Britain you envision," and he replied, "The best example that I've seen of democratic socialism operating in this country was during the second world war. Then we ran Britain highly efficiently, got everybody a job. . . . The conscription of labor was only a very small element of it. It was a democratic society with a common aim."

The American socialist Michael Harrington wrote, "World War I showed that, despite the claims of free-enterprise ideologues, government could organize the economy effectively." He hailed World War II for having "justified a truly massive mobilization of otherwise wasted human and material resources" and complained that the War Production Board was "a success the United States was determined to forget as quickly as possible." He went on, "During World War II, there was probably more of an increase in social justice than at any [other] time in American history. Wage and price controls were used to try to cut the differentials between the social classes. . . . There was also a powerful moral incentive to spur workers on: patriotism."

Collectivists such as Foot and Harrington don't like the killing involved in war, but they love its domestic effects: centralization, the growth of government power, and, not coincidentally, an enhanced role for court intellectuals and planners with Ph.D.'s. The dangers of war in the modern era have encouraged the state and its intellectual allies to look for more trumped-up emergencies and "moral equivalents of war" to rally the citizenry and persuade them to give up more of their liberty and their property to the state's plans. Thus we've had the War on Poverty, and the War on Drugs, and more crises and national emergencies than a planner could count on a supercomputer. One advantage of these "moral equivalents of war" is that real wars eventually end, while the War on Poverty and the War on Drugs can go on for generations. And thus does the alliance between the state and its compliant intellectuals reach its zenith in war or its moral equivalent.

War, then, is Public Choice theory writ large: bad for the people but good for the governing class. No wonder everyone wishes it would stop but no one can stop it.

*Chapter 10*

# CONTEMPORARY ISSUES

*I*t is one thing to agree that freedom is a good thing in the abstract. It is quite another to look around at family breakdown, environmental hazards, and violent crime and conclude that government should have no role in solving problems. That is where many would-be libertarians get off the bus.

But they should stay on. Government cannot solve those problems. In fact, it often causes them. Libertarianism provides a better framework for solving problems than does coercive government. Here's how.

Obviously this is not a complete survey of either policy problems or libertarian answers; more extensive discussion of more issues can be found in the sources listed in the back of this book. Even those books do not address every possible policy topic. The libertarian approach to public policy should be seen not as a catechism but as a set of problem-solving techniques that can be applied to many problems. Many of the proposals in this chapter are attempts to "unscramble the omelet," to apply libertarian principles to real-world problems that have in many cases been *caused* by excessive government. Still, our challenge is not just to state the libertarian goal but to chart a path that leads from where we are to the goal of a free society.

We can begin by identifying three factors that seem to make people skeptical of libertarian ideas and supportive of using government to achieve social and economic goals:

- *A failure to recognize how much liberal society has achieved.* It's easy to point to problems in the world—poverty, pollution, racism, and so on—but we should not lose sight of the real gains, economic and otherwise, that we have realized through free markets and the rule of law.

- *The snapshot view of reality.* Too often we look at a particular part of society, frozen in time, and demand action to remedy a problem. But we need to understand the *processes* by which economic and social change happens. We worry about 40,000 layoffs announced by AT&T, failing to notice that American companies created 2 million jobs in the preceding twelve months, incrementally, day by day, company by company.

- *Paternalism.* The view that other people can't be trusted to make good decisions is all too prevalent. We rarely demand that government make decisions about *our* lives, but many of us worry that *other people* can't select good schools for their children, choose proper drugs for themselves, or make rational economic decisions.

Keeping in mind these fallacies and the principles of individual responsibility, property rights, rule of law, and competitive decision making, we can explore current policy problems and how to solve them.

## Restoring Economic Growth

The biggest issue for most Americans in the 1990s is preserving and increasing economic growth. There are two basic points to be made about prosperity in modern America: First, we have more wealth—including better health and more environmental amenities—than any people in the history of the world have ever had. (People in the other capitalist democracies also enjoy an unprecedented standard of living, but in terms of living space and consumer goods, the average person in Germany or Japan actually consumes about 30 percent less than the average American.) Second, government's discoordination of the market process is making us less prosperous than we could be, and this loss is felt most keenly by those who have the least income and wealth.

## The Good News

To take the first point first: We hear a lot in the 1990s about stagnant wages, the declining middle class, and the fear that baby boomers aren't as well off as their parents and that Generation Xers won't do as well as the boomers. While there are legitimate concerns that we'll address later, we should not forget that since the Industrial Revolution, capitalism has produced a standard of living that earlier generations literally could not have imagined.

Critics of capitalism now concede that living standards increased until 1970 or so; it's during the past two decades, they say, when wages have stagnated and living standards have begun to slip. W. Michael Cox of the Federal Reserve Bank of Dallas and Richard Alm of the *Dallas Morning News* have taken a critical look at such claims and found a different story. It's true that average hourly wages have fallen slightly since the mid-1970s, but total compensation has continued to increase slowly. In the past twenty years, employees have received more of their compensation in the form of health insurance, pension contributions, and other fringe benefits, which are not included in calculations of hourly wages.

Are we working harder to earn that slowly rising income? No. The average American worked 1,903 hours a year in 1950, 1,743 hours in 1973, and 1,562 hours in 1990. We also spend fewer years working, as we start work later and retire earlier than before, and more years in retirement, as life expectancy increases.

What about consumer goods? Those, after all, are the real point of the economic process. We don't work to earn dollars, we work in order to buy more goods and services. According to Cox and Alm, between 1970 and 1990 we saw these changes in our living standards: The average size of a new home increased from 1,500 to 2,080 square feet. The percentage of households with color television rose from 33.9 percent to 96.1 percent. The number of households with cable TV rose from 4 million to 55 million, and the number with VCRs rose from 0 to 67 million. Virtually no one had a microwave oven in 1970; 79 percent of us did in 1990.

Were the poor left out of all this progress? By definition, the poor have less than the nonpoor. That's why people try to become more prosperous. But when products are invented and then become cheaper, they spread throughout society. In 1971, 44.5 percent of *all* households had a clothes dryer; in 1994, 50.2 percent of *poor* households had one. In 1971, 83.3 percent of households had a refrigerator; in 1994, 97.9 percent of poor households had one. No one had a microwave or VCR in 1971; by 1994, 60 percent of the poor had both. Also by 1994, 92 percent of poor households had a color television, compared with 43 percent of all homes in 1971. In 1970, 6.9 percent of American housing units lacked complete plumbing; by 1990 the figure was only 1.1 percent.

Americans today are wealthier, healthier, safer, and more comfortable than people have ever been in history. Sometimes people call such economic growth a "miracle," but it's really just what happens when people are allowed to produce and trade in a world of property rights and the rule of law. What makes it seem miraculous is that in so much of the world, for so much of history, Adam Smith's simple system of natural liberty has been stifled and crushed by state power.

## The Bad News

Despite all this, Americans in the 1990s feel restive. They sense that living standards are not rising as fast as they should and that today's children may not live as well as their parents. Perhaps we've forgotten that a rising living standard is not automatic; it has to be produced, through hard work and capital accumulation.

We do indeed have a problem, with a bigger one down the road. Despite all the new consumer goods in our economy, American economic growth has slowed down dramatically. From 1973 to 1990, per capita GNP in the United States grew by only 1.5 percent a year, while Japanese GNP gained 3.1 percent a year. Real output per worker doubled between 1947 and 1973, then almost stopped growing. Thus after 1973, compensation per worker grew at only one-fifth of the previous rate.

Why has economic growth slowed down? Economists and pundits have offered all sorts of answers, and no doubt the issue is complex. But the most important reason is that government has increasingly taxed, regulated, and interfered in the productive process of market exchange. Every exchange in the market guides resources to be used more effectively to satisfy consumer needs. Every act that impedes voluntary exchange reduces the effectiveness of resource use. When resources are taxed away from those who earn them to be spent by government officials, they do not work as efficiently to satisfy consumer needs as do resources directed by private owners. When regulation prohibits people from making exchanges that they would otherwise find valuable, the economy is inevitably less productive.

Widespread wealth—that is, goods and services for everyone in society—is generated in the marketplace by individuals producing and exchanging with one another. Government can only acquire resources by expropriating them from those who produce them. In the past few decades government has been taking more and more wealth out of the private sector. There are many ways to measure government's depredation of the productive sector of the economy. We can look at the income tax rate or at overall government spending. We can calculate government's expenditures as a percentage of gross domestic product, but since GDP includes government purchases of goods and services in both the numerator and the denominator, that's a form of double counting. Dean Stansel of the Cato Institute has come up with a better approach, seeking to measure government spending at all levels (federal, state, and local) as a percentage of the wealth produced by the American people. All government spending—whether taxed or borrowed—withdraws money from the productive private sector of the economy and spends it according to political dictates. Stansel's calculations look like this table, which we might call the Government Depredation Index. Is it any wonder that the economy slowed down dramatically about the time government's depredation went over 50 percent? Imagine how much stronger and more productive our economy would be if government stopped taking more than half of the wealth produced by working men and women.

*Percentage of Private National Product
Appropriated by the Government*

| Year | Percentage |
|------|:----------:|
| 1929 | 13.7 |
| 1939 | 31.4 |
| 1947 | 26.4 |
| 1960 | 42.5 |
| 1970 | 51.5 |
| 1980 | 52.2 |
| 1990 | 55.8 |
| 1994 | 54.5 |

*Source:* Dean Stansel, "Total Government Spending as a Share of the Private Economy," unpublished paper, Cato Institute, 1995.

It's also instructive to look at government spending. Governments in the United States now spend about $2.6 trillion a year—that's $2,600,000,000,000, or enough to buy all the farmland in the United States *plus* all the stock of the 100 largest corporations in the country. That amounts to $24,000 per household per year. The next table shows how that figure has grown (remember that these numbers are adjusted for inflation). It's hard to believe that any American family gets its money's worth from such spending. But it shouldn't be assumed that all this money is going to "waste, fraud, and abuse," as President Ronald Reagan used to put it. Federal spending purchases some things of real value, including national defense, interstate highways, health care, weather forecasting, and retirement security, as well as some programs that are actually destructive, such as business subsidies, drug prohibition, and costly regulation. No one should assume that if we slashed government spending he would have thousands of dollars more to spend on cars, clothes, and vacations. If government didn't pro-

*Real Total Government Spending per Household*
*(1990 Dollars)*

| Year | Percentage |
|------|-----------|
| 1900 | $1,651 |
| 1930 | 3,301 |
| 1950 | 8,940 |
| 1970 | 17,986 |
| 1994 | 24,400 |

*Source:* Stephen Moore, *Government: America's #1
Growth Industry* (Lewisville, Texas: Institute for
Policy Innovation, 1995), figure 2–5.

vide Social Security, for instance—the largest single federal program—each American would have to decide how much to save for his own retirement. If local governments didn't provide schooling, parents would have to spend some of their no-longer-taxed-away money on education. The libertarian argument is not that all government spending is worthless, but that people can purchase better goods at a better price through voluntary exchanges in the marketplace than they can expect a bureaucratic monopoly to provide.

Government also reduces economic growth through regulation, as discussed in chapter 8. If we added to the Government Depredation Index the $600 billion that the University of Rochester economist Thomas Hopkins estimates that regulation costs our economy, we would find government reducing the real wealth of society by even more than the 55 percent calculated above.

The way to restore economic growth—to boost stagnant wages, raise the standard of living, and restore every American's confidence that the future will be better than the present—is to reduce the size of government and return America's wealth to the people who produce it. Some specific ways of reducing the size of government will be discussed throughout this chapter, but the basic outline is clear:

1. Privatize government services
2. Reduce government spending, borrowing, and taxing
3. Deregulate the market process
4. Restore to individuals the right to make the important decisions in their lives

That's the path to both individual freedom and economic growth. How far along that path should we go? That depends on just how much confidence we have in civil society and the market process. Libertarians argue that we can and should move a long way toward minimal government; outside of the protection of our rights by police, courts, and national defense, it's hard to think of goods and services that could be produced more efficiently by a government bureaucracy than in the competitive marketplace.

Respecting the dignity of working people and the virtue of production, and maximizing economic growth, can be achieved by the same policy: reducing the rate of taxation. Governments and court intellectuals often try to confuse taxpayers by shifting the tax burden from one tax to another or from one group of taxpayers to another, and especially by concealing the impact of taxes, as discussed in chapter 9. Flat tax, graduated tax, sales tax, luxury tax—there are certainly differences among these, but the basic libertarian tax policy is to *reduce* taxes, on everyone.

How far could taxes be reduced? The libertarian goal is a society free of coercion. Any reader who thinks that taxation is not coercive is invited to imagine how much tax revenue the federal government would collect if it announced that there would be no legal penalties—no audits, no fines, no jail terms—for people who chose not to pay their income taxes. The reason the genial advocates of taxation don't propose such a pleasant program is that they know the American people would not willingly turn over half the money they earn to the government. Since taxation is coercive, the ultimate libertarian goal is to eliminate it. How, then, would we pay for the legitimate functions of government—police, courts, and national defense? Several answers to that question have been offered, none of them entirely satisfying. The best we can offer here is that we have a great deal of government spending and taxation to roll back before we get to the point where the only remaining taxation goes to support the legitimate functions of government. At that point, maybe we will be able to see how even the remaining coercive taxation can be eliminated. Perhaps people in a prosperous libertarian society *would* willingly contribute, say, 5 percent of their income to a government that protected their rights and otherwise left them alone. Perhaps the myriad agencies of civil society—businesses, churches, community associations—would be able to produce the necessary revenue. If not, the libertarian goal is to maximize individual freedom and minimize coercion; a government that taxed us 5 percent of our incomes in order to protect us from aggression by fellow citizens or foreign powers would be far closer to the libertarian vision than today's expansive state.

## Cutting the Budget

Libertarians want to reduce spending at every level of government. Throughout this chapter I'll be discussing ways to privatize or eliminate government programs, which would obviously reduce the government budget. Here are a few suggestions for immediate reductions in spending:

- *End corporate welfare.* The federal government spends about $75 billion a year on programs to benefit business, and state and local governments add billions more. Businesses that are serving consumers well can make it without subsidies; businesses that need subsidies shouldn't exist.
- *End farm welfare.* The same principles apply to federal farm programs, which cost about $15 billion a year. Farmers should compete in the free marketplace like other businesses.
- *Spend only what we need on defense.* Now that the cold war is over, the only remaining superpower could defend itself on about half what it now spends for the military, for a savings of about $120 billion a year.
- *Abolish unnecessary and destructive federal agencies.* We got along for almost 200 years without a U.S. Department of Educa-

tion, and there's general agreement that education in the United States has actually gotten worse since the federal department was created in 1979. The Department of Energy doesn't produce any energy. The Department of Commerce impedes commerce. The Drug Enforcement Administration can't stop drug use but creates a lot of prohibition-related crime. The Department of Transportation subsidizes local transportation projects that should be funded either privately or locally.

- *Privatize Social Security,* as I shall discuss in more detail immediately below. This would create a massive savings to taxpayers, but more important, it would prevent the eventual collapse of the system that Americans rely on for their retirement.

- *Privatize other government programs and assets,* from Amtrak to the Tennessee Valley Authority to federal lands to the U.S. Postal Service. The basic argument here is that private owners use resources more carefully and effectively than governments do, so the real advantage is greater economic efficiency. Savings to taxpayers are just icing on the cake.

Congress and the state legislatures could cut government budgets for a long time before they got down to the real duties of government: to protect our rights through police, courts, and national defense. Until then, any government that moans about limited resources or seeks to raise taxes is a government unwilling to take a hard look at unnecessary spending. The budgetary savings from a Congress truly concerned about taxpayers would be immense, and so would the economic boom that such a reduction in government would set off. But the real reason to eliminate such programs is not budgetary at all. It is to expand individual freedom and responsibility and to liberate and invigorate civil society.

## A Secure Retirement

The single biggest federal program—far bigger than national defense—is Social Security, which spent $334 billion in 1995 and is projected to spend $433 billion by the year 2000. Total federal spending on entitlement benefits is $750 billion, or just about half the entire budget (far more than half if you don't count interest payments). Throughout the developed world, the principal activity of government is transferring money from some individuals to others through various kinds of benefits programs. And throughout the developed world, there are soaring deficits and a growing recognition that such programs are unsustainable. Governments have made promises they cannot possibly keep, and there's a real possibility of skyrocketing taxes, economic collapse, generational warfare, or some combination of those frightening prospects.

When Social Security was created in 1935, it seemed like a great idea—benefits for the elderly, very low taxes, and no major government spending for a couple of decades. People came to believe that they were *earning* their Social Security by paying in taxes over the years. In fact, the taxes were never enough to pay for the benefits, but for decades that didn't matter because everyone was paying and few retired people were covered by Social Security. Every election year Congress raised benefits; they made a lot of voters happy, and the eventual problems were still years down the road.

The British economist John Maynard Keynes dismissed a complaint about the long-run effects of his policies by saying, "In the long run we are all dead." Well, as far as Social Security is concerned, the long run is here, Keynes is dead, and we're stuck with the bill.

Right now, with the huge baby-boom generation in its peak earning years, Social Security is running a "surplus" in accounting terms. The excess of income over benefit payments is "invested" entirely in government bonds, which are merely promises to repay borrowers out of future taxes. As early as 1999 the combined Social Security trust funds (including Medicare and disability insurance) will start turning in those bonds to the federal government to pay benefits, which means the government will have to increase its borrowing, raise taxes, or cut other spending. By 2001 Medicare's trust fund will be exhausted. The main Social Security trust fund will start running deficits by 2012, only fifteen years from now, and will be

*What Uncle Sam Has Really Promised You (Latest official projections available as of January 1996)*

| If you were born in . . . | Medicare's main Hospital Insurance Trust Fund is projected to go broke by the time you reach age . . . | Social Security's pension and disability fund is projected to go broke by the time you reach age . . . | Without further cuts, entitlements and interest on the national debt will consume all federal revenue by the time you reach age . . . | To provide you with the Social Security and Medicare benefits you are promised at age 65, the government would have to raise payroll taxes to . . . |
| --- | --- | --- | --- | --- |
| 1935 | 65 | 80 | 77 | 17.8% |
| 1945 | 55 | 70 | 67 | 20.0 |
| 1955 | 45 | 60 | 57 | 26.3 |
| 1965 | 35 | 50 | 47 | 34.1 |
| 1975 | 25 | 40 | 37 | 38.4 |
| 1985 | 15 | 30 | 27 | 41.7 |
| 1995 | 5 | 20 | 17 | 44.6 |

*Sources:* Board of Trustees of the Federal Hospital Insurance Trust Fund, *Annual Report* (Washington, D.C.: U.S. Government Printing Office, April 1995); Bipartisan Commission on Entitlement and Tax Reform, *Final Report to the President* (Washington, D.C.: U.S. Government Printing Office, 1995); Board of Trustees of the Federal Old-Age and Survivors Insurance and Disability Insurance Trust Funds, *Annual Report* (Washington, D.C.: U.S. Government Printing Office, April 1995). Reprinted with permission from *The Return of Thrift* by Phillip Longman (New York: Free Press, 1996), p. 12.

exhausted by 2029. The former chief actuary of the Social Security system, A. Haeworth Robertson, calculates that Social Security currently costs 15 percent of taxable payroll but that by the middle of the next century the cost will be somewhere between 26 and 44 percent of taxable payroll. It is hard to imagine that American workers would stand for the taxes that would be necessary to pay for Social Security then.

Phillip Longman, in *The Return of Thrift,* put all this in a user-friendly table (above). Based on when you were born, the table shows what you can expect from Social Security and Medicare.

The big problem is that, as with any government program, Social Security's designers didn't have to think about the future and weren't required to make their program financially sound. In 1935, when the federal government chose 65 as the retirement age, the average life expectancy for a child born in that year was 61. Today, the average life expectancy is 76, and it's still going up. Meanwhile, people are retiring earlier, so they're spending more years at both ends of retirement. In 1950 there were 16 Social Security taxpayers for 1 recipient. Today the ratio is about 3.3 to 1, and it will likely drop by 2030 to 2 to 1.

Such a system cannot be sustained. We're going to have to make major changes, certainly in the Social Security system and possibly in our own lives. As Longman argues, we're likely to see the return of some old-fashioned virtues in response to the collapse of the middle-class welfare state: thrift, because we're going to have to save more; family, because we're going to need to rely more on our parents and our children as the government's promises are exposed as hollow; and work, because we're probably going to have to spend more years at work as life expectancy increases.

But there is an important policy solution as well, one that can avert the collapse of Social Security and the economic chaos and generational conflict that would ensue: privatization. Social Security is financially unsound because it is run by politicians. It is a pay-as-you-go system that taxes today's workers and transfers the money almost immediately to today's retirees. Like a chain letter or a Ponzi scheme, it can provide big payoffs for those who get in first, but it offers only losses to later participants. A sound retirement system must be built on *savings* and *investment.* Workers put money aside for their retirement, and that money is invested in the creation of new wealth—through stocks, bonds, mutual funds, or other real investments—not transferred directly to other people. Such savings contribute to real economic growth, and the individual worker prospers by participating in that growth.

We could imagine this as a dramatic expansion of the IRA program, allowing people to put not just $2,000 but the entire amount of their Social Security taxes—or more—into tax-exempt retirement accounts. For today's young workers, such a program offers the prospect of much higher benefits than Social Security promises, and the private promises are much more certain to be fulfilled because they're based on investment and economic growth.

Financial analyst William G. Shipman calculates that a worker born in 1970 who earns the maximum income covered by the Social Security tax all his life is promised $1,908 a month (in 1995 dollars) by Social Security. If he invested his Social Security taxes in the stock market, he could expect a monthly income of $11,729. A low-wage worker, making the equivalent of $12,600 all his life, is promised $769 a month by Social Security. A private retirement plan invested in stocks would pay him $2,419 a month—or he could take a smaller payment, from just the interest on his savings, and leave a substantial estate to his children. Stock prices go up and down; sometimes the market crashes; but over the course of a working lifetime, stock investments almost always rise with a growing economy.

Similar programs have been instituted in Singapore, Chile, and New Zealand, and the results have been outstanding. More than 90 percent of Chilean workers chose to leave the government's pension system and open private accounts, and Chile's economy has grown at 7 percent annually since the country implemented its individual retirement plan based on real savings with competitive companies.

Our big mistake was to turn something as important as retirement security over to the coercive and bureaucratic political system. In the world of the future, workers can't count on government to provide them with secure retirement and other benefits. It is time to let people rely on themselves, their families, and their own investments in the dynamic growth of a free market.

## Health Care

Since the election of President Clinton in 1992, health care has been at the center of American policy debates. Newspapers have told us the many problems of our current health-care system: health-care spending has been growing twice as fast as the overall economy; it rose from 6 percent of GNP in 1965 to 14 percent in 1993; on any given day, some 35 million Americans do not have health insurance. Strangely, despite all the evidence about the failure of compulsory and bureaucratic systems, the usual "solution" offered to these problems has been more regulation, more government spending, or outright nationalization of the medical industry.

We can find a better solution by looking at the real source of our health-care problems. First, we should note that the United States does, in fact, have excellent and widely available health care. One way or another, the vast majority of the poor and uninsured do get care. Second, we should recognize that the tremendous technological advances in medical care, such as CAT scans, organ transplants, and other innovations, are expensive; better health care often costs more money. Third, we should realize that increasing life expectancy is a great thing but that an aging population is likely to spend more on health care. Fourth, we might speculate that a wealthier population is likely to spend more of its income on health care. We spend less of our GNP each year on such basics as food and clothing. Where does the money left over go? To things we can now better afford, such as travel, entertainment, and better medical care.

Still, there is a major problem in our health-care system that is driving costs up. The fundamental problem with U.S. health care today is that the consumer isn't making the decisions. Competitive markets produce better goods at lower costs because each participant seeks to satisfy his own needs at the lowest cost. But patients in the American health-care system don't pay directly for their own health care. Out of every dollar spent on health care, 76 cents are paid by someone other than the patient—by the government, insurance companies, or employers. Thus most patients don't benefit by spending wisely or pay the consequences of spending unwisely.

Why don't consumers pay for their own health care? The answer leads us to a great example of the vicious circle of government intervention, one regulation creating problems that lead to another regulation and then another. During World War II the federal government imposed wage-and-price controls to conceal the massive inflation that it was creating by printing money. Wage controls made it hard to hold good employees or to attract new ones. Companies came up with the idea of offering health insurance as an employee benefit not banned by the wage controls. After the war the benefit was so well established that Congress decided not to count health insurance as part of an employee's taxable income, which meant that other companies began to offer it because it was cheaper for both employee and employer to pay for medical insurance with pretax dollars.

Because the employer was paying for health insurance and the insurance was paying for most medical costs, patients became indifferent to costs. What does it matter if the doctor charges you $20 or $40 if you're not paying it anyway? As early as 1965 patients were paying only 17 percent of hospital costs (it's about 5 percent now), so those costs rose especially fast. Costs also rose because politicians kept requiring that more procedures be covered under health insurance—from alcohol and drug abuse treatment to in vitro fertilization to acupuncture and experimental AIDS treatments—instead of letting different insurers and employers offer different plans. The rising costs eventually led employers, who were paying the bills, to start implementing cost controls. Each of us controls our own costs every day, every time we make a decision about what to buy and how much to spend. Every spending decision is weighed: Do I really need that new shirt? Do I want a large drink if it costs a quarter more? Do I need power brakes and a sunroof? No two of us make all the same choices. But third parties, like employer health-benefits experts, can't know our preferences as well as we do. So they limit costs in ways that don't quite fit anybody's needs. That means that employees resist the cost controls and look favorably on the idea of government regulation.

Politicians then forbid certain kinds of cost cutting; for instance, they pass laws to require that mothers get to spend two nights in the hospital after childbirth. Sounds like a good idea, but would every new mother insist on it if she were paying the bill herself? Meanwhile, since consumers don't shop directly for health insurance, they find it difficult to get exactly the benefits they want; they get what everyone in their company gets. If consumers were buying their own health insurance, some might want full pregnancy coverage, mental-health benefits, marriage counseling, acupuncture, and so on. Others might opt for less expensive policies. (The increasingly popular flexible or "cafeteria" benefit plans give employees some options, but generally not the option to take cash instead of benefits; and cafeteria-style health plans are still subject to more than a thousand state laws mandating specific kinds of coverage.) Since consumers aren't paying for the insurance, they have every incentive to want the full, gold-plated, bells-and-whistles plan, so many of them turn to government to mandate it. Of course, each new requirement makes health insurance that much more expensive, and employers feel more pressure either to drop health insurance entirely or to implement managed care or other cost-cutting measures.

Consumer dissatisfaction with managed care and similar policies may lead to pressure for national health insurance, but make no mistake: everywhere in the world, national health insurance means rationing by a bureaucracy far more removed from the consumer than the managed-care gatekeeper. In Britain kidney dialysis is generally denied to patients over age fifty-five, and the National Health Service has suggested denying expensive care to smokers. In Canada the average waiting time to see a specialist after being referred by a general practitioner is about five weeks, often followed by another long wait for surgery recommended by the specialist. The total waiting time from being referred by the general practitioner to treatment ranges from eleven and a half weeks in Ontario to twenty-one weeks on Prince Edward Island. The Canadian system saves money by cutting back on sophisticated equipment: there are more magnetic resonance imaging units in Washington State (population 4.6 million) than in all of Canada (population 26 million), and the United States has seven times as many radiation-therapy units for cancer treatment as Canada, on a per capita basis. In Sweden the wait for heart X rays is more than eleven months. France implemented measures in 1996 to monitor every patient's costs and penalize doctors who exceed government-determined budgets.

How can we get out of this vicious circle? The key is to return control over health care to patients. Individual consumers should decide how much health care—or health insurance—they want to purchase. The way to move in that direction is through Medical Savings Accounts, described in *Patient Power: Solving America's Health Care Crisis* by John C. Goodman and Gerald L. Musgrave. Under the Patient Power plan, people would be allowed to deposit a certain amount of money each year in a tax-free Medical Savings Account, which they could use to pay medical expenses. The logical way to spend the money in an MSA would be to use part of the money to purchase a "catastrophic" insurance policy with a high deductible, say $3,000. Then the money left in the MSA would be used to pay routine medical expenses, and the catastrophic insurance would be there in the event of a major accident or illness.

Such a plan would get back to the real purpose of insurance, which is to insure against unlikely disasters. Using "health insurance" to pay for checkups and minor illnesses is like using automobile insurance to pay for gas and tune-ups. Maintenance of your health should be a normal, budgeted expense. Health insurance, like car insurance, should be purchased to guard against the possibility of a financial problem you can't afford.

Right now, in a city with an average cost of living, employers pay about $5,200 a year to provide an employee and his family with health insurance coverage. The policy has a low deductible, typically $100 or $250, meaning that's what the employee pays each year before insurance kicks in. By contrast, the premium for a catastrophic policy with a $3,000 deductible is only about $2,200 a year. So under the Patient Power plan, an employer could provide a catastrophic policy and then put the $3,000 savings in the employee's MSA. The cost is the same to the employer. The employee comes out ahead if he has less than $3,000 in medical expenses during the year, as about 94 percent of American families do, because he gets to keep the money in his MSA or roll it over into an IRA. Individual control over health-care dollars would also encourage people to practice healthy lifestyles, since a dollar in savings would be a dollar in the consumer's pocket.

The real benefit, though, is that the Patient Power plan would restore consumer choice and consumer cost-control to the health-care business. Consumers would have an incentive to ask how much a procedure cost, whether it was necessary, whether another doctor could do it cheaper—all the things we ask about everything else we buy—because the savings would belong to them. A test of such a plan by the Rand Corporation back in 1976 found that consumers who got free health care spent 45 percent more than people who paid 95 percent of their medical expenses below a catastrophic level. Yet the health of the two groups was the same.

Along with returning health-care financing to the competitive marketplace, libertarians would deregulate the health-care system. Another reason that health care costs so much is that medical licensing limits the number of doctors (lower supply means higher prices, remember) and requires patients to be treated by physicians rather than paraprofessionals, even in cases where other practitioners could provide adequate care at a lower cost. Many studies have shown that qualified nonphysician providers—such as midwives, nurses, and chiropractors—can perform many health and medical services traditionally performed by physicians, with comparable health outcomes, lower costs, and high patient satisfaction. But licensure laws and federal regulations limit their scope of practice and restrict access to their services.

In short, we have to decide whether we want marketplace medicine or government-run medicine. The lesson of economic analysis and of our real-life experience with markets and governments is that markets provide us with better goods and services at lower costs, with more flexibility and innovation, than do bureaucracies.

## Reducing Racial Tensions

Perhaps you agree that markets generally work better than bureaucracies and that less government would lead to more economic growth. But what about social issues? What about the interrelated ills of racial tension, poverty, crime, and the underclass? Millions of Americans are afraid to leave their homes at night; millions of Americans (some of them the same people) feel permanently shut out of the mainstream of society; racial tensions and even racial hatreds are on the rise at a time when they should be disappearing. Let's begin with the hottest social issue: race.

There have been three eras in the treatment of blacks by white people in America: slavery, which lasted for almost 250 years; then, after a brief period of equal treatment, the Jim Crow system, from the late nineteenth century till around 1960; and the contemporary period, in which government policy is characterized by equal voting rights, welfare, and affirmative action.

What did all three eras have in common? Exploitation? Not exactly. Discrimination? Not in the usual sense. What they had in common was a denial of the humanity and individuality of African Americans. From 1619 till 1865, a system devised by white people denied basic individual rights to blacks. Slavery as a system is an attempt to make some people carry out the will of others, as if they were animals or machines. It was called "man-stealing" by the libertarian abolitionists, who saw it as an attempt to steal a person's very self.

Then the Jim Crow laws were created to protect whites from competition with blacks and to limit the ability of blacks to participate in a free labor market. Jim Crow dehumanized blacks by denying each individual the chance to achieve as much as his natural talents would allow.

After Jim Crow was dismantled in the late 1950s and early 1960s, it seemed that blacks might finally be treated with equal dignity in America. Martin Luther King, Jr., enunciated that hope, dreaming of "a nation where [people] will be judged not by the color of their skin, but by the content of their character" and calling the Declaration of Independence and the Constitution "a promise that all men, yes, black men as well as white men, would be guaranteed the unalienable rights of life, liberty, and the pursuit of happiness." But instead of the simple guarantees of the Constitution, the federal government, with the best of intentions, launched the War on Poverty and the system of affirmative action. Both welfare and racial preferences treated black Americans as incapable of making it in American society without help. The white elites who implemented those policies assumed that blacks couldn't get admitted to college or get hired for jobs on their individual merits but would need the paternalistic help of the federal government. The policies treated blacks not as individuals but as members of a group; government once again denied the individual personhood of African Americans. The scholars Glenn C. Loury and Shelby Steele of the Center for New Black Leadership point out that with each transfer payment or racial preference received by a black American, "a little more of his fate is taken out of his hands."

Today, despite civil rights laws, affirmative action, and the clear evidence of black economic progress, racial relations in America seem more acrimonious than ever. White college students scrawl racial epithets on black and Asian students' doors, black entertainers find a wide audience for racist and anti-Semitic lyrics, black churches in the South and white-owned stores in Los Angeles are burned, resentments fester—even though polls indicate that blacks and whites earnestly *want* to get along. Both black and white Americans find that when they talk to each other, they feel like ambassadors from their race, carefully measuring their words to maintain the proper diplomatic balance.

It seems that the welfare state and affirmative action have had sweeping unintended consequences. The welfare state has combined with the War on Drugs to create a horrifying amount of violence in the inner city, leading ghetto residents to suspect a conspiracy to destroy them, and middle-class whites to identify blacks with lawlessness. The coercive, government-mandated form of affirmative action (along with such corollaries as race-norming and contract set-asides) reflects the worst aspects of welfare liberalism: white guilt combined with an unspoken belief that blacks can't make it in a competitive society without such help and a preference for group identification over ability. Racial preferences have done little or nothing for poor and undereducated blacks while causing resentment among white males, who fear that they are losing college and job opportunities that they deserve.

Another problem is the continuing growth of government. As government controls more of society, who controls government becomes more important. If the American government takes half of our income, runs our schools, regulates our businesses, sets quotas for jobs and college admissions, subsidizes art and literature, and interferes in our personal lives, then it becomes vitally important to make sure that "we" control the government. That political struggle plays a role in creating cultural wars in America and real wars in Ireland, South Africa, the former Yugoslavia, and other multiethnic states with centralized governments. We can reduce racial tensions by removing more aspects of life from the political arena, letting people work together—or apart—peacefully in the market process.

The libertarian solution starts with renewing our effort to build a society based on the virtues of choice, responsibility, and respect for self and others. When white elites try to enhance the self-esteem of minorities and the poor by assuring them that they are not responsible for their condition—as when in 1994, the president of Rutgers University defended racial preferences in college admissions by saying that blacks are "a disadvantaged population that doesn't have the genetic hereditary background to have a higher average"—they are denying people the self-respect that can come only from achievement. Government needs at least to give all people, regardless of color, as much opportunity for choice and responsibility—in schools, housing, neighborhoods, and so on—as possible, and then society should grant all people the dignity of being held responsible for the consequences of their actions.

Libertarianism is a political philosophy, not a complete moral code. It prescribes certain minimal rules for living together in a peaceful, productive society—property, contract, and freedom—and leaves further moral teaching to civil society. But on this issue it seems necessary to express a few moral sentiments that go beyond the bare description of libertarian policy. Although we have made great strides toward a society of equal dignity for all, Americans of all races need to affirm their commitment to rise above racial prejudice. We must reject overt and hateful racism from whatever source, whether David Duke or Al Sharpton. We must especially condemn racially motivated violence, from the murder of a young Kentucky man with a Confederate flag on his pickup truck, to the murder of a black man who ventured into the Bensonhurst neighborhood of Brooklyn, to the murder of a Chinese American man in Detroit by two white unemployed autoworkers who thought the victim was Japanese.

White people bear a special burden in this area. Their commitment to a color-blind society is often suspect. Conservatives such as Strom Thurmond and Jesse Helms never complained when black children were bused past white schools to more distant black schools, or when voting rights and good jobs were reserved for whites, so their current denunciations of busing and racial preferences ring hollow.

In many ways race consciousness is slowly declining in America. We can often observe clear generational differences in racial attitudes within one family. Colleges report an increasing and significant number of applicants are refusing to indicate their race on admissions forms, a phenomenon that probably reflects both a fear of "reverse discrimination" on the part of some students and a rejection of race consciousness by others. The number of interracial marriages is rising, one of the clearest indicators of declining prejudice—but that worries some people whose political clout depends on race consciousness. Asked about adding a "multiracial" category to census forms, NAACP officer Wade Henderson replied, "If people are classified or classify themselves outside the established categories, how do we ensure meaningful enforcement of the statutes?" It seems that maintaining a complex system of racial entitlements has become for some people more important than overcoming racism.

Antiracists should trust libertarians over other political groups because the libertarian commitment to government neutrality goes far beyond race. Libertarians reject *all* government-created privileges and entitlements and call for the state to be scrupulously neutral in its enforcement of individual rights. They are far more likely to keep their word than are statists, who assure us that their uses of state power will be entirely benign.

White Americans have denied the individuality of black Americans and treated them as a special class for some 380 years. It's time to try individual dignity, individual rights, and individual responsibility for all Americans.

## Liberating the Poor

The plight of the poor, especially the inner-city poor, is one of the biggest problems confronting modern America. The charge that free markets leave the poor behind is also one of the most common criticisms of libertarianism. It is true, as noted before, that poor people in modern America have a material standard of living much higher than most people throughout history have enjoyed. Forty percent of Americans below the poverty line own their own homes, 92 percent of them have color televisions, and their life expectancy is over seventy years. But "better than the past" is not enough.

There are poor people in America who truly live in wretched poverty, deprived more of hope than of material goods. They cower in fear of criminals in their neighborhood; they have no jobs and no hope of improving themselves; they don't expect their children to have a better life, and they impart to their children the kind of values that make those low expectations self-fulfilling. These people are often called the underclass. Their neighborhoods are marked by unwed motherhood rates that exceed 80 percent, an almost total absence of fathers, overwhelming dependence on welfare, and extraordinary rates of crime. Though there have always been poor people, the plight of the underclass seems to have gotten markedly worse in only a few decades. The distinguished sociologist William Julius Wilson has described how "blacks in Harlem and in other ghetto neighborhoods did not hesitate to sleep in parks, on fire escapes, and on rooftops during hot summer nights in the 1940s and 1950s, and whites frequently visited inner-city taverns and nightclubs." Far better than statistics, that sort of historical reflection reminds us of how unlivable our inner cities have become in little more than a generation.

Many people concerned about the poor argue that government should spend more on programs to help them. Yet since the beginning of the Great Society in 1965, we have spent more than $5 trillion on poverty programs. We're spending more than $300 billion a year today. And the problems have gotten worse. The poverty rate—which fell dramatically from the end of World War II until the 1960s—leveled off after the Great Society began and has remained largely stable since then.

The problem today is that the urban poor are caught in a trap that has two sides. On one side, government regulations such as the minimum wage law and occupational licensing make it difficult for low-skilled people to find jobs. On the other side, welfare programs offer a way to survive without work. It's easy to get trapped in dependency.

Virtually no one in America falls below the poverty line if they do three things: complete high school, don't get pregnant outside marriage, and get a job, any job. The first job may not pay wages above the poverty level, but people with a work history don't stay in minimum-wage jobs for long. The question facing policy makers is, How can we encourage poor Americans, especially poor young people, to make the choices that will lead them out of poverty? We have to recognize that those three simple steps to avoiding poverty don't seem so attractive when you're in high school in a neighborhood where few people work. Welfare can seem a rational choice. In fact, a 1996 study found that welfare benefits (including Medicaid and housing assistance) pay better than a minimum-wage job in all fifty states, and better than a secretary's starting salary in twenty-nine states.

The stark truth is that as long as the welfare state makes it possible for young women—or teenage girls—to have children without a husband and survive without a job, out-of-wedlock births will remain ruinously high (up to 68 percent among blacks and 23 percent among whites in the latest calculation), and the inner city will continue to be marked by crime, poverty, and despair. Tinkering reforms—workfare, learnfare, two-year limits—won't work. The only way to break the cycle of unwed motherhood, fatherless children, poverty, crime, and welfare is to recognize that welfare causes more problems than it cures.

What would happen to potential welfare recipients if welfare weren't available? Many of them would get jobs. To help that process, we should remove the impediments to low-skilled jobs. Repeal the minimum-wage law so people can get that all-important first job and learn the job skills that will enable them to get better jobs. Repeal the occupational licensing laws that prevent people from becoming hairdressers, cabdrivers, and so on. Reduce taxes and red tape so that more people can afford to start businesses. And reduce crime—about which I'll say more below—so people will be more willing to open businesses in inner-city areas. In her classic 1969 book, *The Economy of Cities,* Jane Jacobs wrote, "Poverty has no causes. Only prosperity has causes." She was right; we want to bring more people into the world of work, so they can create prosperity for themselves.

Some teenagers will still get pregnant, of course; some other people will find themselves unable to work or in need of help. Many of those people will rely on their families, the basic institution of civil society. Families can help their down-and-out members in two basic ways: by simply taking them in, of course, or giving them financial or other assistance—but also by imparting values and helping them to learn right conduct. Knowing that welfare won't be available will be a great spur to make mothers impress upon their daughters the importance of avoiding pregnancy and staying in school. No social worker is as likely to supply the right combination of love and toughness as a family member.

When work and family fail, the other institutions of civil society come into play, especially charitable institutions. We discussed mutual aid, which is an important part of poverty avoidance and should be a more important part, in chapter 7; here we'll focus on charity. In the recent discussion of cutting back on government welfare programs, many leading charities have warned that they can't assume all the responsibilities of government; they say they don't have that much money. Well, of course not. But the point is, the government programs have failed. The solution is not to replicate them. If government stopped encouraging irresponsibility, there would be less need for charity. And private charities can do far more with less money than can government bureaucracies. Sister Connie Driscoll's House of Hope in Chicago helps homeless women at a cost of less than $7 a day, compared with $22 a day in government-funded homeless shelters. Yet the House of Hope has a phenomenal success rate, with fewer than 6 percent of women who come there ending up back on the street. The Gospel Mission has been in existence in Washington, D.C., since 1906. It operates a homeless shelter, a food bank, and a drug-treatment center, the underlying principle being that no one should get something for nothing. Men have to either pay $3 a night or work for an hour for a night's shelter. The Reverend John Woods, the mission's director, says, "Compassion is lifting people out of the gutter, not getting down there with them and sympathizing. These people need responsibility." Nearly two-thirds of the addicts completing its drug-treatment program remain drug-free. A nearby government-run treatment center has a 10 percent success rate at twenty times the cost per client.

Across America there are thousands of small, local charitable organizations helping the poor. Americans give more than $125 billion and 20 billion hours a year to charity. If taxes were lower, and people understood that government was turning charitable responsibilities over to the civil society, they would give far more.

If you're not convinced that private charity can replace government welfare, ask yourself this: Suppose you won $100,000 in a lottery. But there's a catch. You have to spend it to help the poor. Would you give it to the U.S. Department of Health and Human Services, your state human services agency, or a private charity? Most people would not hesitate to choose a private charity.

## Crime

America's horrific levels of violent crime make our inner cities unlivable, drive middle-class people out of the city, and increase social tensions. Although we are told that crime has fallen in the past few years, we need to put that claim in perspective. In 1951 New York City had 244 murders; with the same population, it has averaged more than 2,000 a year in the 1990s. In 1965 Milwaukee had 27 murders and 214 robberies; in 1990 it had 165 murders and 4,472 robberies. And the situation may get drastically worse in the next few years. By the year 2000 there will be 500,000 more teenage males than there were in 1995. Criminologists warn that they will be more disposed to crime and more violent than previous generations, largely because more of them than ever have grown up without a father and in communities without fathers. Princeton University professor John DiIulio, Jr., interviewed men in a maximum-security prison and found that *they* fear today's young predators.

The first requirement of civilized society is to protect citizens from violence. Our government is failing dramatically at that task, and we need a new approach to dealing with crime. First, we should remember that under the Constitution, crime fighting is an issue for state and local government. There is no constitutional authority for a general federal criminal code; recent federal "crime bills" are motivated entirely by politics and will *at best* have no influence on the crime rate. Second, we should remember that about 80 percent of the real crimes—murder, rape, assault, and theft—are committed by 20 percent of the criminals. State law enforcement agencies should focus their resources on dangerous repeat offenders and get them off the streets.

In the long run, the most important thing states could do to reduce crime is to change the welfare systems that are ratcheting up the illegitimacy rate. Fatherless boys, especially boys from fatherless communities, are the principal perpetrators of violent crime in our cities today. Fathers teach and show boys how to deal with their natural aggressiveness and how to be strong, self-controlled adult men. Fatherless boys are 72 percent of all adolescent murderers and 70 percent of long-term prison inmates.

More immediately, the most important thing states could do to reduce crime is to legalize drugs. Our current policies drive drug prices sky-high and make drug dealing seem the most profitable and glamorous option available to many inner-city youth. Given the poor quality of inner-city schools, many young people see their options as "chump change" at McDonald's, welfare, or selling drugs. But, like alcohol prohibition in the 1920s, drug prohibition guarantees that drugs will be sold by criminals. Addicts have to commit crimes to pay for a habit that would be easily affordable (and safer) if it were legal. Dealers have no way of settling disputes except by shooting it out. If drugs were produced by reputable firms and sold in liquor stores, fewer people would die from overdoses and tainted drugs, and fewer people would be the victims of prohibition-related robberies, muggings, and drive-by shootings. If there are any limits to the state's power over individuals, surely the state should not be permitted to regulate what we can put into our own bodies. Drug prohibition is both repressive and counterproductive.

If we end drug prohibition, we'll free up police resources, court time, and prison cells for violent criminals. Our goal for such offenders should be swift, sure, and severe punishment. The level of punishment appropriate for violent crimes is related to the degree of a society's crime problem. Because crime in the United States is extremely severe, we should probably increase the level of punishment for real crimes such as robbery, assault, rape, and murder. We might implement truth-in-sentencing laws, so the community knows that a criminal will actually serve the sentence he is given; "three-strikes-and-you're-out" laws for those convicted of three violent felonies; and, given our horrific juvenile-crime problem, tougher sentences than we've been doling out for younger criminals.

In implementing such policies, however, we need to affirm our commitment to civil liberties. Conservatives like to rail against "criminals' rights"; the proper term is "rights of the accused," and that's an important distinction for those of us who intend never to be criminals but can imagine some day being accused of a crime, especially in these days of burgeoning law books. We can improve our anticrime efforts without giving police carte blanche to search our cars, offices, and homes without a warrant or even a knock on the door; without letting police seize property under looser and looser "civil forfeiture" rules;

without becoming the victims of wiretapping and other forms of electronic surveillance.

One popular solution that will *not* reduce crime is gun control. There are more than 200 million privately owned guns in the United States, and no gun-control measure will ever change that. Law-abiding citizens have a natural and a constitutional right to keep and bear arms, not just for hunting but for self-defense and in the last resort for the defense of freedom.

Finally, an often-overlooked solution to crime is privatization. Protection of rights is the fundamental and legitimate purpose of government, but that doesn't necessarily make government much more efficient at it than at other tasks. Already Americans employ about 1.5 million private police officers, about three times as many as are employed by state and local governments. Not long ago I ate in a restaurant after an evening of shopping, so it was quite late when I left the restaurant. As I walked down deserted streets, past shuttered shops, it occurred to me that I was not afraid. Why? Because I was in a private community, a shopping mall. Private communities have more incentive and more ability to maintain order than governments do, which is why people increasingly shop in malls and even live in private, often gated, communities. In this as in so many areas, a narrowing of political society and more reliance on civil society would benefit us all.

## Family Values

The family is the basic institution of civil society, and people on all sides of the political spectrum have begun to express concern about its apparent decline. As the state has expanded and displaced voluntary association, freedom, and responsibility, it has created atomized societies. It is not libertarianism that is "atomistic," but welfare statism.

The problem is most noticeable in the soaring illegitimacy rate, from 5 percent in 1960 to 30 percent today. Two decades of social science research have reminded us of what we had forgotten about millennia of experience: Children need two parents, for both financial and emotional reasons. Mothers

alone—especially unskilled teenage mothers—have great diffi-
culty supporting a family, which is why children living in fatherless homes are five times more likely to be poor. The greater
problem is that mothers alone find it difficult to control—that
is, to civilize—teenage boys. Out-of-control teenage boys have
made our inner cities a nightmare, marked by drive-by shootings and children afraid to play outside.

We have paid less attention to a less dramatic parenting
problem, the effects of divorce on children. More children every
year go through divorce or separation than are born out of wedlock. Most divorced men and women say they are better off out
of the marriage, but many children suffer. Ten years after a divorce, more than two-thirds of children have not seen their father for a year. Children from disrupted families are nearly twice
as likely as those from intact families to drop out of high school;
young adults from disrupted families are nearly twice as likely
to receive psychological help.

Some communitarians and "family advocates" on both left
and right blame capitalism for the family's problems, and
they're not entirely wrong. Freedom means that people can
make their own choices, and affluence gives more people the
means to leave their families and live on their own. (Though,
don't forget, oppression and poverty in Europe impelled millions of people to leave their families and cross the Atlantic
seeking freedom and affluence.) Capitalist wealth and technology produced efficient birth control, which helped to create a
revolution in sexual mores, which in turn may have led to both
delayed marriage for many people and increased rates of divorce. Still, families form and persist, not just because people
have no other choices, but because they need and want the
comfort and structure of family.

In our time, government has undermined families in ways
both obvious and not so obvious. The most obvious is that the
welfare system makes it possible for young women to have children out of wedlock and survive in some degree of comfort. In
earlier generations, mothers taught their daughters that an ille-
gitimate child would be a disaster. Much of the moral stigma
surrounding illegitimacy ultimately stemmed from the very
practical reality that it would impose a financial burden on the

family or the small community. When welfare removed the financial burden, the stigma declined quickly and illegitimacy rates soared.

But that's only the most obvious impact of government on the family. In 1950 the median American family paid 5 percent of its income in federal income taxes; today the figure for the median family is about 24 percent. Women should have the right to work, but high taxes are forcing mothers who would *prefer* to stay home with their children into the workplace. Obscure zoning laws in many cities have outlawed "granny flats," those separate-entrance apartments in the back of houses that might be a great place for a grandparent to find the right combination of closeness and independence. Of course, maybe people don't want their mothers-in-law living around back: After all, the biggest government program of them all, Social Security, has surely loosened family bonds. Before Social Security many older people relied on their children for support, which kept family ties stronger throughout life. Today, we expect the government to support our parents. A friend said to me once, when I was warning of Social Security's dire financial straits, "If it costs $200 billion a year to keep my mother from living with me, it's worth every penny." Understandable, perhaps, in some cases, but a dubious social policy. Of course, we also expect the government to provide us with child care, and to educate our children, and to keep the schools open until 6 P.M. as day-care facilities. Why shouldn't the family decline, when government has usurped responsibility for infants, children, and the elderly?

Libertarians don't think the government needs to support and encourage traditional families, as moralistic conservatives advocate. It just needs to stop undermining families so people can form the kinds of families they want. Ideally, libertarians would like the government to get out of the marriage and family business altogether. Why should government issue marriage licenses? A marriage is a voluntary agreement, a contract, which for many people has a deep religious meaning. What does it have to do with government? We should return to the notion of marriage as a civil contract for everyone and a religious covenant for those who choose it.

Such a policy might even strengthen marriage. The state has

regulated marriage heavily, providing what is essentially a one-size-fits-all contract for all couples. As social mores have changed—with smaller families and more women choosing to work—the state contract has become inappropriate for more families. Couples should be allowed to write their own contracts, and courts should grant them the same respect that commercial contracts receive.

As long as the state does grant marriage licenses, it should grant them on a nondiscriminatory basis. It was wrong for states to deny marriage licenses to racially mixed couples, and it was a travesty of justice that the Supreme Court didn't strike down such discrimination until 1967. Similarly, it is wrong to deny same-sex couples the right to marry today. Jonathan Rauch argues that there are three great social benefits to marriage—the stable upbringing of children, the domestication of men, and the creation of a commitment to care for one's spouse in sickness and old age—and that at least the latter two clearly apply to gay male relationships, while the third and possibly the first would be relevant to lesbian couples. Then, of course, there's also the basic human dignity of being able to make a public affirmation of one's love and commitment. It's hard to see how the acceptance of same-sex marriages would undermine anyone else's marriage, as some conservatives claim; one thing gay couples rarely do is fill the world with fatherless children, and surely *more* people getting married is good for the institution of marriage.


## Education

By now the libertarian position on education should be fairly clear. Education is the process by which we pass on not just the knowledge but the values that are essential to our civilization. Because education involves teaching children about right and wrong, about what is important in life, it must be controlled by individual families, not by politicians or bureaucrats. No monopoly system can adequately reflect the values of all parents in a diverse society, and it is the height of arrogance to suggest that political elites should override parents in deciding what to teach their children.

In addition, of course, a bureaucratic monopoly is a highly inefficient way to deliver valuable services. If we no longer have any confidence in the state's ability to produce steel, why should we expect it to succeed at the far more subtle and complex task of delivering knowledge and values to millions of different children? We should keep in mind Mark Twain's quip that "I never let my schooling interfere with my education." Education happens in many ways; we shouldn't think that our current system of schooling is fixed in stone.

The basic failure of the U.S. public school system can be seen in the following chart. As real spending (adjusted for inflation) tripled in thirty years, test scores plummeted and then leveled off. Ever since World War II, schools and school districts have gotten larger, making them ever more impervious to commu-

*Spending and Achievement in American Schools*

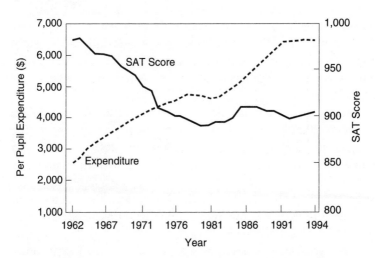

*Sources:* Educational Testing Service, U.S. Department of Education, *Digest of Education Statistics 1994* (Washington: National Center for Education Statistics, 1994), Tables 127 and 165.

*Note:* SAT scores for 1961-67 are means for all students; subsequent scores are averages for college-bound seniors.

nity control and ever more bureaucratic. From 1960 to 1984, enrollment in American public schools rose only 9 percent, while the number of teachers rose by 57 percent and the number of principals and supervisors by 79 percent. Meanwhile, the number of personnel who were neither teachers nor supervisors rose by *500 percent*—yet somehow every school system threatened with budget cuts announces that it would have to lay off teachers, not bureaucrats. The New York City public school system has 6,000 central office bureaucrats, while the Catholic school system of New York serves one-fourth as many students with just 30 central administrative staff.

Not only are test scores declining, but businesspeople complain that graduates of American high schools are not prepared for work. American students tell survey researchers that their reading, writing, and math skills are good, but employers have a different view. In one survey, only 22 percent of employers thought that recently hired high school graduates had sufficient math skills, and only 30 percent were satisfied with new hires' reading abilities. When BellSouth tested technician applicants, only 8 percent passed. Motorola spends $1,350 per employee each year teaching basic skills. Many companies are rewriting manuals to accommodate poor reading skills or designing technology that doesn't require reading or math skills. The schools are not turning out a workforce prepared for global competition.

Every form of communications and information transfer in our society has been revolutionized in the past 20 years, yet the schools still look the same way they did 200 years ago—a teacher lecturing in front of thirty students, with the school day and the school year geared to the rhythms of an agricultural society. We can only imagine the dynamic innovations in learning that profit-seeking companies might have produced had they been delivering education.

Libertarians want to remove education from the bureaucratic state and make it truly responsive to students and parents. Private schools do a much better job at educating students, but most parents find it difficult to pay once for the public school system and then pay again for private school. If they didn't have to pay school taxes, they could afford to purchase education in the marketplace. Or if taxes were lower, more families could afford to have one parent educate children at home.

Many people fear that children wouldn't get educated if schooling weren't free and compulsory. Historical evidence shows that in England and the United States the vast majority of children were educated before the government took over schooling. Even Senator Edward M. Kennedy, no fan of civil society and the market process, has claimed that literacy was higher before the advent of public education than it is today— which makes one wonder why he wants to pour more and more money into a government system that is delivering such poor results.

For people who are sympathetic to these arguments but not quite persuaded that a totally free market would supply enough education, libertarians have offered some halfway steps toward educational freedom. We could take the money we currently spend on public school students—about $6,800 per student per year—and give it directly to families in the form of a scholarship or voucher, to be spent at the public or private school of their choice. That way, education would still be funded by compulsory taxation but at least parents could choose the kind of school they want for their child. Even better would be to expect rich and middle-class families to pay for their own children's education—surely education should be considered a basic cost of bringing up children—but supply a tax-funded voucher for poor children. That would allow a significant reduction in school taxes, which would enable most parents to pay for education on their own.

Like Soviet factories a few years ago, American schools today are technologically backward, overstaffed, inflexible, unresponsive to consumer demand, and operated for the convenience of top-level bureaucrats. We need to open up the $300-billion-a-year education industry and let the market process in. Imagine the ways schools competing for parents' dollars would find to meet the needs of individual students. Educational technology is in its infancy, but create a market and we'll see billions being spent on research and development. We'll see schools that respect parents' values and welcome parents' involvement. We'll learn, as one talented educator puts it, that "we don't need to get kids ready for school, we need to get schools ready for kids." That's what happens in markets.

## Protecting Civil Liberties

As we've said before, libertarianism is the view that each person has the right to live his life in any way he chooses so long as he respects the equal rights of others. Thus libertarians oppose government restrictions on individual behavior as long as one's actions don't infringe on the rights of others. That doesn't necessarily mean approving or endorsing any particular behavior; it just means that the coercive power of the state should be limited to protecting our rights. It would be impossible to make a list of all the civil liberties we have; we tend to identify particular civil liberties as the state attempts to restrict them. The Bill of Rights reflected the Founders' specific experience with British restrictions on individual rights; but, recognizing that it was impossible to enumerate all individual rights, they added the Ninth Amendment—reserving to individuals other rights not enumerated—and the Tenth Amendment—reiterating that the federal government has only those powers set out in the Constitution.

Civil libertarians often find themselves defending an individual's right to engage in actions that they may find reprehensible. As Hayek writes in *The Constitution of Liberty,* "Freedom necessarily means that many things will be done which we do not like." We all benefit from the general condition of freedom, not just because it entitles *us* to do what *we* want, but because civilization progresses through trial and error, through individuals' trying new ways of life. He goes on to say, "The freedom that will be used by only one man in a million may be more important to society and more beneficial to the majority than any freedom that we all use."

Civil society offers room for individuals to live in ways that they choose, even if they may offend the majority. However, it also affords people the opportunity to limit their own freedom of action by entering into contracts and associations with others and to use their property to create an environment they find congenial. For instance, people have a right to smoke tobacco or marijuana even if the majority find smoking both dangerous and disgusting. But other people have a right to forbid smoking in their own homes, restaurants, or businesses. People have a right to paint their houses purple, but not if they have voluntarily entered into an agreement with their neighbors—in a housing development with restrictive covenants, for instance—to paint their house only in pastel colors.

Libertarians defend the right of individuals to freedom of speech, freedom of the press, and freedom of broadcast, even though they may exercise that freedom in ways that offend others in society, whether through sexually explicit language, racist magazines, or communist books. Every new technology brings with it new demands for censorship, and electronic communication is no exception. Fortunately, the fabulously complex, international Internet will prove extremely difficult to censor, and governments will be increasingly hard-pressed to limit what their citizens can know.

Sexuality is another intimate aspect of life that governments have meddled in from time immemorial. As recently as the 1960s, homosexual relations were illegal in almost all states, and about twenty states still have such laws on the books as we approach the twenty-first century. When these laws were vigorously enforced, they drove gay people underground and created much misery. Once gay people stood up for their rights, governments began to back away from enforcing the laws. However, the Supreme Court ruled in 1986 that there was no constitutional right to choose one's own consenting adult sexual partners, and sodomy laws are still used, for instance, to deny gay parents custody of their children. Such laws should be repealed, and all Americans should have equal rights.

In the name of protecting our safety, government restricts our right to make our own decisions and assume responsibility for the consequences of those decisions. Mandatory seatbelt and helmet laws, for instance, deny us the right to choose the risks we want to assume. The Food and Drug Administration denies us the right to choose the vitamins, pharmaceutical drugs, and medical devices that we want. Surely the decision to pursue a particular course of medication is as personal and intimate as any choice could be. Many doctors believe that marijuana has medical benefits, for relief of glaucoma and to reduce the pain and nausea associated with AIDS, cancer, and chemotherapy; those doctors may be right or wrong, but the decision should be up to the patient, not a bureaucratic agency in Washington.

One of the most disturbing trends in civil liberties is the increasing militarization of law enforcement in the United States, much of it—though not all—an attempt to escalate the increasingly futile War on Drugs. Once again, the failure of one government intervention leads to pressure for more intervention. Drug prohibition fails to stop the drug trade, so the government points to that very failure as a reason to hire more police, pressure foreign governments, expand its powers of search-and-seizure and civil forfeiture, deprive law-abiding people of public telephones in drug-trade areas, subject all employees to drug testing, and so on. There are now fifty-two federal agencies whose officers have the power to carry firearms and make arrests. Maybe that's why we've seen an increasing number of violent federal assaults on individual Americans, from the deaths of Vicki and Sammy Weaver at Ruby Ridge, Idaho, to the killing of Donald Scott in a trumped-up marijuana bust in Malibu to the tanks-and-helicopter assault on the Branch Davidians in Waco, Texas, that left more than eighty people dead.

As Thomas Jefferson said, "The price of liberty is eternal vigilance." Constitutions help to protect liberty, but only a society of people determined to guard their freedom against encroachment can, over the long term, resist the natural tendency of power to expand.

## Protecting the Environment

Environmental quality is an important aspect of a good society, and many people are skeptical that the free market can supply it adequately. While there is no perfect solution to environmental problems in any political or philosophical system, libertarianism offers the best available framework for producing the environmental protection that people want.

Economic growth helps to produce environmental quality.

Wealthier people and wealthier societies can afford to demand and pay for better air and water quality. People struggling to survive or to rise above backbreaking labor don't care very much about environmental amenities; when people have reached a comfortable standard of living, they turn their attention to such higher-order "goods." In fact, air and water quality in the United States has improved steadily during this century, and our rising life expectancy is the best evidence that our environment is becoming more, not less, people-friendly.

As economies become more efficient and more technologically advanced, they use fewer resources to produce greater value for consumers. Remember, the basic economic problem is to get more value out of resources. Because soft-drink companies want to save money, they developed ways to use much less tin—and later, aluminum—in each can. In 1974 a pound of aluminum yielded 22.7 beverage cans; in 1994 the same pound yielded 30.13 cans. The same profit incentive impels companies to seek a use for their waste products; the Coca-Cola Company discovered that the sheets of metal out of which they punched bottle caps made ideal furnace filters. When Coca-Cola's Minute Maid division makes orange juice, no part of the orange goes to waste: the company squeezes out every drop of juice, presses oil out of the peel, and feeds the rest to cows.

One of the biggest generators of environmental problems is what the environmentalist Garrett Hardin called "the tragedy of the commons." When resources—such as a common grazing area, forest, or lake—are "owned" by everyone, they are effectively owned by no one. No one has an incentive to maintain the value of the asset or use it on a sustainable basis. It's like six kids sharing a milkshake: each one has an incentive to drain the cup before the others do. When timber companies cut trees in a national forest, their incentive is to cut them all, now, before some other company gets a permit to use the same area. When timber companies cut trees on their own land, they replant as many as they cut, so they'll have a moneymaking asset for years to come. One of the biggest environmental problems today is the depletion of ocean fisheries, a clear example of the tragedy of the commons for which a privatization solution is urgently needed.

So how can a libertarian perspective help to improve environmental quality? First, a free society offers a diversity of approaches to solving problems. Competitive systems—capitalism, democracy, and science—allow ideas to be tested and successful ideas to be emulated. Command-and-control regulation from Washington cannot manage efficiently the environmental issues confronting hundreds of thousands of commercial enterprises any more than it can adequately guide a society's economic activities.

Second, private owners take better care of resources than do public owners. Private property rights mean that lines of authority are clear and that specific people will reap either the benefits or the costs of their actions. The way to avoid the tragedy of the commons is to privatize the commons. As environmental economist Richard Stroup says, property rights must be "3-D": "clearly defined, easily defended against invasion, and divestible (transferable) on terms agreeable to buyer and seller." Why are buffalo an endangered species but not cows? Why did passenger pigeons disappear but not chickens? Because owners have an incentive to maintain what they own. Congress should stop its annual politicized debates over *how* to manage federal lands—timber quotas, mineral rights, grazing fees, offshore drilling—and move toward privatization of natural resources so that private stewards can exercise proper stewardship.

Third, environmental problems should be handled at the most local level possible. Political activists on both sides of environmental issues have run to Washington to get their own agenda imposed on the whole country. But the principles of federalism and subsidiarity would suggest that problems should be handled privately if possible and, if not, then at the local or state level before any federal involvement is considered. We lose the benefits of decentralization and experimentation when we impose one solution on the whole country.

Fourth, where markets don't always work—where property rights are ill defined or goods are hard to divide—common law is an important problem-solving institution. Anywhere people live together, environmental problems will arise—smells, run-offs, factory smoke. As individuals take such disagreements to court, they help to define property rights and the law. Such an

evolving, decentralized production of law leads to better answers than a one-size-fits-all legislative command.

Fifth, the libertarian emphasis on individual responsibility
means that we should avoid the invitation to personal *ir*responsibility entailed by collective liability and adopt a "polluter-
pays" approach to liability issues. Superfund is the classic
mistake here. All producers of hazardous waste are required to
pay into the fund, which is then allocated by a regulatory bureaucracy to clean up specific sites. We should hold individual
polluters responsible for damage they actually do, rather than
impose collective guilt on an entire industry and eliminate
every company's incentive to avoid pollution. The aim of environmental policy should be the protection of persons and their
property, as is true of our legal system generally.

Finally, of course, smaller government means that government itself would stop polluting and encouraging environmental damage. Government environmental destruction was
rampant in the Soviet countries, but it is a real problem in
mixed economies as well. Government subsidies encourage the
clearing of tropical rain forests. Massive hydropower projects
from the United States to China are almost always government
sponsored. Farm programs, especially sugar quotas, have encouraged overuse of agricultural land. Governments without
such powers would do less damage to the environment as well
as to the economy.

The institutions of private property, decentralized decision
making, common law, and strict liability will lead us to better
solutions—solutions that reflect the real costs and benefits of
environmental quality—than command-and-control regulation produced in a political process and implemented by regula-
tors unaccountable for the consequences of their actions.
However, since both common law and property rights are constantly evolving, there are undoubtedly environmental issues
for which we do not yet have adequate solutions. We have developed property rights in water flows, in underground water
pools, in grazing land, in animal herds; but how can we develop
property rights in air? If global warming is a real problem—
and the evidence is still unclear on that point—could property
rights or common law lead us to a solution?

Economists, legal scholars, judges, businesspeople, and property owners are involved in an ongoing search for answers to such questions. Free-market or at least market-oriented institutions that have developed recently to address environmental issues rationally and at the least cost to society include pollution charges, tradeable emission permits, markets for recyclable trading, and performance standards (instead of regulations prescribing technologies and specific kinds of pollution reduction). Those are not perfect libertarian solutions, and more work needs to be done, but they are examples of how we can achieve environmental quality without either politicizing the environment or imposing unnecessary costs on our economy.

A few years ago, at a scholarly conference on environmental issues, I heard a professor of biology who had run a ranch in Montana for twenty years discuss some of the many questions he faced about how best to manage the resources on his ranch. What struck me was that here was a man committed to environmental quality, professionally trained in biological science, with decades of experience in resource management, and he wasn't sure how to answer the questions that came up on his own ranch. The lesson is that no one has all the answers, so no one's answers should be imposed on the whole society. What we need, as Karl Hess, Jr., wrote in *Visions upon the Land,* is "a market of landscape visions, . . . a virtuous republic of independent, caring, and responsible stewards" of their own natural resources.

## Preserving Peace

The classical liberals always regarded war as the greatest scourge that government could visit upon society. They abhorred the killing that war entailed, and they understood something else as well: war destroyed families, businesses, and civil society. Preventing kings from putting their subjects at risk in unnecessary wars was one of their major goals. Adam Smith argued that little else was needed to create a happy and prosperous society but "peace, easy taxes, and a tolerable administration of justice."

The American Founders, happy to be free of the endless European wars, made peace and neutrality a cardinal principle of the new government. In his Farewell Address, George Washington told the nation, "The great rule in conduct for us, in regard to foreign nations, is in extending our commercial relations to have with them as little political connection as possible." And Thomas Jefferson described American foreign policy in his First Inaugural Address this way: "Peace, commerce, and honest friendship with all nations—entangling alliances with none."

In the twentieth century, however, many people came to believe that the United States had to become involved in world affairs and foreign wars. For fifty years U.S. foreign policy was directed at defeating two totalitarian powers, Nazi Germany and Soviet Russia. Today that great crusade is complete; America is secure, and no aggressive ideology threatens U.S. citizens or world peace. But the huge diplomatic and military establishment that grew up during World War II and the cold war refuses to declare victory and return to peacetime status. Instead, the American military remains large and expensive, and American citizens are told that the post–cold-war world is even more dangerous and unstable than the world that was threatened by the Soviet Union. Thus we still have substantial numbers of U.S. troops in Europe, Japan, Korea, and the Middle East.

In just the few short years since the Persian Gulf War, we have sent American troops, or been urged to send troops, to Somalia, Haiti, Bosnia, Liberia, Rwanda, Burundi, Macedonia, and a host of other places. These places have just one thing in common: no vital American interest is at risk there. Less than a generation after the disaster in Vietnam, we seem to have forgotten the lessons of our intervention there. That intervention, too, started small, with good intentions; no one expected that we would end up with 500,000 American troops there and 55,000 American deaths.

We need to remember a few simple rules about war and foreign policy. First, war kills people. Especially in the modern world, it often kills as many civilians as soldiers. War cannot be avoided at all costs, but it should be avoided wherever possible.

Proposals to involve the United States—or any government—in foreign conflict should be treated with great skepticism.

Second, as discussed earlier, war creates big government. Throughout history, it has provided an excuse for governments to arrogate money and power to themselves and to regiment society. During World Wars I and II the United States government assumed powers it could never have acquired in peacetime, powers such as wage-and-price controls, rationing, close control of labor and production, and astronomical tax rates. Constitutional restrictions on federal power were swiftly eroded. That doesn't mean those wars shouldn't have been fought. It *does* mean that we should understand the consequences of war for our entire social order and thus go to war only when absolutely necessary.

Third, the United States can no more police and plan the whole world than it can plan a national economy. Without a superpower threat to rally against, the politico-military establishment wants us to deploy our military resources on behalf of democracy and self-determination around the world and against such vague or decentralized threats as terrorism, drugs, and environmental destruction. The military is designed to fight wars in defense of American liberty and sovereignty; it is not well equipped to be policeman and social worker to the world.

Fourth, our cold-war allies have recovered from the destruction of World War II and are fully capable of defending themselves. Not only is there no longer a Soviet threat to Europe, the countries of the European Union have a collective population of more than 370 million, a gross domestic product of $7 trillion a year, and more than 2 million troops. They can defend Europe and deal with such problems as Serb aggression without U.S. assistance. South Korea has twice the population and eighteen times the economic output of North Korea; it doesn't need our 37,000 troops to protect itself.

Fifth, the communications explosion means that the information imbalance between political leaders and citizens is much reduced. Presidents often watch world events unfolding on CNN, along with all the rest of us. That means that presidents will find it more difficult to expect public deference on matters of foreign policy, so they should proceed cautiously in undertaking foreign commitments without popular support.

The world is still full of potential threats, and the first purpose of government is to protect the rights of citizens. We must maintain an adequate national defense, but we can defend the vital interests of the United States with a military about half the size of the one we have—especially if we reorient our foreign policy to one of strategic independence, not global commitments to collective security agreements. That would still give us about a million active-duty personnel. While we can eliminate some expensive cold-war weaponry designed to project U.S. power far from our shores, we should pursue the possibility of actually *defending* U.S. citizens with an antiballistic-missile defense system.

Libertarians who propose to bring U.S. troops home and concentrate on the defense of the United States are sometimes accused of being "isolationist." That's a misconception. Libertarians are in fact *cosmopolitans*. We look forward to a world bound together by free trade, global communications, and cultural exchange. We believe that military intervention around the world hampers that effort. We also believe that, although the world is growing closer together in many ways, it is inappropriate to view the whole world as a village in which everyone must pitch in to stop every fight. In a dangerous world, with terrorism and nuclear weapons, it is better to keep military conflicts limited and regional rather than to escalate them through superpower involvement.

What may seem to many readers an exhaustive review of contemporary policy issues has hardly scratched the surface of policy analysis, and many questions obviously remain unanswered here. The framework for libertarian policy analysis, however, should be clear: individual liberty, private property, free markets, and limited government create a vibrant and dynamic civil society that best accommodates the needs and preferences of millions of individual citizens.

*Chapter 11*

# THE OBSOLETE STATE

*A*s public services decline and markets get more so-phisticated in the Information Age, people are turning to private provision of everything from education to first-class mail to disaster insurance. Even people who once saw a need for government to provide such services now view the state as an increasingly clumsy and obsolete way to supply most goods and services.

Why does government provide so many goods that could be better provided privately? Some answers, mostly having to do with political imperialism and the dysfunctional nature of politics, were suggested in chapter 9. But there are certainly less sinister reasons, such as the argument that government is needed to supply public goods. Scholars have recently subjected the "public goods" argument to withering examination. Entrepreneurs, however, didn't wait for the scholars to show them the way; from lighthouses and schools to postal service and flood insurance, markets have produced what consumers needed while scholars argued about whether markets *could* work.

## Market Failure and Public Goods

The claim of "market failure" is probably the most important intellectual argument for state intervention in the market.

There is a serious argument developed by economists that in some circumstances, markets fail to supply something that many people want and would be willing to pay for. Outside the economics journals, however, the person claiming a market failure usually means that the market has failed to supply something that *he* wants. A friend of mine likes to poke fun at my dogged faith in the market process by declaring "market failure" every time I complain about my inability to find a particular product or service: There's no good pizzeria in my neighborhood? "Market failure!"

In most cases, of course, if we can't find a good or service that we want, it's for one of two reasons: entrepreneurs are missing an opportunity, in which case we ought to consider supplying it, or there's some good reason that no one is supplying it. These days, it seems that many people would like to go to nonsmoking bars. So why are there almost none in existence? It's possible that this is a great entrepreneurial opportunity. It's more likely that smokers tend to drink more and tip better, so that it's extremely difficult to make a profit on a nonsmoking bar (though this may well change in the next few years).

Most serious claims of market failure are based on the theory of public goods. A "public good" is defined by economists as an economic good with two characteristics: nonexcludability and nonrivalrous consumption. That is, first, it's impossible to exclude nonpaying individuals from enjoying the good. The classic example is the lighthouse, whose beam can be seen by all ships. And second, individuals' ability to enjoy a good or service is not diminished by allowing other individuals to consume it as well. For instance, a broadcast signal or a movie, unlike an automobile or a haircut, can be enjoyed by many people simultaneously.

Economists have argued that people will "free-ride" on the provision of nonexcludable goods; that is, ships won't contribute to the upkeep of a lighthouse because they can enjoy its services as long as other ships contribute. Of course, if many people seek to free-ride, the service may not be provided at all. Some economists therefore argue that government should tax people and provide the service itself to overcome market failure.

There are several problems with this analysis. Goods can be

produced and distributed in many ways, some of which allow for exclusion of nonpayers while others don't. Almost all goods *could* be produced "publicly," that is, in a way that would make it difficult to exclude nonpayers, or privately. It may often be the case that a good's "publicness" reflects the fact that government has produced it without regard to excludability. As Tom G. Palmer wrote in *Cato Policy Report* in 1983,

> The argument for state provision is framed in purely static, rather than dynamic, terms: *given* a good, for which the marginal cost of making it available to one more person is zero (or less than the cost of exclusion), it is inefficient to expend resources to exclude nonpurchasers. But this begs the question. Since we live in a world where goods are not a *given,* but have to be produced, the problem is how best to produce these goods. An argument for state *provision* that assumes the goods are already produced is no argument at all.

The question then becomes whether it is more efficient to let entrepreneurs find ways to supply goods at a profit on the market or to turn the provision of important goods over to government, where we will encounter such problems as a lack of real market signals, an absence of incentives, and a decision-making process dominated by special interests and political influence. The basic argument of this book has been that valuable goods and services are best provided in the competitive marketplace. In this chapter, we'll look at some specific examples of goods and services that people thought the market couldn't provide but found that it not only could but did.

## Some Classic Examples That *Weren't* Public Goods

The traditional example of a public good was the lighthouse. Obviously, economists told generations of students, lighthouses couldn't be supplied privately because it would be impossible to charge everyone who would benefit from the lighthouse. From John Stuart Mill's *Principles of Political Economy* in 1848 to Nobel laureate Paul A. Samuelson's *Economics,* read by millions of modern American college students, textbooks pointed to the lighthouse to show the need for government provision of public goods.

Then in 1974 an economist decided to find out how lighthouses had actually been provided. Ronald H. Coase of the University of Chicago, who would also go on to win a Nobel Prize, investigated the history of lighthouses in Britain and found that they had not been built or financed by government:

> The early history shows that, contrary to the beliefs of many economists, a lighthouse service can be provided by private enterprise. . . . The lighthouses were built, operated, financed and owned by private individuals. . . . The role of the government was limited to the establishment and enforcement of property rights in the lighthouse.

Tolls were collected at ports; recognizing the value of the lighthouses, shipowners were glad to pay. In the nineteenth century, all British lighthouses became the property of Trinity House, an ancient organization that had apparently evolved out of a medieval seamen's guild, but the service was still financed out of tolls paid by ships.

After Coase's article appeared, the economist Kenneth Goldin wrote, "Lighthouses are a favorite example of public goods, because most economists cannot imagine a method of exclusion. (All this proves is that economists are less imaginative than lighthouse keepers.)"

Another classic example of a public good, though much newer than the lighthouse case, was beekeeping. Several distinguished twentieth-century economists argued that apple growers benefit from the presence of bees because they pollinate the apple blossoms; but the beekeepers have no incentive to help the apple growers, and bees can't be confined to particular farms, so there will be less investment in beekeeping than would be good for the economy. Again, it seemed plausible and even obvious—so obvious in theory that no one bothered to check the facts.

When economist Stephen Cheung of the University of Washington went out to examine the Washington apple-growing business, he found once again that businesspeople were already doing what economists said couldn't be done. There was a long history of contractual arrangements between apple growers and beekeepers. Those contracts ensured that beekeepers would have an incentive to supply the bees that apple growers profited from. Informal agreements among the apple growers ensured that all of them paid similar amounts to the beekeepers instead of trying to free-ride off the other growers. Those informal agreements, like the written contracts, are part of the vast network of cooperation that we call the market process or civil society. Economists who wanted to point out examples of market failure were running out of cases, as other economists actually examined the working of the market.

## When Does Government Provide Services?

It's usually assumed that government steps in to provide a service when the private sector fails to supply it. Even if that were true, it would raise the question of why people should be taxed to supply a service that they weren't willing to pay for. Unless a good case can be made that the particular good or service is a public good—and as we've seen, that's difficult to do—then the argument for government provision is simply that some person's preferences should be substituted for the decisions that millions of consumers make by spending their own money.

In fact, however, government usually doesn't supply a service that isn't being provided in the market. Rather, politicians promise to give people something at public expense that people don't like paying for. Provision by a bureaucratic monopoly doesn't actually make the service cheaper, but it does conceal the cost. People no longer connect a specific payment with the service, so they appreciate getting a formerly expensive service apparently for free, even though they wish their taxes wouldn't keep going up. The political opportunity to make gains by offering a new government service seems to come when enough people are paying for the service that many voters would prefer to have the expense taken off their hands.

The economist W. Allen Wallis argues that education in Britain and the United States is a good example of this. He writes, "In 1833, when the government of England first began to subsidize schools, at least two-thirds of the youth of the working class were literate, and the school population had doubled in a decade—although until then the government had deliberately *hindered* the spread of literacy to the 'lower orders' because it feared the consequences of printed propaganda." (Emphasis added.) By 1870, when government education was made free and compulsory, nearly all young people were literate. Their literacy had been achieved in schools that charged fees, including the inexpensive "dames' schools" set up by working-class families. The philosopher James Mill had noted as early as 1813 "the rapid progress which the love of education is making among the lower orders in England."

In the United States, too, Wallis writes, "the government began to provide 'free' schooling only after schooling had become nearly universal." State governments may have decided to make education free, compulsory, and government-run in the late nineteenth century in order to win favor with voters who would no longer pay directly for schools, or in order to impose a particular religious and political agenda on the schools, but it is clear that state action was not needed to make schooling widely available.

Medicare was another example of a service that was being provided privately, at individual expense, until the federal government took it over. A 1957 survey by the National Opinion Research Center found that "about one person in twenty in the older population [aged sixty-five years or older] reported that he was doing without needed medical care because he lacked money for such care." If more than 90 percent of the elderly could afford the medical care they needed, why was a government program needed to provide medical care for all the elderly? Wallis sums up the lessons this way:

> The task of the political entrepreneur, then, is to identify services which are being purchased by substantial and identifiable blocs of his electorate and to devise means by which the cost of these services will be transferred to the public. Successful innovation lies not in getting something done that was not being done before, but in transferring the costs to the public at large. Only if fairly large numbers of voters are already paying for the service

will the offer to relieve them of the cost be likely to influence their votes.

A more recent example might be government subsidies for child care. As more and more parents pay for child care outside the home, there is a larger constituency of people who would like to be relieved of the expense. Thus politicians begin to declare that child care is a national responsibility or that parents "can't afford" child-care expenses. Actually, they *can* afford it—they *are* affording it—but they don't especially like paying for it. The politicians never address exactly why childless people and stay-at-home mothers should be taxed to pay for the care of other people's children, but taxes have become so large and so seemingly inevitable that voters don't seem to connect rising tax burdens with new services from government.

When a service is transferred from the market to the government, of course, its provision is no longer directly responsive to the consumers but will increasingly reflect the preferences of the providers rather than the customers. Recipients of government services can influence them only through the cumbersome political process rather than by the much more efficient process of choosing among competing providers.

## The Contemporary Flight from Government Services

These days government endeavors to supply more goods and services than anyone could count, and people are increasingly disillusioned with the quality of government services. The world is moving rapidly into the Information Age, except for the schools and the post office. Giant financial-services providers offer an array of products designed to meet each customer's needs, with twenty-four-hour customer service, except for Social Security and other government-run systems. Government parks, streets, housing projects, and schools are increasingly dirty and dangerous. That's why more and more Americans seek to flee government services, often to pay extra for products and services that they've already paid for in taxes.

Robert Reich, secretary of labor in the Clinton administration and author of several best-selling books on economic change, has complained about what he calls "the secession of the successful"; in 1995 he told University of Maryland graduates that the richest Americans are walling themselves off from the rest of society—working in the suburbs, shopping in secure suburban malls, and even living in private communities. Worse, he said, they are resisting government efforts to spend their tax dollars outside their own communities. Social democrats like Reich concerned about community values ought to reflect on what their policies have done to divide Americans. They've given government so many tasks, and so undermined the old notions of personal responsibility and morality, that government can no longer perform its basic function of protecting us from physical harm. They have centralized and bureaucratized the schools so that little learning goes on there. They have nationalized and bureaucratized charity. Is it any wonder that people flee the institutions thus created?

## Communications

The U.S. Postal Service is one of the world's largest monopolies, and it displays all the sluggishness we expect from a government-run monopoly. Every other form of information transfer has been changed beyond recognition in the past generation, but the Postal Service still chugs along with 800,000 employees delivering letters the old-fashioned way, just a little bit slower each year. The price of a megabit of memory in a personal computer has fallen from $46,000 to $1 in fifteen years, but the price of stamps keeps rising. We've heard all sorts of horror stories about the post office—200 pounds of mail found under a viaduct in Chicago, 800,000 pieces of first-class mail stashed in tractor-trailer trucks near a Maryland postal facility because mail isn't counted as "delayed" unless it's inside a facility—but the big issue is speed and reliability of communications.

In areas where competition is allowed, the U.S. Postal Service has lost almost all its market share. Its share of the parcel post market fell from 65 percent twenty-five years ago to 6 percent in 1990, and its share of overnight deliveries fell from 100 percent to 12 percent or less (industry estimates vary). Even postal boxes and counter service are increasingly provided by firms like Mail Boxes Etc., which was described by one customer as "just what you'd like the post office to be"—friendly, efficient service with helpful accessories like boxes and packing tape. Given a choice, businesses and individuals overwhelmingly opt to have their letters and packages delivered by competitive private firms.

With first-class mail, however, there is no choice. The U.S. Postal Service has a legal monopoly, which means it is illegal for a private firm to offer to carry a letter to its recipient, except for "urgent" communications, for which private firms must charge at least $3. The USPS takes that "urgent" exception seriously; it conducts surveillance, with binoculars and telescopes, of shipments and delivery trucks, and sends agents into private firms to audit what they're sending out by Federal Express or United Parcel Service. It imposes hundreds of thousands of dollars in fines each year on firms whose privately delivered packages are deemed not to be urgent. One would think a firm's willingness to pay several dollars to get a piece of mail delivered the next day would be adequate evidence of its urgency, but the Postal Service believes it is the best judge of what's urgent for private businesses.

Meanwhile, private firms and individuals are increasingly looking for ways to get around the postal monopoly. In a sense, faxes and electronic mail are eroding the Postal Service's share even of a market where it has a legal monopoly. Already, it is estimated that 50 percent of telephone traffic across the Atlantic and 30 percent of U.S.-Pacific traffic is fax messages. Electronic mail will be even more revolutionary. Steve Gibson of the Bionomics Institute points out that Gutenberg's invention of movable type cut the cost of copying written information a thousandfold in just forty years. By contrast, he says, in the first twenty-five years after the invention of the microprocessor in 1971, the cost of copying information dropped ten-million-fold. During the next decade, computing power is expected to rise 100 times; and bandwidth, the size of the "pipe" that carries digital information like e-mail, will increase 1,000 times. Letter mail will soon be left in the dustbin of history.

In the late 1970s the Postal Service tried to protect its monopoly by moving to monopolize electronic mail. That's the natural reaction of a monopolist to potential competition, and we can all be glad the plan failed. Now the question is why a clunky bureaucracy should have a monopoly on letter mail. Maybe if the postal monopoly were eliminated, private firms could find an efficient way to go on delivering mail house-to-house for a few more years. Otherwise, the economy will treat the Postal Service like a disruption in a telephone line and route important traffic around it.

## Education

We spend more money every year on the public schools—three times as much in real terms as we spent in 1960—yet test scores decline and many urban schools are actually dangerous. According to Keith Geiger, president of the National Education Association, about 40 percent of big-city public school teachers send *their* children to private schools. They must know something. Yet the NEA bitterly resists making such choices easy for other families; it spent $16 million to defeat just one school-choice initiative, in California in 1993.

Many Americans have chosen to take their children out of government schools and send them to private schools, in effect paying twice for education. Among those parents are President Clinton, Vice President Gore, Senator Edward M. Kennedy, the Reverend Jesse Jackson, and Children's Defense Fund founder Marian Wright Edelman, all staunch opponents of school choice. Less wealthy families find it difficult to pay high taxes and then pay again for private education. Nevertheless, some families think private education is worth whatever sacrifice it takes. The Institute for Independent Education has identified 390 small black-run schools across the country and finds that 22 percent of their students come from families making less than $15,000 a year, while another 35 percent of families earn $15,000 to $35,000.

Other families, often those with more political skills, try to game the system, sneaking their children into better schools in another part of town or a nearby town. Families use friends' and relatives' addresses to enroll their children in other school districts, establish mail drops, or get school officials to grant them waivers so their children can go to better schools. In response, school officials have taken to videotaping children coming off the subway to find out-of-district students, and they've asked legislatures to stiffen the penalties for "school enrollment fraud."

Many families have given up on organized schooling altogether and begun teaching their children at home. Families choose home schooling for a variety of reasons. Many object to what they see as aggressive secularism in the government schools and want to give their children a religiously based education. Others dislike the conformity and authoritarianism that are probably inherent in the process of grouping small children in classes of twenty to thirty and trying to teach all of them the same thing at the same time. "Public schools as we know them are an aberrant bureaucracy," says David Colfax, who has sent three home-schooled sons to Harvard University. Mothers who want to stay home with their children may find home schooling a less expensive alternative than private education. And some families just think the schools don't do a good job of teaching the basics.

Estimates on the number of children being home-schooled vary widely, from about 500,000 to as many as 1.5 million, but all observers agree that the number has grown rapidly in the past twenty years. There are newsletters for Christian, Jewish, black, and sixties-secular home-schooling families. There are on-line services for home schoolers and sports leagues to bring them together for physical activity and social interaction. Home schooling means opting out of government, not civil society.

Despite the good test scores earned by home schoolers, school systems have bitterly resisted letting parents educate their own children. A Michigan education official defended the state's arrest of a mother who wasn't a certified teacher by saying, "The state has an interest in the future of the state, and the children are the future of the state." School officials seem to regard home schooling as a rejection of their schools, which of course it is. In addition, school districts receive an average of $4,000 to $7,000 per student in state and federal aid, so each home-schooled child means less money for school administrators. Most states have liberalized their laws, but some 2,500 home-schooling families a year seek legal advice from the Home School Legal Defense Association (there were seventy-five cases contested in court in 1991, up from fifty-five in 1987).

The next big challenge to the education establishment will be the entry of for-profit firms into the education business. Americans spend about $600 billion a year on education, half of that for kindergarten through twelfth-grade schools. If that money were all spent by families, it seems likely that for-profit companies could provide education that would be far superior to stultified monopoly school systems. But the money is spent collectively, of course, which means that for-profit firms have largely been kept out of the field, so educational technology has remained at eighteenth-century levels. But schools are becoming so inefficient that 60 percent of school boards have considered hiring firms to run some part of the school operation. The First Annual Education Industry Conference was held in 1996, and a new newsletter, the *Education Industry Report,* has compiled a list of twenty-five education companies in an Education Industry Index like the Dow-Jones Index; it's soaring. Companies like Sylvan Learning Systems and Huntington Learning Centers are making a profit teaching children what the schools have failed to teach them. Hooked on Phonics advertises, "We have a money-back guarantee. Don't you wish the schools did?"

The problem is not that civil society and the market *can't* supply education. The problem is that special interests that benefit from the current tax-supported system won't let parents keep their own money and purchase education where they find the best product. But in the next few years, as government schools continue to deteriorate and new learning technologies become available even in a severely stunted market, families will increasingly bypass state schooling to get the education they need.

### Private Communities

Despite Robert Reich's advice, 4 million Americans have chosen to live in some 30,000 private communities. Another 24 million live in locked condominiums, cooperatives, or apartment houses, which are small gated communities. Why do people choose to live in private communities? First, to protect themselves from crime and the dramatic deterioration of public services in many large cities. A college professor complains about "the new Middle Ages . . . a kind of medieval landscape in which defensible, walled and gated towns dot the countryside." People built walls around their cities in the Middle Ages to protect themselves from bandits and marauders, and many Americans are making the same choice.

Private communities are a peaceful but comprehensive response to the failure of big government. Like their federal counterpart, local governments today tax us more heavily than ever but offer deteriorating services in return. Not only do police seem unable to combat rising crime, but the schools get worse and worse, garbage and litter don't get picked up, potholes aren't fixed, panhandlers confront us on every corner. Private communities can provide physical safety for their residents, partly by excluding from the community people who are neither residents nor guests.

But there's a broader reason for choosing to live in a private community. Local governments can't satisfy the needs and preferences of all their residents. People have different requirements in terms of population density, type of housing, presence of children, and so on. Rules that might cater to some citizens' preferences would be unconstitutional or offensive to the free-wheeling spirit of other citizens.

Private communities can solve some of these public goods problems. In the larger developments, the homes, the streets, the sewers, the parklands are all private. After buying a house or condominium there, residents pay a monthly fee that covers security, maintenance, and management. Many of the communities are both gated and guarded.

Many have rules that would range from annoying to infuriating to unconstitutional if imposed by a government: regulations on house colors, shrubbery heights, on-street parking, even gun ownership. People choose such communities partly because they find the rules—even strict rules—congenial.

In a 1989 issue of *Public Finance Quarterly,* economists Donald J. Boudreaux and Randall G. Holcombe offer a theoretical explanation for the growing popularity of private communities, which they call contractual governments. Having constitutional rules drawn up by a single developer, who then offers the property and the rules as a package to buyers, reduces the decision-making costs of developing appropriate rules and allows people to choose communities on the basis of the kind of rules they offer. The desire to make money is a strong incentive for the developer to draw up good rules.

Boudreaux and Holcombe write, "The establishment of a contractual government appears to be the closest thing to a real-world social contract that can be found because it is created behind something analogous to a veil [of ignorance], and because everyone unanimously agrees to move into the contractual government's jurisdiction."

Fred Foldvary points out that most "public goods" exist within a particular space, so the goods can be provided only to people who rent or purchase access to the space. That allows entrepreneurs to overcome the problem of people trying to "free-ride" off others' payments for public goods. Entrepreneurs try to make their space attractive to customers by supplying the best possible combination of characteristics, which will vary from space to space. Foldvary points out that private communities, shopping centers, industrial parks, theme parks, and hotel interiors are all private spaces created by entrepreneurs, who have a much better incentive than governments to discover and respond to consumer demand. And many private entrepreneurs competing for business can supply a much wider array of choices than governments will.

Private communities—including condominiums and apartment buildings—come in virtually unlimited variety. Prices vary widely, as does the general level of amenities. Some have policies banning children, pets, guns, garish colors, rentals, or whatever else might be perceived to reduce residents' enjoyment of the space. The growing "cohousing" movement responds to the need many people feel for a closer sense of community by offering living spaces centered around a common house for group meals and activities. Some people create cohousing arrangements based on a shared religious commitment.

Private communities are a vital part of civil society. They give more people an opportunity to find the kinds of living (or working, or shopping, or entertainment) arrangements they want. They reflect the understanding of a free society as not one large community but a community of communities.

## Law and Justice

Libertarians believe that the one proper function of government is to protect our rights. To that end, governments hire police to protect us from aggression by our neighbors and establish courts to settle legal disputes. Yet, perhaps because they are distracted by all the additional tasks they have taken on, governments aren't doing even these basic functions well, and people are forced to find alternatives in the marketplace.

As courts become backlogged and people find litigation both costly and unpleasant, more people are taking disputes to private arbitrators. Decisions by arbitrators are legally binding and, if necessary, can be enforced in the public courts, although the whole point of private arbitration is to avoid the costs and delays of going to court. The next wave in alternative dispute resolution (ADR) is likely to be mediation, a nonbinding, less formal process in which a neutral party helps disputants to reach a settlement among themselves. Many people prefer mediation because it helps to avoid the adversarial atmosphere and lingering bad feelings of both courts and binding arbitration. Since most disputes are among people who will go on dealing with one another—family members, neighbors, businesses that have ongoing relationships—it makes sense to try to work problems out without having a third party impose a solution.

There are about 200,000 cases filed in the federal courts each year, while the private, nonprofit American Arbitration Association handles about 60,000 arbitrations and mediations. JAMS/Endispute, a for-profit firm, handled about 20,000 cases in 1995, double the number three years earlier. AAA, JAMS/Endispute, and other arbitration firms have large networks of "neutrals"—impartial third parties available to settle disputes for customers. Those employed by JAMS/Endispute are all lawyers, many of them retired judges, while AAA offers both lawyers and business professionals. Providers argue that, compared to the government courts, ADR saves time and money, allows procedural flexibility, gives disputants more control over the arbitration process, preserves relationships, offers confidentiality, and provides closure, because arbitration and mediation agreements cannot be appealed except in extraordinary circumstances. Many business contracts provide that any dispute arising from the contract will be settled by a representative of a particular ADR firm. Arbitrators make decisions based on the terms of the contract and on common law, which was itself originally a private institution and is still a process of case-by-case lawmaking rather than legislative edict.

Meanwhile, concerns over crime have also spurred Americans to rely more on private police officers. There are about 550,000 officers serving on state and local police forces; there are about 1.5 million private police officers. Many of those are employed by businesses to guard the firm's property, shipments, and so on. Others work for security firms such as Brink's, which contract their services out to banks, businesses, housing developments, and event organizers. There would be fewer private police officers if the government did a better job of preventing crime and punishing criminals, but private guards also provide services that would not be appropriately provided by government, such as round-the-clock protection for factories, offices, and housing developments.

In some areas, businesses and individuals have paid for extra police protection in a sort of public-private partnership. Merchants and residents in the Koreatown–West Adams neighborhood of Los Angeles raised about $400,000 and obtained a building for a neighborhood police station. Some people complained that taxpayers shouldn't have to pay extra to get basic services, others that not every neighborhood could afford to pay for police service. But at least such privately funded efforts avoid the problem of agreeing to pay higher taxes to a vast jurisdiction like Los Angeles in the hope that *your* neighborhood *might* get some additional services.

## Insurance and Futures

People have often thought that insurance is a valuable service for government to provide. Many of the largest federal programs are intended to insure Americans against economic and other risks: Social Security, Medicare and Medicaid, deposit insurance, flood insurance, and more. The general argument for insurance is to spread risks; a loss that would be disastrous for a single individual can be absorbed by a large group of individuals. We pool our money in an insurance plan to guard against the small possibility of a catastrophic event.

The argument for government insurance, as opposed to competitive private insurers, is that you can spread the risk over a larger number of people. But as George L. Priest of the Yale Law School points out, government insurance has had many unfortunate results. There's no economic advantage to creating an insurance pool larger than necessary, and there are definite disadvantages to large monopolies. Government is very bad at charging risk-appropriate premiums, so its insurance tends to be too expensive for risk-averse people and too cheap for those who engage in high-risk activities. And government dramatically compounds the "moral hazard" problem—that is, the tendency of people who have insurance to take more risks. Insurance companies try to control this by having deductibles and copayments, so the insured will still face some loss beyond what insurance covers, and by excluding certain kinds of activities from coverage (like suicide or behavior that is more risky than the insurance pool is designed for). For both economic and political reasons, government usually doesn't employ such tools, so it actually encourages more risk taking.

Priest cites several specific examples: Federal savings-and-loan insurance increased the risk level of investments; the savings-and-loan companies would reap the profits from high-risk ventures, but the taxpayers would make up the losses, so why not go for the big return? Government-provided unemployment insurance increases both the extent and the duration of unemployment; people would find new jobs sooner if they didn't have unemployment insurance, or if their own insurance rates were affected by how much they used, as car insurance rates are. Priest writes, "I will not go so far as to claim that government-provided insurance increases the frequency of natural disasters. On the other hand, I have no doubt whatsoever that the government provision of insurance increases the magnitude of *losses* from natural disasters." Flood insurance, for instance, provided by the government at less than the market price, encourages more building on flood plains and on the fragile barrier islands off the East Coast.

The desire to reduce one's exposure to risk is natural, and markets provide people with means to that end. But when people sought to reduce risk through government insurance programs, the result was to channel resources toward *more* risky activities and thus to increase the level of risk and the level of losses suffered by the whole society.

Still, the market has provided many opportunities for people to choose the level of risk with which they're comfortable. Many kinds of insurance are available. Different investments—stocks, bonds, mutual funds, certificates of deposit—allow people to balance risk versus return in the way they prefer. Farmers can reduce their risks by selling their expected harvest before it comes in, locking in a price. They're protected against falling prices, but they lose the opportunity to make big profits from rising prices. Commodities markets give farmers and others the opportunity to hedge against price shifts. Many people don't understand commodities and futures markets, or even the simpler securities markets; in Tom Wolfe's novel *The Bonfire of the Vanities,* the bond trader Sherman McCoy thought of himself as Master of the Universe but couldn't explain to his daughter the value of what he did. Politicians and popular writers rail against "paper entrepreneurs" or "money changers," but those mysterious markets not only guide capital to projects where it will best serve consumer demand, they also help millions of Americans to regulate their risks.

A new twist for farmers is the opportunity to contract with food processors to grow specific crops. More than 90 percent of vegetables are now grown under production contracts, along with smaller percentages of other crops. The contracts give farmers less independence but also less risk, which many of them prefer.

Meanwhile, major commodities markets like the Chicago Board of Trade, the Chicago Mercantile Exchange, and the New York Mercantile Exchange (Nymex) are looking for new investment options to offer to customers. The Chicago Merc recently began offering milk price futures—allowing people to lock in milk prices or bet on price shifts—in response to deregulation, which will likely mean lower but fluctuating prices. The Nymex established a market in electricity futures, which will come in handy as electric utilities are deregulated.

The Board of Trade is one of the players looking for new ways to protect insurance companies—and by extension, everyone who buys insurance or invests in insurance companies—from the threat posed by megadisasters. According to the *New York Times,* "Two of the most destructive natural disasters in American history have occurred" in the past few years: Hurricane Andrew in 1992, which cost insurers $16 billion in South Florida, and the 1994 Los Angeles earthquake, which cost $11 billion. (Note that the reason these were the "most destructive" disasters ever is that Americans own more wealth than ever, so financial losses are greater.) Insurers fear a disaster of $50 billion magnitude, which could put insurance companies out of business and even be too much for the reinsurance business, which sells policies to protect insurers from large losses. They are looking for new ways to spread the risk, including catastrophe futures on the Board of Trade, with which insurers could hedge against the possibility of large losses. Investors would make money by, in effect, betting that there would be no such catastrophe.

Reinsurers are also offering "act of God" bonds that would pay very high interest but would require bondholders to forgo repayment in the event of disaster. Catastrophe futures and "act of God" bonds will help keep insurance coverage available and reasonably priced. They also raise the question: If the market can adequately deal with even the prospect of multi-billion-dollar financial disasters, why does government need to intervene in the economic system at all?

## Bypassing the State

The twentieth century has been a failed experiment in big government. Every day more people see more ways that problems could be better solved by profit-seeking companies, mutual-aid associations, or charities than by government. Private capital markets can provide actuarially sound insurance and offer better retirement benefits than Social Security. One of the world's largest engineering projects, the $12 billion tunnel under the English Channel, was designed, financed, built, owned, and operated by a private consortium. A company called Human Capital Resources wants to sell equity investments in the future earning power of college students as an alternative to student loans—better return for investors, less postgraduation burden on students, and no cost to the taxpayers.

Private communities, based on governance by consent, can be better tailored to the needs and preferences of 250 million diverse Americans than can local governments. Private schools provide a better education at lower cost than government schools, and in the next few years information technology and for-profit companies will revolutionize learning. Private charities get people *off* welfare rather than snaring them *in* it.

Some day soon we may be able to bypass governments to get all the goods and services we need. But in the meantime, our $2.5 trillion federal-state-local governments are not going to give up their power without a fight. The U.S. Postal Service tenaciously clings to its legal monopoly. School boards and teachers' unions declare that they won't let children "escape" from their schools, and they spend millions to prevent the implementation of school-choice plans. The people who benefit from the existing system won't willingly downsize government even if all the customers desert it. As school enrollment in the District of Columbia fell by 33,000—about 25 percent—the system actually *added* 516 administrators. The 800,000 postal employees are not going to quietly accept layoffs even if we send all our communications electronically.

We cannot simply wait for "social forces" or technology to automatically replace bloated government. To ensure that such changes happen, individuals will have to demand their *right* to choose schools for their children, to compete with the U.S. Postal Service, to invest their money in a secure private retirement fund. And then taxpayers will have to work to ensure that government stops producing services no one uses anymore.

## Chapter 12

# THE LIBERTARIAN FUTURE

𝒫olitical society has failed to usher in the new age of peace and plenty it promised. The failure of coercive government has been proportional to the level of coercion and the grandiosity of its promises. Fascist and communist governments that sought to eliminate civil society and to subsume individuals entirely in a larger cause are now recognized as abject failures; they promised community and prosperity but delivered poverty, stagnation, resentment, and atomism.

The libertarian critique of socialism, long derided by left-leaning intellectuals, has been proven correct. Now the challenge to libertarianism is greater. With fascism and socialism largely off the political scene, the conflict in the twenty-first century will be between libertarianism and social democracy, a watered-down version of socialism whose advocates accept the necessity of civil society and the market process but find constant reasons to limit, control, shape, and obstruct the decisions individuals make. (Social democracy is often called liberalism in the United States, but I prefer not to tarnish the memory of a word that once stood for individual freedom.) As for modern American conservatism, we can expect to see its adherents divide into supporters of civil society and advocates of political intervention to bring about a particular social order. Eventually, the statist conservatives will find themselves aligned with the social democrats as defenders of political society against civil society, a trend that has already begun with the protectionist Buchanan movement and the growing tendency among conservatives not to limit government but to use it to impose conservative values.

Because social democracy in the United States and Western Europe never entirely replaced civil society and markets, its failures have been less obvious. That is good news for the American and European peoples, but it presents a bigger challenge for libertarians who want to point out the problems of intervention and make the case for greater individual freedom and strictly limited government. Still, the evidence of the failure of political society has become overwhelming, and new examples appear every day.

Welfare-state transfer programs are becoming unsustainable around the world, and the impending retirement of the baby boomers will make Social Security's commitments impossible to meet, even after massive tax increases. Information technology is being revolutionized, except for those forms monopolized by the state—the schools and the post office—which get a little less efficient and a lot more expensive every year. Examples from Watergate to Whitewater, from Waco to the War on Drugs, remind us that power corrupts. Taxes and regulation have dramatically slowed down economic growth, just when improved technology, better communications, and more efficient capital markets ought to give us *increased* rates of growth. Slower growth and the increasing perception that rewards are handed out by government on the basis of identity politics and political pull, rather than earned in the competitive marketplace, encourage group resentments and social conflict.

## The Washington That Roosevelt Built

The widespread disillusionment with big government, and the growing attraction of the libertarian critique, have caused the defenders of political society to launch a counterattack. What's interesting about the most popular recent defenses of activist government is their modesty. Gone are the sweeping calls for social change of the 1930s and the starry-eyed crusades of the

1960s. Although such old-fashioned models can still be found among tenured professors, politicians and authors who want to appeal to a wide audience now make only modest claims for what government can do.

Consider the 1992 book by David Osborne and Ted Gaebler, *Reinventing Government: How the Entrepreneurial Spirit Is Transforming the Public Sector,* which was widely hailed by such "new Democrats" as Bill Clinton and Al Gore. Osborne and Gaebler recognize that "the kinds of governments that developed during the industrial era, with their sluggish centralized bureaucracies, their preoccupations with rules and regulations, and their hierarchical chains of command, no longer work very well." They lay out ten things government should become: catalytic, community owned, competitive, mission driven, results oriented, customer driven, enterprising, anticipatory, decentralized, and market oriented. The striking thing about that list is that it's very close to a description not of government but of the market process. The leading theorists of government activism in our time promise that we can make government act like the market.

Or consider Jacob Weisberg's 1996 book *In Defense of Government,* which sets forth five principles for "resurrecting government": (1) accept that life is risky and stop trying to legislate risk out of existence; (2) stop promising more than government can deliver; (3) be willing to abolish failed, outdated, or low-priority programs; (4) stop delegating Congress's lawmaking authority to the bureaucracy; and (5) promise that government won't get any bigger than it is now, in terms of government share of GNP. While Weisberg retains a touching belief in a "wise, effective, and benevolent federal government," his policy program is restrained compared with those of previous generations of enthusiasts for state activism.

Despite these chastened interventionists, however, and despite President Clinton's proclamation that "the era of big government is over," government in fact remains bigger than ever. The federal government forcibly extracts $1.6 trillion a year from those who produce it, and state and local governments take another trillion. Every year, Congress adds another 6,000 pages of statute law and regulators print 60,000 pages of new regulations in the *Federal Register.* Lawyers agree that no business can possibly be in full compliance with federal regulation.

Most of our political leaders are still living in the Washington that Roosevelt built, the Washington where, if you think of a good idea, you create a government program. Consider a few examples:

- Senator Bob Dole reads the Tenth Amendment ("The powers not delegated to the United States by the Constitution, nor prohibited by it to the States, are reserved to the States respectively, or to the people") on the campaign trail but introduces bills to federalize criminal law, welfare policy, and the definition of marriage.
- Vice President Gore announces a plan to tear down public housing projects, saying, "These crime-infested monuments to a failed policy are killing the neighborhoods around them." He reminds his listeners, "In years past, Washington told people around the country what to do, dictating wisdom from on high. And let's be honest: some of that wisdom really wasn't very wise." Then he announces a plan to . . . build new public housing projects.
- Senator Dan Coats (R-Ind.) says that Republicans "need to offer a vision of rebuilding broken communities—not through government, but through those private institutions and ideals that nurture lives" and argues that "even if government undermined civil society, it cannot directly reconstruct it." Then he proposes nineteen federal laws to establish a model school for at-risk youth, implement a waiting period for divorcing couples, fund religious maternity shelters, set up savings accounts for the poor, and more.
- Secretary of Housing and Urban Development Henry Cisneros promises to "decentralize with a vengeance" because churches, neighborhood groups, and small businesses "know at least as much and are better positioned than the organizationally encumbered government in Washington" to improve their own communities. But then he proposes to set up classrooms in public housing units and require all residents

to attend class every day in prenatal training, educational day care, high school equivalency sessions, or seminars for the elderly.

• Christian Coalition executive director Ralph Reed writes that America is united around "a vision of a society based on two fundamental beliefs. The first belief is that all men, created equal in the eyes of God with certain inalienable rights, are free to pursue the longings of their heart. The second belief is that the sole purpose of government is to protect those rights." But his political program includes banning abortion, forbidding gay people to marry, and censoring the Internet.

And on and on it goes, in any day's newspaper: the president has a plan to reduce the price of gasoline and to raise the price of beef; the administration wants Japan and China to set specific targets for U.S. imports; a panel of experts wants to reduce the number of doctors; county planners require developers to build "affordable" housing, then a few years later develop a plan to encourage "upscale" housing. The era of big government is over, but the government doesn't seem to know it yet.

Meanwhile, activists organize marches and rallies for all good things under the sun: jobs, children, housing, health care, the environment. It's hard to organize a rally for civil society and the market process—the source of the ideas and the wealth that allow us to provide better jobs, health care, child care, and homes and use scarce resources more efficiently.

## Centralization, Devolution, and Order

Two competing tendencies can be seen in world politics in the 1990s: centralization and devolution. Despite the talk in Washington about devolution and the Tenth Amendment, both Republicans and Democrats in Congress continue to offer federal solutions to the problems that concern them, eliminating local control, experimentation, and competing solutions. State courts increasingly demand that all the schools in the state be funded equally and be regulated by state guidelines. The bureaucrats of the European Union in Brussels try to centralize regulation at the continental level, partly to prevent any European government from making itself more attractive to investors by offering lower taxes or less regulation.

Paradoxically, nation-states today are too big *and* too small. They're too big to be responsive and manageable. India has more than 1 million voters for each of its more than 500 legislators; can they possibly represent the interests of all their constituents or write laws that make sense for almost a billion people? In any country larger than a city, local conditions vary greatly and no national plan can make sense everywhere. At the same time, even nation-states are often too small to be effective economic units. Should Belgium, or even France, have a national railroad or a national television network, when rails and broadcast signals can so easily cross national boundaries? The great value of the European Union is not the reams of regulation produced by Eurocrats but rather the opportunity for businesses to produce and sell across a market larger than the United States. A common market doesn't require centralized regulation; it only requires that national governments not prevent their citizens from trading with citizens of other countries.

Meanwhile, as centralized governments from Washington to Ottawa to Brussels to New Delhi try to centralize control and squelch regional differences and small-scale experiments, another trend is also visible. Businesspeople try to ignore government and find their natural trading partners, be it across the street or across national borders. Businesses in the triangle between Lyon, France; Geneva, Switzerland; and Turin, Italy, do more business among themselves than with the political capitals of Paris and Rome. Dominique Nouvellet, one of Lyon's leading venture capitalists, says, "People are rebelling against capitals that exercise too much control over their lives. Paris is filled with civil servants, while Lyon is filled with merchants who want the state to get off their back." Other cross-border economic regions include Toulouse and Montpellier, France, and Barcelona, Spain; Antwerp, Belgium, and Rotterdam, the Netherlands; and Maastricht, the Netherlands, with Liege, Belgium, and Aachen, Germany. National governments and national borders impede the creation of wealth in those areas.

Many regions are coming up with an old solution to the

problems of out-of-touch, out-of-control government: secession. The French-speaking people of Quebec agitate for independence from Canada. So do a growing number of people in British Columbia, who see that their trade ties to Seattle and Tokyo are greater than those with Ottawa and Toronto. The Lombard League has achieved rapid electoral success with its call for the secession of productive northern Italy from what it regards as Mafia-dominated, welfare-addicted southern Italy. There's an increasing likelihood of devolution or even independence for Scotland. National breakup may well be a solution to some of the problems of Africa, whose national boundaries were carved by colonial powers with little regard to ethnic identity or traditional trading patterns.

Even in the United States, we see more agitation for secession than we've seen in a long time. Staten Island voted to secede from New York City in 1993, but the state legislature blocked its path. Nine counties in western Kansas have petitioned Congress to be split off as a separate state. Activists in both northern and southern California have proposed that the giant state be split into two or three more manageable units. The San Fernando Valley of *American Graffiti* fame is brimming with demands to secede from the city of Los Angeles.

One of the most important lessons of America's economic success is the value of broadening the geographic area in which trade can flow freely while keeping government close to the communities that will have to live with its decisions. Switzerland may be an even better example of the benefits of free trade and decentralized power. Although it has only 7 million people, Switzerland has three major language groups and people with distinctly different cultures. It has solved the problem of cultural conflict with a very decentralized political system—twenty cantons and six half-cantons, which are responsible for most public affairs, and a weak central government, which handles foreign affairs, monetary policy, and enforcement of a bill of rights.

One of the key insights offered by the Swiss system is that cultural conflicts can be minimized when they don't become political conflicts. Thus, the more of life that is kept in the private sphere or at the local level, the less need there is for cultural groups to go to war over religion, education, language, and the like. Separation of church and state and a free market both limit the number of decisions made in the public sector, thus reducing the incentive for groups to vie for political control.

People around the world are coming to understand the benefits of limited government and devolution of power. Even a student from faraway Azerbaijan recently said at a conference, "My friends and I have been thinking, couldn't we solve the conflict between Armenians and Azerbaijanis not by moving the borders but by making them unimportant—by abolishing internal passports and allowing property ownership and the right to work on both sides of the border?"

Still, the centralists will not give up easily. The impulse to eliminate "inequities" among regions is strong. President Clinton said in 1995, "As president, I have to make laws that fit not only my folks back home in Arkansas and the people in Montana, but the whole of this country. And the great thing about this country is its diversity, its differences, and trying to harmonize those is our great challenge." A *Washington Post* columnist says that America "needs badly . . . a single education standard set by—who else?—the federal government." Kentucky governor Paul Patton says that if an innovative education program is working, all schools should have it, and if it isn't, none should.

But why? Why not let local school districts observe other districts, copy what seems to work, and adapt it to their own circumstances? And why does President Clinton feel that his challenge is to "harmonize" America's great diversity? Why not enjoy the diversity? The problem for centralizers is that appreciating diversity means accepting that different people and different places will have different situations and different results. The bottom-line question is whether centralized systems or competitive systems produce better results—that is, arrive at more solutions that although not perfect, are better than they might have been. Libertarians argue that our experience with competitive systems—whether that means democracy, federalism, free markets, or the vigorously competitive Western intellectual system—shows that they find better answers than imposed, centralized, one-size-fits-all systems.

Two large companies—ITT and AT&T—both announced in

1995 that they would split themselves into three parts because they had become too large and diverse to be managed efficiently. ITT had sales of about $25 billion a year, AT&T about $75 billion. If corporate managers and investors with their own money at stake can't run businesses that size effectively, can it really be possible for Congress and 2 million federal bureaucrats to manage a $1.6 trillion government—to say nothing of a $6 trillion economy?

## The Information Age

One big reason that the future will be libertarian is the arrival of the Information Age. Information is getting cheaper and cheaper and thus more widespread; increasingly, our problem is not a dearth but a glut of information. The Information Age is bad news for centralized bureaucracies. First, as information gets cheaper and more widely available, people will have less need for experts and authorities to make decisions for them. That doesn't mean we won't consult experts—in a complex world, none of us can be expert in everything—but it does mean we can choose our experts and make our own decisions. Governments will find it more difficult to keep their citizens in the dark about world affairs and about government malfeasance. Second, as information and commerce move faster, it will be increasingly difficult for sluggish governments to keep up. The chief effect of regulation on communications and financial services is to slow down the pace of change and keep consumers from receiving the full benefits that companies are striving to offer us. Third, privacy is going to be easier to maintain. Governments will try to block encryption technology and demand that every computer come with a government key—like the "Clipper Chip"—but those efforts will fail. Governments will find it increasingly difficult to pry into citizens' economic lives. Finally, as techno-entrepreneur Bill Frezza puts it, "coercive force cannot be projected across a network." As digital bits become more valuable than coal mines and factories, it will be more difficult for governments to exert their control.

Some people worry that the cost of computers and Internet

access creates a new divide between the haves and the have-nots, but in fact an adequate used computer and on-line access for a year can be had for the cost of a year's subscription to the *New York Times*—and nobody worries about the newspaper have-nots. In any case, the cost of computers is falling and will continue to fall, as did that of telephones and televisions, once the playthings of the rich. By mid-1996 entrepreneurs were offering free e-mail to any customer willing to put up with advertisements on the computer screen. There will be no haves and have-nots, says Louis Rossetto, editor of *Wired,* the libertarian bible of the Information Age: "Better to think of the haves and the have-laters. And the haves may be the ones who are really disadvantaged, since they are the guinea pigs for new technology, paying an arm and a leg for stuff that in a couple of years will be widely available for a fraction of its original price." Attempts to force companies to supply their technology to everyone at once or at a below-market cost will just reduce every entrepreneur's incentive to come up with a new product and thus slow down the pace of change.

As more of the value in our world reflects the products of our minds embedded in digital bits, traditional natural resources will become less relevant. Institutional structures and human capital will become far more important to wealth creation than oil or iron ore. States will find it more difficult to regulate capital and entrepreneurship as it becomes easier for people and wealth to move across borders. Countries will prosper by reducing taxes and regulation in order to keep innovators and investors at home and attract them from abroad.

Some visionaries of the Information Age have overstressed its differences from the industrial age. Many of the wealthiest countries of the seventeenth through the twentieth centuries—the Netherlands, Switzerland, Great Britain, Japan, Singapore—have been notably lacking in natural resources. They got rich the old-fashioned way—actually the new-fashioned, capitalist way—through the rule of law, economic freedom, and a hard-working and well-educated populace.

Still, the importance of free markets and individual effort will indeed be enhanced by the more open, participatory economy made possible by cyberspace. Peter Pitsch of the Hudson

Institute writes that "Hayek and Schumpeter are prophets for the Innovation Age," his term for the new economy. Hayek's analysis of spontaneous order and the immense dangers of coercive tampering with its complex workings is more relevant than ever in an era of unbounded opportunity and fast-paced change. And Schumpeter's point that "creative destruction is the essential fact about capitalism" will be more true than ever, as entrepreneurs have learned and will continue to learn to their chagrin. The overthrow of the mainframe by the personal computer, which cost IBM 70 percent of its market value in just five years, was a dramatic example of creative destruction. Will the PC itself be overthrown by the network? Will Microsoft be rocked as IBM was? As Hayek and Schumpeter would tell us, no one knows.

People have always had trouble seeing the order in the apparently chaotic market. Even as the price system constantly moves resources toward their best use, on the surface the market seems the very opposite of order—businesses failing, jobs being lost, people prospering at an uneven pace, investments revealed to have been wasted. The fast-paced Innovation Age will seem even more chaotic, with huge businesses rising and falling more rapidly than ever, and fewer people having long-term jobs. But the increased efficiency of transportation, communications, and capital markets will in fact mean even more order than the market could achieve in the industrial age. The point is to avoid using coercive government to "smooth out the excesses" or "channel" the market toward someone's desired result. Let the market work—let billions of people seek happiness in their own ways—and the second edition of this book will probably be composed on technology undreamed of in 1997.

## Toward a Framework for Utopia

Lots of political movements promise utopia: Just implement our program, and we'll usher in an ideal world. Libertarians offer something less, and more: a framework for utopia, as Robert Nozick put it.

My ideal community would probably not be your utopia.

The attempt to create heaven on earth is doomed to fail, because we have different ideas of what heaven would be like. As our society becomes more diverse, the possibility of our agreeing on one plan for the whole nation becomes even more remote. And in any case, we can't possibly anticipate the changes that progress will bring. Utopian plans always involve a static and rigid vision of the ideal community, a vision that can't accommodate a dynamic world. We can no more imagine what civilization will be like a century from now than the people of 1900 could have imagined today's civilization. What we need is not utopia but a free society in which people can design their own communities.

A libertarian society is only a framework for utopia. In such a society, government would respect people's right to make their own choices in accord with the knowledge available to them. As long as each person respected the rights of others, he would be free to live as he chose. His choice might well involve voluntarily agreeing with others to live in a particular kind of community. Individuals could come together to form communities in which they would agree to abide by certain rules, which might forbid or require particular actions. Since people would individually and voluntarily agree to such rules, they would not be giving up their rights but simply agreeing to the rules of a community that they would be free to leave. We already have such a framework, of course; in the market process we can choose from many different goods and services, and many people already choose to live in a particular kind of community. A libertarian society would offer *more* scope for such choices by leaving most decisions about living arrangements to the individual and the chosen community, rather than government's imposing everything from an exorbitant tax rate to rules about religious expression and health care.

Such a framework might offer thousands of versions of utopia, which might appeal to different kinds of people. One community might offer a high level of services and amenities, with correspondingly high prices and fees. Another might be more spartan, for those who prefer to save their money. One might be organized around a particular religious observance. Those who entered one community might forswear alcohol, tobacco, nonmarital sex, and pornography. Other people might prefer something like Copenhagen's Free City of Christiana, where cars, guns, and hard drugs are banned but soft drugs are tolerated and all decisions are at least theoretically made in communal meetings.

One difference between libertarianism and socialism is that a socialist society can't tolerate groups of people practicing freedom, but a libertarian society can comfortably allow people to choose voluntary socialism. If a group of people—even a very large group—wanted to purchase land and own it in common, they would be free to do so. The libertarian legal order would require only that no one be coerced into joining or giving up his property. Many people might choose a "utopia" very similar to today's small-town, suburban, or center-city environment, but we would all profit from the opportunity to choose other alternatives and to observe and emulate valuable innovations.

In such a society, government would tolerate, as Leonard Read put it, "anything that's peaceful." Voluntary communities could make stricter rules, but the legal order of the whole society would punish only violations of the rights of others. By radically downsizing and decentralizing government—by fully respecting the rights of each individual—we can create a society based on individual freedom and characterized by peace, tolerance, community, prosperity, responsibility, and progress.

Can we achieve such a world? It is hard to predict the short-term course of any society, but in the long run, the world will recognize the repressive and backward nature of coercion and the unlimited possibilities that freedom allows. The spread of commerce, industry, and information has undermined the age-old ways in which governments held men in thrall and is even now liberating humanity from the new forms of coercion and control developed by twentieth-century governments.

As we enter a new century and a new millenium, we encounter a world of endless possibility. The very premise of the world of global markets and new technologies is libertarianism. Neither stultifying socialism nor rigid conservatism could produce the free, technologically advanced society that we anticipate in the twenty-first century. If we want a dynamic world of prosperity and opportunity, we must make it a libertarian world. The simple and timeless principles of the American Revolution—individual liberty, limited government, and free markets—turn out to be even more powerful in today's world of instant communication, global markets, and unprecedented access to information than Jefferson or Madison could have imagined. Libertarianism is not just a framework for utopia, it is the essential framework for the future.

*Appendix*

# ARE YOU A LIBERTARIAN?

*L*ibertarianism starts with a simple statement of individual rights, but it raises hard questions. The fundamental political question is, do you make the decisions that are important to your life, or does someone else make them for you? Libertarians believe that individuals have both the right and the responsibility to make their own decisions. Nonlibertarians of all political stripes believe that the government should make some or many of the important decisions in an individual's life.

For instance, consider whether you agree with the following:

As long as I respect the rights of others, I should have the right to
    Read whatever I want to—even if it offends others in the community.
    Choose the medical treatment I think is best—even if it's risky.

If you answer yes to these questions, then you probably agree with some basic libertarian positions on personal freedoms: the government has no business establishing a particular religion, enforcing moral codes, or regulating pornography or hate speech. That doesn't mean libertarians endorse any of those particular choices, but it does mean they respect the right of adults to make their own choices. Now consider some other issues:

> As long as I deal with others honestly, I should have the right to
> Earn more money than others even if I don't contribute money to charity.
> Leave my wealth to my children even though other children will be born with less.

If you answer yes to these questions, then you agree with the basic libertarian goal of economic freedom. Now consider another way of looking at freedom:

Should the government protect each individual's right to life, liberty, and the pursuit of happiness, even though some people will earn more than others, or use its power to try to make people more equal in monetary terms by transferring money from some people to others?

If you are still in favor of freedom—as opposed to government coercion—to bring about a desired result, then you're ready to measure your libertarianism.

Again using the diamond chart described in chapter 1, we now give you the opportunity to place yourself on the political spectrum. In the modern American context, we frequently find conservatives endorsing government restrictions on people's personal choices, and liberals endorsing restrictions on their economic decisions. Of course, that distinction is by no means clear; conservatives may be more likely than liberals to favor subsidies for big business, and many liberals support restrictions on smoking, gun ownership, and contributions to political candidates.

The following questionnaire asks whether you think it should be *your decision* or *the government's decision* whether you engage in a variety of activities, which have been divided into "Personal Freedoms" and "Economic Freedoms." (It should be noted, however, that the division of individual choices into "personal" and "economic" is somewhat arbitrary. Every choice involving your life is personal, and most choices involve property rights and economic exchange.)

*Give yourself 10 points if you think that you decide, 5 points if you're not sure, and 0 points if you think the government decides. Then plot your score on the diamond chart.*

### Personal Freedom

Who should decide whether or not you

wear a seatbelt? _____

own a gun? _____

serve in the military? _____

smoke marijuana? _____

use a risky medical treatment? _____

engage in a homosexual relationship? _____

buy a pornographic video? _____

buy a sexist book? _____

send your child to a particular school? _____

have uncensored access to the Internet? _____

    Total Personal Freedom score _____

### Economic Freedom

Who should decide whether or not you

buy a foreign car? _____

put your retirement savings in Social Security? _____

give money to help the poor? _____

drive a taxicab without a license? _____

hire a worker of another race? _____

build a home without a permit? _____

pay subsidies to farmers? _____

work for less than minimum wage?                    _____

set up a mail-delivery company to compete          _____
   with the Postal Service?
                                                    _____
purchase flood or earthquake insurance?

   Total Economic Freedom score    _____

Now plot your Personal Freedom score on the left scale of the diamond chart and your Economic Freedom score on the right. The intersection of your scores reveals your position on the political spectrum.

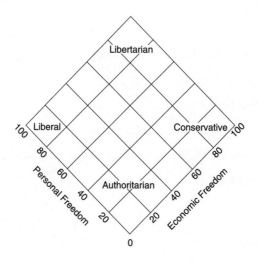

Very few people will have "perfect" scores in any direction. If you've read this book, I hope that you've become convinced that people can make most of the decisions about their lives better than any legislator or regulator could and that you scored near the top of the chart, in the Libertarian quadrant. (And if you haven't read the book yet, I hope you'll do so and then take the quiz again.) If so, welcome to the political movement that will change the twenty-first century. If not, I hope you were at least challenged and intrigued by the argument and that in the future you'll notice more and more examples of the benefits of spontaneous order and the difficulties with coercive government.

# FOR FURTHER READING

## Chapter 1

A basic introduction to libertarian ideas can be found in Murray N. Rothbard, *For a New Liberty: The Libertarian Manifesto* (New York: Collier, 1978). A more current and less radical presentation is Charles Murray, *What It Means to Be a Libertarian* (New York: Broadway, 1997). For contemporary libertarian policy ideas, see David Boaz and Edward H. Crane, eds., *Market Liberalism: A Paradigm for the 21st Century* (Washington, D.C.: Cato Institute, 1993). Other introductory libertarian works include F. A. Hayek, *The Road to Serfdom* (Chicago: University of Chicago Press, 1944); Milton Friedman, *Capitalism and Freedom* (Chicago: University of Chicago Press, 1962); and David Friedman, *The Machinery of Freedom* (La Salle, Ill.: Open Court, 1989). British readers might want to consult Geoffrey Sampson, *An End to Allegiance* (London: Temple Smith, 1984). And for a light-hearted libertarian look at big government, see P. J. O'Rourke, *Parliament of Whores* (New York: Atlantic Monthly Press, 1991).

## Chapter 2

For an introduction to the history of liberty, see Lord Acton, *Essays in the History of Liberty* (Indianapolis: Liberty Classics, 1985); Alexander Rustow, *Freedom and Domination* (Princeton, N.J.: Princeton University Press, 1980); and Ralph Raico, "The Epic Struggle for Liberty" (New York: Laissez Faire Books, 1994), audiotape series. Many of the works discussed in this chapter are excerpted in David Boaz, ed., *The Libertarian Reader: Classic and Contemporary Writings from Lao-tzu to Milton Friedman* (New York: Free Press, 1997). A different selection of documents and excerpts from classical liberal writings is E. K. Bramsted and K. J. Melhuish, eds., *Western Liberalism: A History in Documents from Locke to Croce* (New York: Longman, 1978). On the rise of liberty and commerce in Europe, see E. L. Jones, *The European Miracle* (Cambridge: Cambridge University Press, 1981); Douglas Irwin, *Against the Tide: An Intellectual History of Free Trade* (Princeton, N.J.: Princeton University Press, 1996); and Nathan Rosenberg and L. E. Birdzell, Jr., *How the West Grew Rich* (New York: Basic Books, 1986). On the libertarian origins of the United States, see Bernard Bailyn, *The Ideological Origins of the American Revolution* (Cambridge: Harvard University Press, 1967) and Arthur Ekirch, *The Decline of American Liberalism* (New York: Atheneum, 1967).

The key books of classical liberalism are available in many editions, including John Milton, *Areopagitica;* John Locke, *The Second Treatise of Government;* David Hume, *A Treatise of Human Nature;* Adam Smith, *The Theory of Moral Sentiments* and *The Wealth of Nations;* Thomas Paine, *Common Sense* and *The Rights of Man;* Alexander Hamilton, James Madison, and John Jay, *The Federalist Papers;* Alexis de Tocqueville, *Democracy in America;* John Stuart Mill, *On Liberty;* Herbert Spencer, *Social Statics* and *The Man versus the State;* Wilhelm von Humboldt, *The Sphere and Duties of Government;* and various writings of Thomas Jefferson, Benjamin Constant, Frederic Bastiat, William Lloyd Garrison, and Mary Wollstonecraft. Leveller writings can be found in G. E. Aylmer, ed., *The Levellers in the English Revolution* (Ithaca, N.Y.: Cornell University Press, 1975), and Cato's Letters are now available in Ronald Hamowy, ed., *Cato's Letters* (Indianapolis: Liberty Press, 1995).

Important twentieth-century libertarian books include Ludwig von Mises, *Socialism* (1922; Indianapolis: Liberty Classics, 1981), *Human Action* (New Haven, Conn.: Yale University Press, 1963), and other works; F. A. Hayek, *The Road to Serfdom* (1944), *The Constitution of Liberty* (1960), *The Fatal Conceit* (1988) and *Law, Legislation, and Liberty* (1973, 1976, 1979) (all from the University of Chicago Press), and many other works; Isabel Paterson, *The God of the Machine* (1943; New Brunswick, N.J.: Transaction, 1993); Rose Wilder Lane, *The Discovery of Freedom* (1943; New York: Laissez Faire Books, 1984); Ayn Rand, *The Fountainhead* (New York: Bobbs-Merrill, 1943), *Atlas Shrugged* (New York: Random House, 1957), *Capitalism: The Unknown Ideal* (New York: New American Library, 1967), and other works; Milton Friedman, *Capitalism and Freedom* (Chicago: University of Chicago Press, 1962); Milton and Rose Friedman, *Free to Choose* (New York: Harcourt Brace Jovanovich, 1980); Murray Rothbard, *Man, Economy, and State* (Los Angeles: Nash, 1972), *For a New Liberty* (New York: Collier, 1978), and *The Ethics of Liberty* (Atlantic Highlands, N.J.: Humanities Press, 1982); and Robert Nozick, *Anarchy, State, and Utopia* (New York: Basic Books, 1974).

Contemporary libertarian scholarship is too voluminous to list. A basic list might include work in economics (Thomas Sowell, *Knowledge and Decisions;* Israel Kirzner, *Competition and Entrepreneurship),* law (Richard Epstein, *Simple Rules for a Complex World;* Ellen Frankel Paul, *Property Rights and Emi-*

*nent Domain)*, history (Robert Higgs, *Crisis and Leviathan: Critical Episodes in the Growth of American Government)*, philosophy (Loren Lomasky, *Persons, Rights, and the Moral Community;* Tara Smith, *Moral Rights and Political Freedom;* Tibor Machan, *Individuals and Their Rights;* Jan Narveson, *The Libertarian Idea)*, psychology (Thomas Szasz, *Law, Liberty, and Psychiatry)*, feminism (Joan Kennedy Taylor, *Reclaiming the Mainstream;* Wendy McElroy, *Sexual Correctness)*, economic development (P. T. Bauer, *Dissent on Development;* Hernando de Soto, *The Other Path;* Deepak Lal, *The Poverty of Development Economics)*, civil rights (Walter Williams, *The State against Blacks;* Clint Bolick, *Changing Course)*, the First Amendment (Jonathan Emord, *Freedom, Technology, and the First Amendment)*, education (Myron Lieberman, *Beyond Public Education;* Sheldon Richman, *Separating School and State)*, the environment (Julian Simon, *The Ultimate Resource;* Terry Anderson and Don Leal, *Free-Market Environmentalism)*, social theory (Charles Murray, *In Pursuit: Of Happiness and Good Government)*, bioethics (Tristram Engelhardt, *The Foundations of Bioethics)*, civil liberties (Stephen Macedo, *The New Right v. the Constitution;* James Bovard, *Lost Rights)*, foreign policy (Earl Ravenal, *Defining Defense;* Ted Galen Carpenter, *A Search for Enemies)*, new technologies and the Information Age (Michael Rothschild, *Bionomics: The Economy as Ecosystem;* Lawrence Gasman, *Telecompetition: The Free Market Road to the Information Highway)*, and more.

## Chapter 3

For more on the libertarian view of rights, see Robert Nozick, *Anarchy, State, and Utopia* (New York: Basic Books, 1974); Murray N. Rothbard, *The Ethics of Liberty* (Atlantic Highlands, N.J.: Humanities Press, 1982); and Ayn Rand, "Man's Rights," in *Capitalism: The Unknown Ideal* (New York: New American Library, 1967). More recent treatments include Douglas B. Rasmussen and Douglas J. Den Uyl, *Liberty and Nature* (La Salle, Ill.: Open Court, 1991); Jan Narveson, *The Libertarian Idea* (Philadelphia: Temple University Press, 1988); David Conway, *Classical Liberalism: The Unvanquished Ideal* (New York: St. Martin's, 1996); and Richard Epstein, *Simple Rules for a Complex World* (Cambridge: Harvard University Press, 1995). Of course, the works of Locke, Hume, Paine, Spencer, and others cited in chapter 2 are also essential to an understanding of libertarian rights theory.

## Chapter 4

On individualism, see Felix Morley, ed., *Essays on Individuality* (Indianapolis: Liberty Press, 1977). See also Wendy McElroy, ed., *Freedom, Feminism, and the State* (Washington, D.C.: Cato Institute, 1982); Joan Kennedy Taylor, *Reclaiming the Mainstream: Individualist Feminism Rediscovered* (Buffalo:

Prometheus, 1992); and Clint Bolick, *Changing Course: Civil Rights at the Crossroads* (New Brunswick, N.J.: Transaction, 1988).

## Chapter 5

On the appropriate rules for a free society, see F. A. Hayek, *The Constitution of Liberty* (Chicago: University of Chicago Press, 1960). On the meaning of toleration and pluralism in specific areas, see George H. Smith, "Philosophies of Toleration," in *Atheism, Ayn Rand, and Other Heresies* (Buffalo: Prometheus, 1991); Sheldon Richman, *Separating School and State* (Fairfax, Va.: Future of Freedom Foundation, 1994); and H. Tristram Engelhardt, Jr., *The Foundations of Bioethics* (Oxford: Oxford University Press, 1986).

## Chapter 6

On law and liberty, see F. A. Hayek, *The Constitution of Liberty* (Chicago: University of Chicago Press, 1960) and *Law, Legislation, and Liberty,* vols. 1 and 2 (Chicago: University of Chicago Press, 1973 and 1976); and Bruno Leoni, *Freedom and the Law* (Indianapolis: Liberty Press, 1991). On modern constitutional law, see Richard Epstein, *Simple Rules for a Complex World* (Cambridge: Harvard University Press, 1995) and *Takings: Private Property and the Right of Eminent Domain* (Cambridge: Harvard University Press, 1985); Henry Mark Holzer, *Sweet Land of Liberty?* (Costa Mesa, Calif.: Common Sense, 1983); Stephen Macedo, *The New Right v. the Constitution* (Washington, D.C.: Cato Institute, 1987); Roger Pilon, "Freedom, Responsibility, and the Constitution: On Recovering Our Founding Principles," in David Boaz and Edward H. Crane, eds., *Market Liberalism: A Paradigm for the 21st Century* (Washington, D.C.: Cato Institute, 1993) and "A Government of Limited Powers," in *The Cato Handbook for Congress* (Washington, D.C.: Cato Institute, 1995). See also, of course, *The Federalist Papers* and Herbert Storing, ed., *The Anti-Federalist* (Chicago: University of Chicago Press, 1985), a collection of Anti-Federalist writings.

## Chapter 7

On civil society, see (once again) F. A. Hayek, *The Constitution of Liberty* (Chicago: University of Chicago Press, 1960); Ernest Gellner, *Conditions of Liberty: Civil Society and Its Rivals* (New York: Viking Penguin, 1994); and Charles Murray, *In Pursuit: Of Happiness and Good Government* (New York: Simon & Schuster, 1988). For earlier treatments, see Adam Ferguson, *An Essay on the History of Civil Society* (1773); Alexis de Tocqueville, *Democracy in America* (1835); and Benjamin Constant, "The Liberty of the Ancients Compared with That of the Moderns" (1833) in *Benjamin Constant: Political Writ-*

*ings,* Biancamaria Fontana, ed. (New York: Cambridge University Press, 1988). On mutual aid, see David Green, *Reinventing Civil Society: The Rediscovery of Welfare without Politics* (London: Institute of Economic Affairs, 1993); David Green and Lawrence Cromwell, *Mutual Aid or Welfare State: Australia's Friendly Societies* (Sydney: Allen & Unwin, 1984); and David Beito, "Mutual Aid for Social Welfare: The Case of American Fraternal Societies," *Critical Review* 4, no. 4.

### Chapter 8

There are three short books that provide an easy introduction to economics: Henry Hazlitt, *Economics in One Lesson* (New York: Crown, 1979); Faustino Ballvé, *Essentials of Economics* (Irvington, N.Y.: Foundation for Economic Education, 1963); and James D. Gwartney and Richard L. Stroup, *What Everyone Should Know about Economics and Prosperity* (Tallahassee, Fla.: James Madison Institute, 1993). The serious student should consult two outstanding treatises: Ludwig von Mises, *Human Action* (New Haven, Conn.: Yale University Press, 1963) and Murray Rothbard, *Man, Economy, and State* (Los Angeles: Nash, 1972), along with its sequel, *Power and Market* (Menlo Park, Calif.: Institute for Humane Studies, 1970). Two good textbooks are Paul Heyne, *The Economic Way of Thinking* (Chicago: Science Research Associates, 1983) and James D. Gwartney and Richard L. Stroup, *Economics: Private and Public Choice* (Orlando, Fla.: Dryden Press, 1992). Of course, the classic source for economics is Adam Smith, *An Inquiry into the Nature and Causes of the Wealth of Nations* (1776).

### Chapter 9

On the libertarian view of coercive government, see Thomas Paine, *Common Sense* (1776); Albert Jay Nock, *Our Enemy, the State* (1935); Herbert Spencer, *The Man versus the State* (1884); and Murray N. Rothbard, *For a New Liberty: The Libertarian Manifesto* (New York: Collier, 1978). On Public Choice economics see James M. Buchanan and Gordon Tullock, *The Calculus of Consent* (Ann Arbor: University of Michigan Press, 1962) and James L. Payne, *The Culture of Spending* (San Francisco: Institute for Contemporary Studies, 1991). On war and the growth of the state, see Robert Higgs, *Crisis and Leviathan: Critical Episodes in the Growth of American Government* (New York: Oxford University Press, 1987) and Bruce D. Porter, *War and the Rise of the State* (New York: Free Press, 1994). On how the U.S. government presently deprives Americans of their rights, see James Bovard, *Lost Rights* (New York: St. Martin's, 1994).

*Chapter 10*

On libertarian approaches to public policy issues, I can heartily recommend David Boaz and Edward H. Crane, eds., *Market Liberalism: A New Paradigm for the 21st Century* (Washington, D.C.: Cato Institute, 1993) and *The Cato Handbook for Congress* (Washington, D.C.: Cato Institute, 1995).

*Chapter 11*

On the problem of market failure and public goods, see Tyler Cowen, ed., *The Theory of Market Failure* (Fairfax, Va.: George Mason University Press, 1988), which includes, among other essays, both Coase on lighthouses and Cheung on beekeepers. Allen Wallis's analysis can be found in *Welfare Programs: An Economic Appraisal* (Washington, D.C.: American Enterprise Institute, 1968). On the Postal Service, see Edward L. Hudgins, ed., *The Last Monopoly: Privatizing the Postal Service for the Information Age* (Washington, D.C.: Cato Institute, 1996). On education, see Sheldon Richman, *Separating School and State* (Fairfax, Va.: Future of Freedom Foundation, 1994); Lewis Perelman, *School's Out: Hyperlearning, the New Technology, and the End of Education* (New York: Morrow, 1992); and Myron Lieberman, *Public Education: An Autopsy* (Cambridge: Harvard University Press, 1993). On private communities, see Fred Foldvary, *Public Goods and Private Communities: The Market Provision of Social Services* (Brookfield, Vt.: Edward Elgar, 1994).

*Chapter 12*

For libertarian perspectives on the Information Age, see Lawrence Gasman, *Telecompetition: The Free Market Road to the Information Highway* (Washington, D.C.: Cato Institute, 1994); Peter Huber, *Orwell's Revenge* (New York: Free Press, 1994); and Norman Macrae, *The 2025 Report: A Concise History of the Future, 1975–2025* (New York: Macmillan, 1985).

A good resource for libertarian books and general information on free-market economics and libertarian political theory is Laissez-Faire Books, 938 Howard Street, San Francisco, CA 94103, (800) 326-0996.

# ACKNOWLEDGMENTS

For whatever success I have achieved in the intellectual arena I am grateful to my father, who taught me about right and wrong, and to my mother, who instilled in me an excitement about learning. In the writing of this book my greatest debts are to Edward H. Crane, president of the Cato Institute, for building an institution in which I have been able to develop the knowledge to produce this book and for generously allowing me time to work on it; and to Tom G. Palmer, whose indispensable advice, critiques, and recommended readings went well beyond the call of duty. I also appreciate the advice on various parts of the manuscript of Jonathan Adler, Stephen Chapman, Chris Hocker, Karen Lehrman, Ross Levatter, Deroy Murdock, Eric O'Keefe, Ralph Raico, Jonathan Rauch, Andrea Rich, and Mario Rizzo. The book is dedicated to Roy Childs and Don Caldwell, who could have done it better, and to Stephen H. Miller.

# INDEX